U.S.-Czech Missile Defense Cooperation

Alliance Politics in Action

Michaela Dodge, Ph.D.

National Institute Press®

Published by
National Institute Press®
9302 Lee Highway, Suite 750
Fairfax, Virginia 22031

Library of Congress Control Number: 2020946333

Copyright © 2020 by National Institute Press®

All rights reserved. No part of this book may be reprinted or reproduced or utilized in any form or by an electronic, mechanical or other means, now known or hereafter invented, including photocopying, and recording or in any information storage or retrieval system, without permission in writing from the publisher. The views expressed in this book are the author's alone and do not represent any institution with which she is or has been affiliated.

Table of Contents

List of Abbreviations v

List of Figures vii

Preface ix

Acknowledgements xix

Chapter One. Alliance Politics and Selected International Relations Theories 1

Chapter Two. Brief History of the U.S. Ballistic Missile Defense Program 25

Chapter Three. Early U.S.-Czech Ballistic Missile Defense Cooperation 41

Chapter Four. The Rise and Fall of U.S.-Czech Ballistic Missile Defense Cooperation 83

Chapter Five. Russia's Influence Operations on Czech Territory During the Radar Debate 159

Chapter Six. Assessing the Importance of Different Factors in U.S.-Czech Ballistic Missile Defense Cooperation 183

Index 213

About the Author 231

List of Abbreviations

Anti-Ballistic Missile ....ABM
Ballistic Missile Defense Agreement ....BMDA
Ballistic Missile Defense Review ....BMDR
Ballistic Missile Defense Organization ....BMDO
Civic Democratic Party ....ODS
Christian and Democratic Union-Czechoslovak
   People's Party .... KDU-ČSL
Communist Party of Bohemia and Moravia .... KSČM
Czech Social Democratic Party ....ČSSD
European Phased Adaptive Approach .... EPAA
Freedom Union-Democratic Union .... US-DEU
Global Protection Against Limited Strikes .... GPALS
Ground-Based Midcourse Defense .... GMD
Intercontinental Ballistic Missile ....ICBM
Missile Defense Agency .... MDA
National Missile Defense Act ....NMDA
National Security Council ....NSC
North Atlantic Council .... NAC
North Atlantic Treaty Organization .... NATO
Status of Forces Agreement .... SOFA
Strategic Defense Initiative .... SDI
Strategic Defense Initiative Organization .... SDIO
Strategic Offensive Reductions Treaty ....SORT
Visa Waiver Program ....VWP

List of Figures

Figure 1. Levels of Czech Republic Cooperation with U.S. on Ballistic Missile Defense .... 5 & 156

Figure 2. Support for a U.S. Missile Defense Site in the Czech Republic .... 21 & 197

Figure 3. Likely Consequences of Public and Government Perceptions of Allies 22

Figure 4. Poll on Happiness with Czech Membership in NATO 121

Figure 5. Czech Republic Defense Spending 185

Figure 6. Attitudes Toward a Missile Defense Base/Radar in the Czech Republic, by Party Preference 200

Preface

The book you are about to read is a product of more than a decade of research; professional work on missile defense issues; numerous interviews with people who participated in events that the book describes; and thousands of hours of reading, writing, revising, writing some more, rewriting, and rewriting again. The book advances understanding of factors that contribute to, or hamper, ballistic missile defense cooperation between two states in the context of alliance cooperation and management by opening the "black box" of decision-making. The book is a case study of U.S.-Czech ballistic missile defense cooperation between 2002 and 2011.

More generally, the book develops a methodology to help policymakers assess and evaluate the progress their countries are making on missile defense cooperation, and alerts them to potential pitfalls that can derail it.[1] Improving such an understanding is critical not only for U.S. national security and foreign policy decision-making, and but also for alliance management. Alliances are one of the most important tools for advancing states' defense and foreign policy goals and securing their interests. That is why a case study that can shed light on their cooperative behavior is valuable from a policy perspective.

The book advances a theoretical understanding of alliance behavior, which has been a relatively understudied subject since the end of the Cold War. Much has changed since the era of U.S.-Soviet Union confrontation, and alliances have had to adapt to the realities of a new situation in which one of the two superpowers no longer

---

[1] The terms "missile defense" and "ballistic missile defense" are used, by and large, interchangeably throughout the book, even though the former is broader than the latter.

exists. While literature addresses the question of why alliances form, particularly in the Cold War context, it is less developed with respect to explaining the behavior of member states once alliances are formed, and with respect to analyzing how alliance behavior is managed. Even then, the work that has been done on the topic is generally too academic to be read by busy policymakers, and does not consider policymakers' day-to-day environment within which they conduct and execute foreign and defense policy. Policymakers must deal with real-world scenarios, rather than with broadly defined sanitized hypotheticals that are common in academic discourse. Additionally, this case study shows just how important it is to understand the personalities of diplomats and politicians who represent an ally internationally, as well as the domestic politics within which these actors operate—considerations that most international theories treat as less important than structural attributes of the system (such as distribution of power among states).

The United States is formally allied with more than 40 countries around the world. It cooperates on ballistic missile defense with many countries in regions as different as Poland to Japan to Saudi Arabia. The North Atlantic Treaty Organization (NATO), of which the Czech Republic is a member, is America's most mature multilateral alliance.[2] Under Article V of the North Atlantic Treaty, each member state agrees that "an armed attack against one or more of them in Europe or North America shall be considered an attack against them all," and pledges to take "action as it deems necessary, including the use of armed force, to restore and maintain the security of the North Atlantic area."[3] Most NATO member states cannot defend their

---

[2] "NATO" and "Alliance" are used interchangeably.

[3] North Atlantic Treaty Organization, "The North Atlantic Treaty," April 4, 1949,
http://www.nato.int/cps/en/natohq/official_texts_17120.htm.

territories on their own. They rely on other NATO allies, be it in form of joint military exercises, arms procurement cooperation, or via a pursuit of complementary military capabilities. The United States is arguably NATO's most important member and is definitely its most capable one, as it is currently the organization's largest contributor in terms of both the total defense budget and military capabilities.[4] Other NATO allies look to the United States for leadership and consider it a principal guarantor of their security, particularly on Europe's eastern flank. NATO's geographic scope and its members' level of commitment make it one of today's most predominant military alliances.

The focus on ballistic missile defense as an area of international cooperation is timely because ballistic missile threats to U.S. and allied interests are increasing.[5] In December 2001, the United States announced its decision to withdraw from the 1972 Anti-Ballistic Missile (ABM) Treaty. Six months later, the treaty-imposed constraints on U.S. ballistic missile defense development, testing, and deployment were gone. The reason behind the withdrawal—ballistic missile proliferation by hostile actors—was strategically sound. Increasingly sophisticated and ever-longer-range ballistic missiles in openly adversarial countries, such as North Korea and Iran, have threatened the U.S. population, allies, and forward-deployed forces; so the U.S. government decided to protect

---

[4] NATO itself does not possess any military capabilities; it relies on the contributions of its member states.

[5] Defense Intelligence Ballistic Missile Committee, "Ballistic and Cruise Missile Threat," 2017,
https://www.nasic.af.mil/Portals/19/images/Fact%20Sheet%20Images/2017%20Ballistic%20and%20Cruise%20Missile%20Threat_Final_small.pdf?ver=2017-07-21-083234-343.

its citizens "against limited ballistic missile attack (whether accidental, unauthorized, or deliberate)."[6]

Tactical and strategic advantages that ballistic missiles provide as tools of coercion and warfare drive both state actors and non-state actors to obtain them; this trend is unlikely to change in the future. Ballistic missiles offer an adversary an unprecedented element of surprise because they travel hundreds of miles in minutes. They may carry weapons of mass destruction or conventional payloads. They threaten populations as well as economic centers and military installations in the U.S. and in allied nations. This can put U.S. alliances under pressure in the case of a conflict, particularly in Europe, the Middle East, and the Asia-Pacific region. Consequently, missile defense cooperation will continue to be one of the most important factors in international relations in general, and in America's alliances with other countries around the world in particular.

Countries that are at a greater risk of being targeted by ballistic missiles are likely to be more interested in defending themselves against them, particularly those that value their populations over, for example, leadership survival.[7] But these countries can also be interested in protecting their other key assets, including military and economic centers. Ballistic missile defense systems help to assure U.S. allies because they help to protect their territory, allow for strengthening of U.S. military operations in support of allies if needed, and help to "counter adversary strategies attempting to coerce the United States, allies and

---

[6] National Missile Defense Act of 1999, Public Law 106-38, § 2, July 22, 1999, https://www.congress.gov/106/plaws/publ38/PLAW-106publ38.pdf.

[7] It is safe to assume that some states value their populations more than others. For example, Israel obviously values its citizens' lives more than North Korea.

partners with missile threats."[8] The need to occasionally deploy some ballistic missile defense components, such as radars, on allied territory (closer to the threat) further underscores the need to see ballistic missile defense as a cooperative endeavor.[9] Forward deployments require bilateral or multilateral arrangements, which provide opportunities for allied cooperation and burden-sharing.[10]

At the same time, issues of ballistic missile defense and offense are not trivial from a technological point of view. Ballistic missiles can travel hundreds of miles in minutes making options to respond to them rather limited and technologically challenging. Because of these attributes, ballistic missiles can serve as a tool of coercion and limit a state's option to respond to conflicts with a ballistic missile-armed adversary even before he decides to deploy them. The United States and its allies and partners are concerned with ballistic missile threats to Europe, the Middle East, and in the Asia-Pacific region.[11]

U.S.-Czech ballistic missile defense cooperation is theoretically interesting because its levels fluctuated over time. This makes it possible to ascertain which factors were more important than others. If some of them remained constant even as levels of cooperation changed, it means that they were not as impactful as others that fluctuated during the period of change.

---

[8] U.S. Department of Defense, "2019 Missile Defense Review," January 17, 2019, https://www.defense.gov/Portals/1/Interactive/2018/11-2019-Missile-Defense-Review/The%202019%20MDR_Executive%20Summary.pdf.

[9] Unless these components are space-based, in which case the existing treaty architecture would likely be sufficient to support ballistic missile defense deployments.

[10] U.S. Department of Defense, "2019 Missile Defense Review."

[11] For a more detailed treatment of the issue, see, for example, Bradley Thayer, *American National Security Policy: Essays in Honor of William R. Van Cleave* (Fairfax, VA: National Institute Press, 2007).

The Czech Republic emerged as a key partner state in early post-ABM-Treaty efforts by the U.S. to deploy ballistic missile defenses for the protection of the U.S. homeland and allies. Starting as an ally interested in contributing to these efforts, the Czech Republic negotiated with the United States to host an X-band radar, a critical component of its ballistic missile defense system, in 2007 and 2008.[12] Along with interceptors in Poland, the two missile defense sites in Europe were intended to protect the U.S. homeland and parts of Europe from Iranian ballistic missiles.[13] The Czech Republic also became an important diplomatic partner in getting NATO to acknowledge ballistic missile defense's critical role for allied security at NATO's Bucharest summit in 2008. After U.S. missile defense plans changed in 2009 and the Obama Administration cancelled the deployment of an X-band radar to Europe and Ground-Based Midcourse Defense interceptors to Poland, the Czech Republic turned down an opportunity to host a U.S. early warning ballistic missile defense data center in 2011.

The U.S.-Czech ballistic missile defense cooperation offers several important lessons for alliance cooperation and management, and for how governments discuss complex national security issues with their populations.

First, while U.S. and Czech threat perceptions differed, their cooperation proceeded as if they were the same. That is a significant finding because international relations literature on alliance management makes an implicit assumption that threat perceptions ought to be shared in order for allies to cooperate with each other.

Second, economic benefits of cooperation were not a primary driver of defense cooperation between the Czech

---

[12] Throughout the text, the words "X-band radar" and "radar" are used interchangeably if the context is a U.S. ballistic missile defense component in the Czech Republic.

[13] The United States deployed long-range interceptors at two additional sites in California and Alaska.

Republic and the United States, although the Czech government tried to use economic incentives on the domestic level to help to obtain the population's support for its preferred foreign policy choice. But when employing economic incentives on the domestic level, a government runs the risk of appearing as if it wants to bribe its way into the public's grace.

Third, a government must be extremely careful with respect to the timing of discussions about complex national security issues. In an era of social media and its sophisticated exploitation by adversaries, falling behind the communications curve may put a government on the defensive, with little prospect of shaping the narrative favorably once opponents frame the issue in a negative light in the public discourse.

Fourth, the book provides one of the first accounts of the Russian Federation's influence operations and active measures campaigns on Czech territory. In doing so, this book is intended to inform a debate about Russia's continued influence operations worldwide. It underscores the need to invest in educated and resilient societies, so that they will not be easily susceptible to adversarial influence operations.

Fifth, governments' communications strategies must be kept as simple as possible. Parallel narratives about why a country cooperates on defense with another country must be managed carefully, as they can become counterproductive to the goals of communication campaigns. A favorable perception of NATO among the Czechs did not make a U.S. radar on Czech territory more acceptable to them. Introducing overlapping arguments created confusion as the Czech government tried to frame the issue in NATO terms to the Czech public.

Sixth, domestic politics matters, including its nuances. A detailed understanding of an alliance partner's domestic politics ought to inform the timing of major announcements, visits, and contents of major speeches, and make politicians and diplomats sensitive to what is said in off-hand comments. The United States must develop government career paths that build (and reward) regional expertise over time.

Seventh, small countries run a risk when they center bilateral relations with a larger country on a single issue. The Obama Administration announced the cancellation of a radar site in the Czech Republic after years of discussions and negotiations with the Czech Republic, after thousands of workhours put in by many in both the U.S. and the Czech governments, and after the United States invested significant resources in educating constituencies in the United States and the Czech Republic on the merits of the plan. After the cancellation, the Czech Republic found itself in a difficult situation in which it promptly had to find new themes and topics on the basis of which bilateral cooperation with the United States would continue.

The book is organized in the following manner. Chapter One provides a brief overview of international relations theories relevant to alliance politics. Chapter Two introduces the reader to an abbreviated history of the U.S. ballistic missile defense program to provide context for the chronologically organized case study that follows in Chapter Three. Chapter Three examines the Czech government's early exploratory efforts to discuss ballistic missile defense cooperation with the United States between 2002 and 2011. The chapter documents unofficial but significant discussions between the two governments before the launch of official ballistic missile defense negotiations in early 2007. Chapter Four discusses the official negotiations between 2007 and 2009 about the Czech Republic potentially hosting an X-band radar on its territory. The Obama Administration changed its missile defense plans for Europe in September 2009. After the cancellation, the Czech Republic turned down an opportunity to host a missile defense early warning data center in June 2011. This event marked an official end of direct bilateral U.S.-Czech ballistic missile defense collaboration. Chapter Five offers one of the first comprehensive accounts of Russia's influence operations on Czech territory in the context of U.S.-Czech ballistic missile defense cooperation. Russia's activities contributed in no small measure to politicization of the issue, as well as polarization of the Czech public and political scene over whether the Czech Republic should host a U.S. radar, and, more broadly, over a pro-Western course in Czech foreign policy.[14] This was Russia's first successful influence campaign on the territory of a new NATO member state after the end of the Cold War. Its lessons are worth heeding given Russia's activities on this front today. Chapter Six concludes the book with policy-relevant lessons and offers recommendations for other states that cooperate on ballistic missile defense with the United States.

---

[14] Except for the Communist Party.

Acknowledgements

In the fall of 2007, a young student walked into a professor's office at the International Institute of Political Science in Brno in the Czech Republic, to ask a question about differences between the United States' and the European Union's lists of designated terrorist organizations. The professor didn't have an answer, but said he was looking for someone to help with logistics for a conference on U.S.-Czech ballistic missile defense cooperation. The student was excited to help and to learn more about a topic that was raising so many emotions in the Czech Republic. While the student is not as young anymore, and no U.S. radar was built on Czech territory, this book is an extension, though not a conclusion, of the author's interest in missile defense.

That meeting more than a decade ago changed the course of that student's life—mine. At the April 2008 conference in Černín Palace in Prague, I had the privilege of meeting the late Professor William Van Cleave. Known for his steadfast dedication to educating the next generation of U.S. national security practitioners (and for his love of beer and football), he influenced U.S. national security policy through his students perhaps more than any other U.S. professor. He and Ambassador J.D. Crouch, Professor Van Cleave's former student, told me about the Defense and Strategic Studies Program at Missouri State University in Fairfax, Virginia. I started the program in 2009 and the rest is history, as we Americans sometimes say. I miss Professor Van Cleave dearly and hope my work would make him proud.

This book is based on my doctoral dissertation, which I defended at George Mason University in March 2019. I am grateful to the members of my committee for their invaluable feedback and help in seeing the dissertation through: Professors Colin Dueck, Mark Katz, and Ed Rhodes. My supportive bosses at The Heritage Foundation and in the Senate gave me time and space to complete the doctoral program: Steve Bucci, Jim Carafano, Tom Spoehr, and Senator Jon Kyl. Without their support, I would probably still be writing my dissertation. Břetislav Dančák and Peter Suchý at Masaryk University provided me with incredible opportunities and shared their immense knowledge of the topic at hand with me. The project would be much less comprehensive without their help. I owe special thanks to Keith Payne and Amy Joseph at the National Institute for Public Policy. Without their nudging, this book would not have existed. I am grateful to my former Heritage colleagues Karina Rollins and Bill Poole, whose careful editorial work made the final product that much better, and to John Fleming, also a former Heritage colleague, whose talent in creating graphics to tell a story is unparalleled. I would also like to thank the Smith Richardson Foundation and the Sarah Scaife Foundation for their generous support of this project.

I am grateful to many friends and colleagues scattered around the world. They were generous with their time and never hesitated to share their knowledge of U.S.-Czech ballistic missile defense cooperation. Their insights stemming from participation in important matters that the book analyzes, and their willingness to share their knowledge with me allowed me to understand the issue on a much more detailed level than otherwise would be the case. Any errors, however, are mine alone.

In completing this book, I have drawn from several of my previously published works. I appreciate the permission to do so granted by the publishers of the following: "U.S. Czech Ballistic Missile Defense Cooperation: Policy Implications," Issue No. 445 National Institute for Public Policy, September 24, 2019; "Russia's Influence Operations in the Czech Republic During the Radar Debate," *Comparative Strategy*, Vol. 39, No. 2, March 2020, copyright the National Institute for Public Policy, available online, https://doi.org/10.1080/01495933.2020.1718989; and "U.S.-Czech Ballistic Missile Defense Cooperation: Lessons Learned and Way Forward for Others," *Comparative Strategy*, Vol. 39, No. 3, April 2020, copyright Taylor & Francis, available online, http://tanfonline.com, https://doi.org/10.1080/01495933.2020.1740573.

This book is dedicated to the most important men in my life. My father, whose incredible work ethic has inspired me over the years, and on whose wisdom and experience I've drawn when I tried to understand what the Evil Empire of the past can teach us about evil empires of today. My husband, who works tirelessly to prevent today's evil empires from gaining an edge on the United States in the future. And our two sons, for whom we hope to leave the world better than we found it.

Chapter One
Alliance Politics and Selected International Relations Theories

History is clear: Nations with strong allies thrive, and those without them wither.

James Mattis
swearing-in as U.S. Secretary of Defense
January 20, 2017

Alliances—their formation, management, and politics—have been of enduring interest to scholars, foreign policy practitioners, and the general public. This interest stems in part from the fact that, at a first glance, alliances seem to defy the logic of the international system. They are cooperative endeavors, albeit to various degrees. It may be said that "among states, the state of nature is a state of war,"[15] but alliances are a present and tangible reminder that some of the most prominent and influential international theories do not fully capture the richness of the empirical world.

For purposes of this book, alliances are defined as "formal associations of states for the use (or nonuse) of military force, in specified circumstances, against states outside their own membership."[16] This definition captures several important attributes: a formal, sustained agreement between allies, that allies possess and manage military capabilities, that they coordinate with each other, and that they share an understanding of which states outside an

---

[15] Kenneth N. Waltz, *Theory of International Politics* (Reading, MA: Addison-Wesley Pub. Co., 1979), p. 102.

[16] Glenn H. Snyder, *Alliance Politics* (Cornell University Press, 2007), p. 4.

alliance constitute an external threat. Alliances can be distinguished by several attributes, including number of participants (bilateral or multilateral) and issues of focus (active promotion of cooperation on a single issue between allies or a broader agenda).

Whether alliance relationships arise from factors outside or inside a state's borders is an important analytical distinction, particularly for policymakers as they navigate a dynamic and multifaceted web of international relations. Although alliance cooperation has decidedly positive connotations, alliance politics involves a spectrum of relationships, including those that might include conflict and negotiations. After all, allies need not agree on everything to be allies.

Alliances are created by sovereign states, and the governments of those states are made up of individuals who do not necessarily share the same goals, even within the same state. Under the best of circumstances, alliance interests are bound to diverge, and this can be a reason for conflict.

This chapter conceptualizes ballistic missile defense cooperation. Figure 1 (page 5) graphically depicts different levels of ballistic missile defense cooperation by analyzing its different stages and analytically distinguishing among them. Additionally, Figure 1 shows the varying levels of cooperation between the United States and the Czech Republic from 2002 to 2011. There was no significant ballistic missile defense cooperation in 2005 because the Czech government was entangled in a domestic scandal, and the U.S. government was in the process of analyzing its own ballistic missile defense options. Similarly, there were no notable ballistic missile defense activities between the two countries after the Czech rejection of hosting a U.S. early warning center in June 2011.

Figure 1 ranks levels of cooperation from the most involved to the least involved. Such a conceptualization can help policymakers to assess whether ballistic missile defense cooperation with a state is advancing or regressing and where to place it on different rungs of the ladder. It can also help policymakers to decide how to tailor their strategies in order to advance missile defense cooperation, including using tools such as economic incentives, public relations, and subject matter expertise. This chapter grounds the case study theoretically and identifies factors that are important for alliance politics and ballistic missile defense cooperation.

Conceptualizing Ballistic Missile Defense Cooperation

Before proceeding to the case study itself, it is important to conceptualize ballistic missile defense cooperation. Such conceptualization will provide a baseline for assessing whether ballistic missile defense cooperation is advancing or stagnating, and help to organize and categorize the many steps that comprise such cooperation.

A country can advance ballistic missile defense cooperation in many ways and on many levels. Naturally, some of them are more involved than others and require larger investments in political and diplomatic capital, manpower, and financial resources. In order to better understand why different countries choose different levels of engagement when it comes to ballistic missile defense cooperation, one must clarify what different levels of cooperation entail.

A few words of caution are warranted. The distinction between different levels of cooperation may not be as clear cut as Figure 1 suggests. Different levels might blend and overlap, particularly when negotiations are ongoing. For example, nations might debate the nature of the threat while conducting separate negotiations on ballistic missile defense force deployments. As the case study shows, they might even disagree about the degree of a ballistic missile threat, yet cooperate as if they agreed.

Ranging from ballistic missile threats consultations to exploring the potential of technologies for addressing threats, to more involved ways to participate in another country's ballistic missile defense programs, states have plenty of options from which to choose when deciding how involved they want to be in ballistic missile defense cooperation. More involved efforts might include providing territory to host elements of the system, contributing funding for the development of the system, or jointly developing a ballistic missile defense system as equal partners. Other efforts might entail informal discussions about the nature of ballistic missile threats or potential options for including a country's assets in another state's ballistic missile defense architecture. A state might offer to provide physical security for assets deployed on its territory, fund infrastructure supporting ballistic missile defense deployments, or participate in ballistic missile defense research and development efforts. Ballistic missile defense cooperation does not have to be limited to military hardware, and in fact its political aspects are very much intertwined with its operational aspects. For states' joint efforts to be considered cooperation, they must be consistent to some degree, and continuous. This means that discrete one-off arms transfers with no, or very little, follow up would not be considered ballistic missile defense cooperation.

Figure 1 visualizes degrees of ballistic missile defense cooperation: the more advanced it is, the more involvement in terms of manpower, diplomatic resources, and economic resources between countries. The burden of missile defense cooperation does not need to be shared by all the participating countries equally. Such a situation would be unrealistic in the real world, given significant disparities between countries in size; technological development;

priorities; and resources that a country can devote to ballistic missile defense research, development, and deployment.

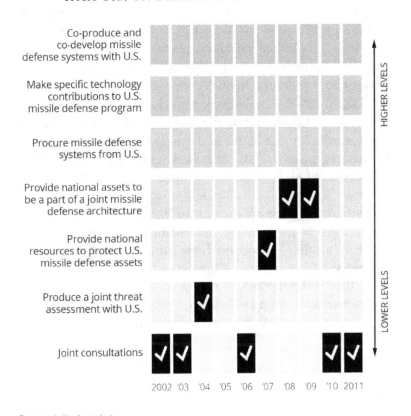

Fig. 1. **Levels of Czech Republic Cooperation with U.S. on Ballistic Missile Defense**

Source: Author's analysis.

At the most basic level, a nation can hold consultations with an ally about the status of a ballistic missile threat and jointly explore options to respond to it. Such consultations can be held at different levels of the government and require different degrees of leadership attention, manpower, and resources. They might be prompted by international events or be a part of overall cooperative efforts within an alliance. They might quickly advance toward more involved cooperative endeavors or continue on a basic and even superficial level for a long time. Interacting on this level does not presuppose that countries have the same view of ballistic missile threats, what the important missile defense issues are, or that they agree which solutions they ought to pursue jointly or separately. But without even discussing the issue, ballistic missile defense cooperation would simply not be on the agenda between countries at all, making any potential further progress impossible.

Consultations on ballistic missile threats are a part of day-to-day diplomatic (and sometimes intelligence) efforts between the United States and other states and are the most common type of ballistic missile defense cooperation. After all, the United States, as a global power with a global alliance network, faces a variety of actors with a variety of ballistic missile capabilities in different parts of the world. This means it needs allies, since some of its ballistic missile defense systems must be forward deployed to operate properly.

Other countries might be interested in purchasing U.S. ballistic missile defense systems. The United States is one of the most technologically advanced countries in the world, and ballistic missile defense is rocket science. But the United States is not the only one with ballistic missile defense systems. For example, Turkey, a NATO ally, purchased a Russian S-400 missile defense and air defense system despite widespread objections from other NATO member states.[17] Consultations between Turkey and the Russian Federation that preceded this purchase would be a part of a

---

[17] "Turkey Has Completed Purchase of Russian Missile Defense: Defense Minister," Reuters, November 12, 2017,
https://www.reuters.com/article/us-turkey-defence/turkey-has-completed-purchase-of-russian-missile-defense-defense-minister-idUSKBN1DC0H7.

consultation category (although the countries are not formally allied). If the Russian-Turkish ballistic missile defense exchange does not continue, activities between the two countries would be considered an arms transfer rather than cooperation.

Producing a shared threat assessment with an ally represents a more involved ballistic missile defense cooperation type. A shared threat assessment requires more coordination than consultations, as well as a joint view regarding what constitutes a threat on the official level. This is not to say that their understanding has to be uniform. Countries might pursue different objectives while cooperating with each other or value different aspects of ballistic missile defense cooperation unequally. But unless they agree that there is a ballistic missile proliferation challenge to their shared interests, it would be more difficult, although not impossible, to progress toward more involved ballistic missile defense cooperation types.

A consistent and coordinated joint position regarding which countries or actors constitute a ballistic missile threat makes it more difficult for an adversary to exploit a gap between countries' official positions and their potentially opposed domestic constituencies (if there is such a gap). Countries might disagree on the urgency of a threat but continue their ballistic missile defense cooperation on more involved levels for a variety of other reasons. For example, NATO agreed to "develop the capability to defend our populations and territories against ballistic missile attack as a core element of our collective defence," at the Lisbon summit in 2010 despite different member states having different ideas about which other states are a threat to the Alliance and how urgent such a threat might be.[18] It follows,

---

[18] North Atlantic Treaty Organization, "Active Engagement: Modern Defence. Strategic Concept for the Defence and Security of the Members of the North Atlantic Treaty Organization," November 19, 2010,

then, that member states' contributions to ballistic missile defense capabilities will range from substantive to little depending on their own threat perceptions and domestic politics.

On the next level of cooperation, a country might provide forces to protect U.S. (or another country's) ballistic missile defense assets deployed on this nation's territory or, in a more complicated instance, on territory of a third country that hosts ballistic missile defense assets. U.S. ballistic missile defense forces operating on another country's territory generally operate under a Status of Forces Agreement (SOFA) with a host nation. A SOFA is intended to define the legal status of U.S. Department of Defense personnel, "activities, and property in the territory of another nation and set forth rights and responsibilities between the United States and the host government."[19] A SOFA may require ratification by a host country's parliament (or an equivalent institution) and thus require consideration of domestic politics on the part of a host government and the United States. Audience costs matter in these negotiations.[20] To the extent that ballistic missile defense cooperation is a salient issue among the presumed host country's population, its government must not only make a case for ballistic missile defense cooperation to key stakeholders, but it ought to be transparent regarding SOFA negotiations and a ballistic missile defense cooperation process. The need for transparency is likely more pertinent

---

https://www.nato.int/strategic-concept/pdf/Strat_Concept_web_en.pdf.

[19] U.S. Department of State, "Report on Status of Forces Agreement" International Security Advisory Board, January 16, 2015, https://2009-2017.state.gov/t/avc/isab/236234.htm.

[20] See, for example, James Fearon, "Domestic Political Audiences and the Escalation of International Disputes," *American Political Science Review*, Vol. 88, No. 3 (1994), and Robert Putnam, "Diplomacy and Domestic Politics: The Logic of Two-Level Games," *International Organization*, Vol. 42, No. 3 (1988).

to democracies than other types of government. An example of this kind of cooperation is Denmark's and the United Kingdom's hosting U.S. early warning radars (components of a U.S. missile defense architecture) on their territories.

The next level of ballistic missile cooperation involves a continuous integration of a national asset or assets, for example a radar or a ship, into a ballistic missile defense system of another nation. Such an endeavor requires not only a close coordination between two nations, but also extensive continuous sensitive operational information sharing, which does not have to be symmetrical. Arrangements involving military assets' integration into other nation's ballistic missile defense architectures require extensive negotiations about appropriate command and control, conditions under which assets would be used, and priorities assigned to areas they are meant to defend in the event of a large attack. An example of this type of cooperation would be an integration of data from Danish ship-based radars into a U.S. missile defense sensor architecture.

On the next level, a country can seek to procure a missile defense system from another country while integrating it to a joint ballistic missile defense architecture. A shared threat assessment is not required for this type of ballistic missile defense cooperation per se. A country may or may not share another's threat assessment or views regarding the threat's urgency but might still choose to make ballistic missile defense technology available for other reasons, such as to boost its diplomatic standing with another country, secure investments for its defense industrial base, or secure agreements with respect to other types of cooperation. As a general rule, however, a country will not provide advanced technologies, particularly those as sensitive as ballistic missile defense, to its adversaries or to countries openly allied with their adversaries. It will also not integrate its systems with their networks. The more advanced the technology, the more strictly it will be guarded in its origin country. The high-tech sensitivity related to ballistic missile defense systems makes it categorically different from less technologically advanced arms transfers. It is one thing to transfer small arms; it is another thing entirely to transfer a Theatre High Altitude Area Defense (THAAD) battery.

Advanced technology transfers might also trigger domestic politics dynamics in both an origin and a recipient nation. A nation might require authorizations from domestic political bodies to transfer advanced technologies to other states. For example, the U.S. Congress must authorize certain technology transfers from the United States to another country. A recipient nation might need an approval of an appropriations body (or its equivalent) to secure funding for advanced technology purchases. The process might involve placating vested players with different domestic interests.

A country might pursue an independent ballistic missile defense research and development program and then make new technologies available to other allied nations. A nation might, for example, share data about its program and its development, including, but not limited to, telemetry produced during ballistic missile defense tests. It can provide scientists or testing facilities for different elements of another state's missile defense program. Negotiations on this level go beyond usual diplomatic interactions because they require access to very sensitive and often-classified information. They may require business cooperation among different countries that research and develop these technologies. An example of this type of cooperation is an early U.S.-Israeli effort on the Israeli Iron Dome air and ballistic missile defense system.

Lastly, countries might choose to pursue the most involved ballistic missile defense cooperation option: a joint co-production and co-developmental program or its parts.

Such a collaboration can be mutually beneficial because ballistic missile defense is a particularly difficult and expensive technological endeavor, involving a range of capabilities from powerful radars, to kill vehicles, to directed energy research, to powerful rocket motors needed to deliver a kinetic kill or an explosive kill vehicle close to an incoming missile in order to destroy it. Sharing developmental costs of these sophisticated systems might permit nations to realize inefficiencies in the program and potentially come up with better technological solutions. An example of this type of cooperation is a U.S.-Japanese effort to develop and deploy the Standard Missile-3 Block IIA interceptor for the U.S. Aegis missile defense system.

Alliance Cooperation and What Affects It

The following section provides a brief overview of some of the dominant strands of international relations theory regarding cooperation among states and what they tell us about factors that affect cooperation among states. These theories identify potentially important factors with an impact on international cooperation: threat, economic considerations, dependence on other countries, and public perceptions. These factors are general enough that they can be utilized to analyze other cases of cooperation among states. This section is not meant to be academic or exhaustive. It is meant to provide a conceptual framework for this discussion of U.S.-Czech ballistic missile defense cooperation and illustrate different theoretical approaches to matters related to international cooperation. The following pages elaborate on each of them in greater detail.

Threats

For centuries, scholars have been interested in patterns of international politics that appear to have a timeless quality.

From the Melian Dialogue's themes of the weak doing what they must and the strong doing what they will, to Clausewitz's thoughts in his unfinished treatise *On War*, scholars and practitioners of international relations have been quick to point out that international relations share patterns that seemingly transcend the personalities of decision-makers or individual attributes of actors in historical events. "The enduring character of international politics accounts for the striking sameness in the quality of international life through the millennia," argues Kenneth Waltz in his *Theory of International Politics*.[21] As he states in his book *Man, the State, and War*:

> With many sovereign states, with no system of law enforcement among them, with each state judging its grievances and ambitions according to the dictates of its own reason or desire—conflict, sometimes leading to war, is bound to occur. To achieve a favorable outcome from such conflict a state has to rely on its own devices, the relative efficiency of which must be its constant concern.[22]

Obtaining allies and managing relations with them is one such a device. What do select international relations theories tell us about international cooperation? Neo-realists, for instance, argue that at the heart of an alliance is a desire to balance against an external threat. A threat consists of two components: capability and intent.[23] How serious the threat is depends on its and a state's own

---

[21] Waltz, *Theory of International Politics*, p. 66.

[22] Kenneth N. Waltz, *Man, the State, and War: A Theoretical Analysis* (New York: Columbia University Press, 1959), p. 159.

[23] J. David Singer, "Threat-Perception and the Armament-Tension Dilemma," *The Journal of Conflict Resolution*, Vol. 2, No. 1 (1958), pp. 90–105.

attributes, including "size of population and territory, resources endowment, economic capability, military strength, political stability and competence."[24] The more capable a threatening state is, the more cohesive an alliance against it will be, that is if countries do not chose to align themselves with the source of the threat.

While capabilities take years to develop, intentions can change overnight and are much more difficult to measure reliably, which is why the temptation is to conflate the first with the second. But relying on the distribution of military capabilities as the only factor for determining whether a nation is a threat to another would be foolish. What matters most is allying against a state that is perceived as posing the greatest threat to one's survival.[25] Instead of focusing on the balance of power, states ought to focus on what Stephen Walt calls "balance of threat," which captures aggregate power, geographic proximity, offensive capabilities, and intentions.[26] The United States is a case in point. It has more allies than any other country in the world, despite its superior military capabilities and a level of defense spending that no other country currently matches. Yet it is not considered a threat by nearly as many states as some international relations theories might lead one to assume.

Understanding whether another nation feels threatened, by whom, and whether its leadership perceives it as such is essential to understanding the dynamic of ballistic missile defense cooperation—and is discernible to some extent from a country's national security strategies and its leaders' and political representatives' public statements. In this context, it is worth keeping in mind that not all ballistic missiles are created equal. Allied ballistic

---

[24] Waltz, *Theory of International Politics*, p. 131.

[25] Stephen M. Walt, *Origins of Alliances* (Ithaca, NY: Cornell University Press, 1987), p. 21.

[26] Ibid., pp. 22–26.

missile capabilities are not concerning the same way other states' ballistic missiles are. For example, the Czech Republic is within range of several NATO allies' ballistic missiles, and this proximity was not a factor in its decision to cooperate on ballistic missile defense with the United States.

A stronger ballistic missile threat perception ought to result in higher degrees of ballistic missile defense cooperation with another nation if given a chance to pursue ballistic missile defense cooperation. In needing to address ballistic missiles, countries face a challenging technological problem. Ballistic missiles are unlike other conventional weapons. Given their special nature, ability to carry potentially devastating payloads, and very short flight times, it is justifiable to consider enemy states' ballistic missile capabilities separately from their overall military capabilities. For example, because of its long-range ballistic missile and nuclear weapons program, North Korea is a threat to the U.S. homeland in a way to which its conventional capabilities cannot aspire.

In the face of a significant threat, states have an option to ally with others to counter the threat (balance) or ally with the source of the threat (bandwagon).[27] The key problem with these distinctions is that whether a state balances or bandwagons is entirely in the eye of the beholder. What might look like balancing to one is bandwagoning to another. To obtain a better understanding of the dynamic at play, it is important to understand how leaders and governments think about the choices they make. This book, based on interviews with policymakers and decision-makers among others, highlights the thinking behind Czech, and, to a more limited degree, U.S., strategic choices regarding ballistic missile defense cooperation.

---

[27] Ibid., p. 27.

Alliances matter to the extent that they affect "the decision of the allies to intervene on one another's behalf in the event of war," and if they lead "states outside the alliance to determine that the allies will intervene to support one another."[28] The first is an instance of commitment; the second, of signaling. Ballistic missile defense cooperation between two countries can be considered an example of both commitment and signaling — and the more mature it is, the more credible these signals will be considered by a potential adversary. When a state places its military assets on an ally's territory in a cooperative manner, the state is indicating that it is more likely to come to its ally's defense because its own assets or forces would be engaged in the case of an attack on this ally. Maintaining a forward-deployed presence is also a visible and tangible reminder to a potential adversary that one is committed to defend allies because one's forces would suffer in case of an adversary's attack on this ally, too. Such was the "trip-wire" logic of U.S. deployments to Europe during the Cold War.

Economic Considerations

Alliances that are defined by profound asymmetries in economic, military, or diplomatic resources are said to be characterized by an asymmetry of expectations: A stronger member seeks to exercise its influence while a weaker member seeks unilateral guarantees.[29] As will be shown below, this was only partially true in U.S.-Czech ballistic missile defense cooperation. While the Czech Republic wanted security guarantees in excess of the U.S. commitment to NATO, it did not feel pressured into ballistic missile defense cooperation with the United States;

---

[28] James D. Morrow, "Alliances: Why Write Them Down?" *Annual Review of Political Science* Vol. 3, No. 1 (June 2000), pp. 63 and 67.

[29] Snyder, *Alliance Politics*, p. 12.

neither did it reportedly feel the pressure of asymmetry during negotiations themselves. "The Americans were fair and serious negotiating partners. We never felt as if it was a superpower negotiating with a smaller state," stated Ambassador Veronika Kuchyňová-Šmigolová, then-member of the Czech negotiation team for the potential missile defense site in the Czech Republic.[30] Indeed, the Czech government saw cooperation with the United States as something desirable and valuable in its own right, not as something that has to be done because the United States is bigger and more powerful than the Czech Republic.

Examining a policymaker's perspective makes clear that individuals and their relationships are a more relevant consideration when trying to understand a current issue than abstract theories of how a nation state would act in a given situation. Events like the fall of the Soviet Union and the central role that Mikhail Gorbachev played in it highlighted the importance of both internal and external factors in the conduct of a state's foreign policy.[31] Richard Neustadt's seminal work on alliance politics provides a useful bridge between the systemic and individual level of analysis and develops a framework for enriching one's understanding of alliance crises escalation and alliance management. Upon a close examination of two crises in U.S.-UK relations, Neustadt found that they were marked by common attributes: muddled perceptions, stifled communications, disappointed expectations, paranoid reactions, and bureaucratic politics at home.[32] Interesting for this book topic, the U.S. announcement to terminate the

---

[30] Author interview with Ambassador Veronika Kuchyňová-Šmigolová on U.S.-Czech missile defense cooperation, Skype, January 22, 2019.

[31] Gideon Rose, "Neoclassical Realism and Theories of Foreign Policy," *World Politics*, Vol. 51, No. 1 (1998), pp. 144–72, https://doi.org/10.1017/S0043887100007814.

[32] Richard E. Neustadt, *Alliance Politics* (New York: Columbia University Press, 1970), pp. 56 and 65.

placement of an X-band radar on Czech territory in 2009 shared all the markings of an alliance crisis.

To complicate matters further, the modern environment in which international affairs are conducted challenges a traditional understanding of military power as a dominant military tool of coercion and its impact on relations between states. Neo-liberalists point out that states today are interdependent, which refers to "situations characterized by reciprocal effects among countries or among actors of different countries."[33] This means that factors other than raw military strength can bear upon cooperation among states.

Democratic governments care for the economic well-being of their citizens because their re-election depends on it.[34] (This interest is not limited to democracies. Some authoritarian states are also interested in the economic well-being of their citizens because it allows them to buy the citizens' compliance with a lack of democratic reforms and freedoms.)[35] Attracting foreign capital in today's competitive global economy is challenging and requires countries to use all tools at their disposal in order to be successful. Ballistic missile defense cooperation (and defense cooperation in general) can potentially improve an

---

[33] Robert O. Keohane and Joseph S. Nye, *Power and Interdependence*, 3rd ed. (Harlow, UK: Longman, 2000), p. 7.

[34] Nita Rudra and Stephan Haggard, "Globalization, Democracy, and Effective Welfare Spending in the Developing World," *Comparative Political Studies*, Vol. 38, No. 9 (November 1, 2005), pp. 1015–49, https://doi.org/10.1177/0010414005279258.

[35] See, for example, Steven Heydemann, "Upgrading Authoritarianism in the Arab World," Brookings Institution Saban Center for Middle East Policy *Analysis Paper* No. 13, October 2007, https://www.brookings.edu/wp-content/uploads/2016/06/10arabworld.pdf.

image of a host nation in the eyes of international businesses and attract further investments.[36]

Dependence on Allies

Smaller nations like the Czech Republic often depend on their allies for their defense needs. Their military dependence can be judged high, moderate, or low and must take into account a smaller state's need for military assistance, the degree to which another ally fills that need, and alternative ways of meeting the need.[37] An ally can meet the need through increasing its own military preparedness, allying with someone else, acquiring additional resources by military action, and conciliating an adversary.[38] These options need to be weighed against an adversary's military power and a probability of conflict with him.[39] None of these options is currently realistically available to the Czech Republic, which makes it highly dependent on NATO for its security, and on the United States, as NATO's principal guarantor.

Historically, the Czech Republic often chose the route of conciliation with a threat rather than fighting it. Sometimes, the Czech Republic's choices were made in a geopolitical context of other European allies' failure to uphold their security commitments (such as France and the United Kingdom prior to World War II). While one can argue that the more acutely an ally perceives a threat, the more militarily dependent on another ally it will be, the two are not the same. A perception of a threat does not

---

[36] Admittedly, many factors affect whether a country can be judged "safe" for international investments. Similarly, states have other tools, such as tax incentives, to attract foreign capital.

[37] Snyder, *Alliance Politics*, p. 175.

[38] Ibid.

[39] Ibid.

automatically translate into military dependence on others, particularly since the most assured way to guarantee one's survival is to prioritize advancing one's own military capabilities.

Public Perceptions

The last salient factor that the book analyzes, and that has the potential to affect international cooperation in democratic countries, are the general public's perceptions. According to James Fearon, who analyzes the impact of domestic political audiences on the escalation of international conflicts, negotiations between governments of different states can be understood on two levels: (1) the international level, where the focus is on the nation-state, and (2) the domestic level, where the focus is on a variety of domestic actors, including political parties, social classes, interest groups, legislators, and public opinion.[40] Democracies in general face a higher audience cost relative to authoritarian regimes when negotiating issues of interest because they need to sustain their constituents' support throughout several election cycles, while the authoritarian regimes are accountable to a much smaller set of privileged groups and individuals.[41]

The policymakers' perceptions play a critical role in understanding alliance bargaining power. A position that a government will take on a particular issue, then, is said to be determined by the structure of coalitions that pressure that government. The goal of the government is to achieve its foreign policy aims without major impact on domestic

---

[40] Fearon, "Domestic Political Audiences and the Escalation of International Disputes."

[41] Ibid.

actors and their distribution of power.⁴² After negotiators discuss tentative agreements among themselves on the international level, they approach their domestic constituents to build a coalition large enough to get the agreement ratified on the domestic level. In the case of the United States, the domestic balance of power and partisanship are central to the U.S. negotiating position.⁴³

Fearon's emphasis on two-level games—domestic and international—differs from a systemic-level analysis in three critical ways. First, it focuses on the theory of international bargaining rather than on giving analytical primacy to impacts of the international system on a state's foreign relations. Second, it emphasizes the statesman as the central strategic actor rather than focusing solely on nation-states. Third, it analyzes an actor's calculations of constraints and opportunities in both the domestic and international realms.⁴⁴ For this approach to be theoretically viable, specifications of domestic politics (the nature of the "win sets"), of the international negotiating environment (the determinants of interstate bargaining outcomes), and of the statesman's preferences must be clarified.⁴⁵ The two-level game dynamic is apparent from the way the Czech government navigated ballistic missile defense cooperation with the United States. What the Czechs thought about U.S.-Czech ballistic missile defense cooperation over time can be discerned from public polling data, as Figure 2 shows.⁴⁶

---

⁴² Putnam, "Diplomacy and Domestic Politics: The Logic of Two-Level Games."

⁴³ Peter B. Evans, Harold K. Jacobson, and Robert D. Putnam, *Double-Edged Diplomacy International Bargaining and Domestic Politics* (Berkeley, CA: University of California Press, 1993).

⁴⁴ Ibid., pp. 16 and 17.

⁴⁵ Ibid., p. 23.

⁴⁶ See for example Jan Červenka, "Americké protiraketové základny v ČR a Polsku z pohledu domácí veřejnosti" (U.S. Misisle Defense Bases in the Czech Republic and Poland from the Perspective of the Public),

Fig. 2. Support for a U.S. Missile Defense Site in the Czech Republic

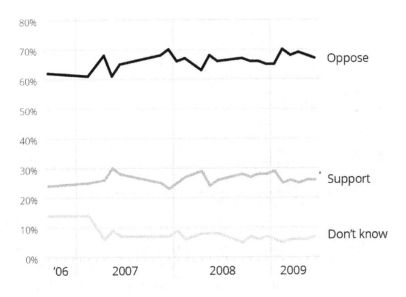

Note: Some figures have been interpolated.
Source: Centrum pro výzkum veřejného mínění (Public Opinion Research Centre).

Figure 3 illustrates several possible combinations of public opinion of an ally and the government's view of missile defense cooperation with that ally, and what these views mean for the likelihood of missile defense cooperation with another ally.

Centrum pro výzkum veřejného mínění (Public Opinion Research Center), September 10, 2007,
https://cvvm.soc.cas.cz/media/com_form2content/documents/c3/a1
136/f28/%c4%8cervenka,%20Jan.%20Americk%c3%a9%20protiraketov
%c3%a9%20z%c3%a1kladny%20v%20%c4%8cR%20a%20Polsku%20z%
20pohledu%20dom%c3%a1c%c3%ad%20ve%c5%99ejnosti.pdf.

Fig. 3. **Likely Consequences of Public and Government Perceptions of Allies**

	Government's View of Cooperation with Ally	
	NEGATIVE	POSITIVE
Public's View of Ally — POSITIVE	Government does not consider public perceptions important	Higher degree of cooperation
Public's View of Ally — NEGATIVE	Lower degree of cooperation	Cooperation not a factor in domestic politics

If a nation's leadership supports ballistic missile defense cooperation with its ally despite the population having a negative view of this ally, it would indicate that a government values an alliance with this ally more than it fears the domestic costs incurred by this cooperation. It could also indicate that the issue is not important or salient enough for the general public to care about in elections, so the government is free to pursue cooperation regardless of domestic politics considerations.

A government might have a negative view of defense cooperation with an ally despite the general public's overall positive view of this ally. This would be an indication that factors other than public perception are more significant in explaining ballistic missile defense cooperation among states.

A positive view of an ally and cooperation with it should result in higher degrees of missile defense cooperation. A negative view of both, then, ought to result in lower degrees of missile defense cooperation.

Lastly, if the two lines trend in different directions over time, it likely means that a nation's population treats an ally's image as distinct from the general question of the feasibility of cooperating with it. This would open an opportunity for the government to treat issues of alliance politics and defense cooperation with an ally separately. If the two lines trend in the same direction but at a different rate, it could indicate that the two issues are only tangentially related.

Conclusion

This brief foray into important theoretical perspectives on alliance cooperation and management paints a complicated picture of possible ways to organize thinking about how nations approach alliance formation and management. Yet, to one degree or another, they all leave out an important part of the picture: how people executing foreign policy think about their decisions, how their environment shapes those decisions, and how they approach their execution.

After all, relationships matter, and politics is people. Disregarding personalities involved in important national security decisions misses a critical element of the process. The case study of early U.S.-Czech missile defense cooperation in Chapter 3 illustrates as much.

Chapter Two
Brief History of the U.S. Ballistic Missile Defense Program

In any case, the whole ABM question touched off so intense and emotional a debate in this country as to be virtually without precedent on any issue of weaponry.

Bernard Brodie and Fawn Brodie
From *Crossbow to H-Bomb: The Evolution of the Weapons and Tactics of Warfare*, 1973

Before one introduces personalities involved in U.S.-Czech ballistic missile defense cooperation, one has to understand the state of U.S. ballistic missile defense efforts from a technological standpoint on the eve of December 2001, when the George W. Bush Administration announced its intent to withdraw from the 1972 Anti-Ballistic Missile (ABM) Treaty with the Russian Federation. Before that fateful decision was made, the treaty presented a legal impediment to any significant ballistic missile defense efforts.

U.S. Pre-ABM Treaty Missile Defense Efforts

Just like U.S. interest in nuclear weapons can be traced to what the United States learned about German plans for developing such weapons, U.S. interest in ballistic missile defense systems was sparked by the German use of V-2 rockets against Great Britain during World War II.[47] Many German scientists who worked on ballistic missile programs in Germany went on to participate in U.S. efforts after the end of the war.[48] A few visionary rocket scientists foresaw a future in which rocket fuel will be able to generate enough energy to propel humans to space—and to propel deadly payloads to targets thousands of miles away from their original launch sites. Considering how to defend oneself against such attacks was a natural extension of these trends.

Ballistic missile defense efforts led to the U.S. Army's first successful intercept of a dummy intercontinental-range ballistic missile warhead in 1962.[49] The first U.S. strategic missile defense interceptors were nuclear-armed, but the United States was aware of hit-to-kill technologies that would be politically more acceptable to the general public, particularly as negative effects of radiation fallout became more widely understood in the 1950s and 1960s.

As the Cold War with the Soviet Union threatened to turn into a hot war, the United States debated whether and how missile defense systems would affect strategic stability between the two main nuclear-armed superpowers. Much of this discussion was rooted in deterrence theory with questions focusing on whether missile defenses incentivized nuclear first strikes, stimulated an arms race, affected the arms control process, and destabilized relations between the United States and the Soviet Union. Unprecedented destructive power of nuclear weapons, increases in the number of warheads in the worlds' nuclear-

---

[47] Donald Baucom, "Origins of the Strategic Defense Initiative: Ballistic Missile Defense, 1944–1983," Strategic Defense Initiative Organization, December 1989, http://www.dtic.mil/dtic/tr/fulltext/u2/a242465.pdf.

[48] Perhaps most notable among them was Werhner Von Braun, a chief architect of the Saturn V rocket.

[49] Lawrence Kaplan, "Missile Defense: The First Sixty Years," Missile Defense Agency, August 15, 2008, p. 8.

armed countries' stockpiles, increasing diversity of delivery platforms, attack timelines shortened to minutes, increasing sophistication and yield of nuclear warheads, rising nuclear weapons costs, and nuclear weapons proliferation made these issues extremely salient in the late 1960s.[50]

Ballistic missile defenses have always been technologically challenging, and defense budgets limited. The United States started to develop a nation-wide ballistic missile defense system in the 1960s, but as Soviet long-range ballistic missiles advanced, it soon became clear that U.S. defenses would not be able to keep up with the threat. The Johnson Administration limited its missile defense program, the Sentinel, to addressing Chinese (rather than Soviet) ballistic missiles because the Soviet Union was building up long-range ballistic missile capabilities too quickly for the system to keep up at a politically acceptable cost. The Johnson Administration's limitations reflected its belief that the U.S. ballistic missile defense program was destabilizing because it contributed to an arms race, and that a better investment of U.S. dollars was in offensive forces to ensure that the United States has an assured second-strike capability.[51]

President Lyndon Johnson's Secretary of Defense Robert McNamara's view (also shared by many opponents of U.S. missile defense) that ballistic missile defenses were destabilizing because they incentivized a first nuclear strike was initially not shared in Moscow. "An antimissile system may cost more than an offensive one, but it is intended not for killing people but for saving human lives," said Soviet

---

[50] Keith Payne, *The Great American Gamble: Deterrence Theory and Practice from the Cold War to the Twenty-First Century* (Fairfax, VA: National Institute Press, 2008).

[51] Herbert Scoville and Robert Osborn, *Missile Madness* (Boston: Houghton Mifflin, 1970), https://books.google.com/books?id=GZcsAAAAYAAJ.

Prime Minister Aleksey Kosygin in 1967.[52] The Soviets had a vested interest in supporting the U.S. narrative that ballistic missile defenses are destabilizing because it helped to keep the United States from developing them. A significant ballistic missile defense capability would negate the Soviet Union's large investments in a land-based missile force.

Missile Defenses during the Nixon Administration

The Nixon Administration scaled down the Sentinel program and pursued more limited missile defense efforts under the banner of the Safeguard program. In defending the decision before Congress, President Richard Nixon's Secretary of Defense Melvin Laird stated:

> [T]he Sentinel system was ambiguous, at best. It was interpreted by some as the beginning of a 'thick' defense of our cities against Soviet attack. In fact, it could have been used for precisely that purpose. It could also have been construed as a system designed to protect our cities from surviving Soviet missiles after a surprise attack by the United States. Our review, therefore, convinced us that the original Sentinel was potentially provocative. As such, it appeared to us to be a step toward, rather than away from, an escalation of the arms race.[53]

---

[52] David S. Yost, *Soviet Ballistic Missile Defense and the Western Alliance* (Cambridge, MA: Harvard University Press, 1988), p. 98.

[53] United States Congress Senate Committee on Foreign Relations Subcommittee on International Organization and Disarmament Affairs, *Strategic and Foreign Policy Implications of ABM Systems: Hearings Before the United States Senate Committee on Foreign Relations, Subcommittee on International Organization and Disarmament Affairs, Ninety-First Congress, First Session,* Parts 1–3 (Washington DC: U.S. Government Printing

This negative view of ballistic missile defense programs as something that made the Soviet Union more aggressive rather than something that moved it toward a more defensive posture was formally codified in the 1972 ABM Treaty. The ABM Treaty imposed qualitative and quantitative restrictions on missile defense system research, development, and deployment, stating that "effective measures to limit anti-ballistic missile systems would be a substantial factor in curbing the race in strategic offensive arms and would lead to a decrease in the risk of outbreak of war involving nuclear weapons."[54] The treaty was controversial—as was the idea that a government ought to just give up on defending its citizens in the face of a ballistic missile threat.

The ABM Treaty experience illustrated an often-ignored effect of arms control on U.S. weapon programs: Because arms control treaties limit knowledge of the systems they are purported to control, they make it more difficult to understand how adversaries that do not comply with their treaty obligations generate advantages through uses of these systems against the United States. The ABM Treaty also made it more difficult to obtain congressional support and funding for even a limited Safeguard missile defense system in compliance with the treaty because it made Safeguard compete with other weapons systems that were not limited by arms control and therefore could get developed and fielded with few or no restrictions.[55] Safeguard's only operational site was active from October

---

Office, 1969), p. 169, https://books.google.com/books?id=UAo4ugEACAAJ.

[54] "Treaty Between the United States of America and the Union of Soviet Socialist Republics on the Limitation of Anti-Ballistic Missile Systems," U.S. Department of State, 1972, https://www.state.gov/t/avc/trty/101888.htm#text.

[55] Baucom, "Origins of the Strategic Defense Initiative: Ballistic Missile Defense, 1944–1983," p. 201.

1975 to February 1976 before Congress decided to stop funding it altogether.[56]

Despite the ABM Treaty, the United States continued limited treaty-compliant ballistic missile defense research and development. Over time, major technological advances and breakthroughs in fields like miniaturization, optics, and electronics made non-nuclear missile defense systems technologically possible and cheaper (although still not cheap). The United States was able to leverage these new technologies and developments for conceptually exploring hit-to-kill interceptors and directed energy weapons.[57]

The Reagan Administration and the Strategic Defense Initiative

The role of U.S. missile defense systems was to some extent reconsidered in the late 1970s and early 1980s as a consequence of a perceived Soviet drive for nuclear superiority and technological advances.[58] In a rebuke to proponents of action-reaction theories that stipulated that the U.S. is a first mover in an arms race with the Soviet Union, President Jimmy Carter's Secretary of Defense Harold Brown described the dynamic between U.S. defense and Soviet offense in the following manner: "Soviet spending has shown no response to U.S. restraint—when we build, they build; when we cut, they build."[59]

---

[56] Ibid., pp. 176 and 177.

[57] Ibid., p. 224.

[58] Donald Baucom, "The Rise and Fall of Brilliant Pebbles," *The Journal of Social, Political and Economic Studies*, Vol. 29, No. 2 (Summer 2004), p. 144.

[59] "Hearings before the Commitee on the Budget United States Senate," Senate Budget Committee, April 18, 1979,
https://books.google.com/books?id=i0hLAQAAIAAJ&pg=PA140&lpg=PA140&dq=%E2%80%9CSoviet+spending+has+shown+no+response+to+U.S.+restraint%E2%80%94when+we+build+they+build;+when+we+

President Ronald Reagan took office dissatisfied with the mutual vulnerability paradigm and became a staunch proponent of the United States advancing its ability to defend itself from Soviet (and potentially other states') ballistic missiles. In his 1983 address to the nation, President Reagan stated:

> What if free people could live secure in the knowledge that their security did not rest upon the threat of instant U.S. retaliation to deter a Soviet attack, that we could intercept and destroy strategic ballistic missiles before they reached our own soil or that of our allies? I know this is a formidable, technical task, one that may not be accomplished before the end of this century.[60]

President Reagan's speech marked a new era of ballistic missile defense advancements. The Reagan Administration created the Strategic Defense Initiative Office (SDIO), responsible for ABM Treaty-compliant missile defense research in April 1984.[61] Three years later, President Reagan approved a program involving six major acquisition initiatives: (1) a boost-phase surveillance and tracking system, (2) a space-based interceptor, (3) a battle management/command-and-control and communications

---

cut+they+build,%E2%80%9D&source=bl&ots=JqsyNhE5QS&sig=ACfU3U0JZRL8YINyxK6YxNOQIOOg1ksbdQ&hl=en&ppis=_e&sa=X&ved=2ahUKEwi_2cvd3qvmAhUiqlkKHdQ3C-8Q6AEwAHoECAkQAg#v=onepage&q=%E2%80%9CSoviet%20spending%20has%20shown%20no%20response%20to%20U.S.%20restraint%E2%80%94when%20we%20build%20they%20build%3B%20when%20we%20cut%20they%20build%2C%E2%80%9D&f=false.

[60] Ronald Reagan, "From the Address to the Nation by President Ronald Reagan March 23, 1983 'Peace and National Security,'" *Daedalus* Vol. 114, No. 3 (1985), p. 370.

[61] Baucom, "Origins of the Strategic Defense Initiative: Ballistic Missile Defense, 1944–1983," p. 145.

system, (4) a space-based surveillance and tracking system, (5) a ground-based surveillance and tracking system, and (6) the Exoatmospheric Reentry-vehicle Interceptor Subsystem (ERIS), also called a ground-based interceptor.[62]

If the United States seriously pursued a development and deployment of these systems, it would have to renegotiate or withdraw from the ABM Treaty. Such steps would require the Reagan Administration to spend its political capital and convince a reluctant Congress to support its efforts. And, while the United States continued debating ABM Treaty-related matters throughout the late 1980s, real-world events interfered in a largely unexpected manner.

For a majority of U.S. policymakers, who were hesitant about withdrawing from the ABM Treaty to begin with, the fall of the Soviet Union in 1991 provided an additional rationale that, with its main adversary gone, the United States no longer needed to develop and deploy a large-scale layered comprehensive ballistic missile defense system.

End of the Cold War and U.S. Missile Defense Efforts

President George H. W. Bush reduced the Strategic Defense Initiative (SDI) to a more limited Global Protection Against Limited Strikes (GPALS) program. The latter was meant to address smaller and more primitive ballistic missile attacks against the U.S. homeland, allies, and potentially even the Soviet Union.[63] Eventually, the GPALS program was further scaled down to intercept ballistic missiles launched by third world states, and about 200 re-entry vehicles (because that is how many the United States believed a rogue

---

[62] Baucom, "The Rise and Fall of Brilliant Pebbles," p. 147.
[63] Kaplan, "Missile Defense: The First Sixty Years," p. 15.

Soviet/Russian submarine commander could launch).[64] Even that scope was far greater than what is meant today by "limited ballistic missile defense system."

During the first Persian Gulf War (1990–1991) millions of Americans watched the events unfold in real-time on their televisions.[65] The war showcased U.S. technological superiority—and more important for missile defense, included Scud (a short-range missile of Soviet/Russian origin) versus Patriot (a U.S. short-range missile and air defense system) engagements that captured the imagination of the American public. For members of Congress and the general public, the war underscored the importance of regional (shorter-range) ballistic missile defense.

This experience and the Clinton Administration's desire to preserve the ABM Treaty contributed to a perception that the United States needed to address more-pressing and less-controversial shorter-range theater ballistic missiles rather than focusing on a robust SDI or GPALS-type missile defense program. Additionally, congressional opposition to the GPALS program, and particularly to its space-based interceptor component called Brilliant Pebbles, made the pursuit of the program politically costly.[66] The Clinton Administration cancelled the Brilliant Pebbles program, arguing that the funding levels (and political guidance) provided by Congress meant that the United States could deploy only a single Exoatmospheric Kill Vehicle.[67]

---

[64] Thomas Karako and Ian Williams, "Missile Defense 2020: Next Steps for Defending the Homeland," Center for Strategic and International Studies, April 2017, http://missilethreat.csis.org/wp-content/uploads/2017/04/170406_Karako_MissileDefense2020_Web.pdf.

[65] Baucom, "The Rise and Fall of Brilliant Pebbles," p. 170.

[66] Ibid., pp. 176–180.

[67] Ibid., p. 184.

The Clinton Administration conducted a major re-evaluation of the U.S. ballistic missile defense efforts, renamed the SDIO the Ballistic Missile Defense Organization (BMDO) to better reflect its new priorities, and decreased funding for long-range ballistic missile defense programs. President Clinton's Secretary of Defense Les Aspin, who reportedly prided himself for taking the "stars out of Star Wars," declared "the end of the 'Star Wars' era" in 1993.[68] The Clinton Administration focused on the theater missile defense and air defense development in its first term, and attributed only secondary importance to a national missile defense system.[69] The U.S. homeland missile defense program was initially reduced to being able to intercept five relatively less-sophisticated long-range ballistic missiles, and later, scaled back up to address 20 long-range ballistic missiles equipped with more advanced countermeasures.[70] The Clinton Administration assessed such an endeavor as requiring a deployment of initially 20, and later 250, Ground-Based Midcourse Defense (GMD) interceptors, a notably larger number than the 44 GMD interceptors that the United States deploys today.[71]

The GMD deployment-number re-evaluation reflected the Clinton Administration's concerns over ballistic missile proliferation and increasing range and sophistication of these systems, particularly in the light of North Korea's nuclear weapon and ballistic missile programs. The Clinton Administration considered the "assured destruction" paradigm undesirable with North Korea, which highlighted that much of the Cold War thinking about ballistic missile

---

[68] Melissa Healy, "'Star Wars' Era Ends as Aspin Changes Focus," *Los Angeles Times*, May 14, 1993, https://www.latimes.com/archives/la-xpm-1993-05-14-mn-35185-story.html.

[69] Kaplan, "Missile Defense: The First Sixty Years," p. 16.

[70] Karako and Williams, "Missile Defense 2020: Next Steps for Defending the Homeland," p. 17.

[71] Ibid.

defense was not easily applied to a post-Cold War world with multiple ballistic-missile-armed and nuclear-armed adversaries and potential adversaries. Congress agreed.

The 1999 National Missile Defense Act (NMDA) balanced the need to protect the U.S. homeland from less-sophisticated, less-predictable, and less-numerous long-range ballistic missile threats with abiding by the restrictions in the ABM Treaty. The NMDA stated:

> It is the policy of the United States to deploy as soon as is technologically possible an effective National Missile Defense system capable of defending the territory of the United States against limited ballistic missile attack (whether accidental, unauthorized, or deliberate) with funding subject to the annual authorization of appropriations and the annual appropriation of funds for National Missile Defense, while continuing to seek negotiated reductions in Russia's nuclear forces.[72]

The word "limited" meant that U.S. missile defense efforts would not undermine Russia's nuclear deterrent, which would be perceived as destabilizing.

In his signing statement to the NMDA, President Clinton emphasized that any future missile defense program must be "be operationally effective, cost-effective, and enhance our security," and indicated his preference for maintaining the ABM Treaty framework.[73] The Clinton Administration, however, decided to defer the decision about a national missile defense deployment and dealing

---

[72] National Missile Defense Act of 1999, Public Law 106–38, §2.

[73] "Statement on Signing the National Missile Defense Act of 1999 (Pres Bill Clinton Speech)(Transcript)," *Weekly Compilation of Presidential Documents*, Vol. 35, No. 30 (1999), p. 1471.

with its potential implications for the ABM Treaty to its successor.[74]

The Clinton Administration was aware of potentially negative impacts of homeland ballistic missile deployments on allied security, as such deployments could create a perception that the United States is pursuing a "fortress USA," while leaving allies vulnerable to ballistic missiles. "Origins of the European missile defense go back to the Clinton Administration and rose out of concerns over decoupling of U.S. and European security in the light of an advancing ballistic missile threat. The Clinton Administration directed the BMDO to develop options to defend Europe," according to the Honorable Frank Rose, who worked at the Department of Defense during the initial missile defense discussions between the United States and the Czech Republic.[75]

ABM Treaty Dead... At Last

The George W. Bush (Bush 43) Administration "inherited" the results of the BMDO's efforts and made one of its top priorities the development of a limited national missile defense system.[76] In order to do so, the Bush 43 Administration withdrew from the ABM Treaty in June 2002.[77] The withdrawal removed a legal obstacle to ballistic missile defense research, development, and deployment. It

---

[74] Kaplan, "Missile Defense: The First Sixty Years," p. 17.

[75] Author interview with the Honorable Frank Rose, formerly of the Office of the Secretary of Defense, on U.S.-Czech missile defense cooperation, in person, January 15, 2019.

[76] News release, "Secretary Rumsfeld Interview with CNN Late Edition," U.S. Department of Defense, September 13, 2001, http://archive.defense.gov/Transcripts/Transcript.aspx?TranscriptID=1624.

[77] The Bush-43 Administration gave the official notice to withdraw six months prior, in December 2001.

also made it somewhat easier to make the case for ballistic missile defenses before Congress because research and development resources would not be "wasted" by pursuing systems that could never be deployed due to U.S. arms control obligations.

The Bush Administration coordinated its decision to withdraw from the treaty with domestic players in the United States, the Russian Federation, and U.S. allies, particularly in the North Atlantic Treaty Organization (NATO). The Russian Federation was unable to convince the Bush Administration to stay within the legal framework of the ABM Treaty, although it received the news of the ABM Treaty's demise rather calmly. "Therefore I fully believe that the decision taken by the president of the United States does not pose a threat to the national security of the Russian Federation," stated Russian President Vladimir Putin in December 2001.[78] Then in February 2002, he accused the United States of causing an arms race and undermining global stability by pursuing its missile defense plans.[79] Nevertheless, not even three months later, in May, Russia went on to sign the Strategic Offensive Reductions Treaty (SORT, or Moscow Treaty), which mandated the largest strategic offensive arms reductions in arms control history.

"Once the Bush Administration got out of the ABM Treaty, it started to solve the problem of how to cooperate with allies on missile defense," according to the Honorable

---

[78] Terence Neilan, "Bush Pulls Out of ABM Treaty; Putin Calls Move a Mistake," *The New York Times*, December 13, 2001, https://www.nytimes.com/2001/12/13/international/bush-pulls-out-of-abm-treaty-putin-calls-move-a-mistake.html.

[79] Thomas Shanker and Mark Landler, "Putin Says U.S. Is Undermining Global Stability," *The New York Times*, February 10, 2007, https://www.nytimes.com/2007/02/11/world/europe/11munich.html.

Frank Rose.[80] Russia voiced its objections to U.S. missile defense efforts more vocally when it became clear that the United States was considering Eastern European countries that used to be a part of the Soviet bloc for ballistic missile defense deployments.[81] Never mind that the missile defense system "was not aimed at Russia or China. The part we tried to negotiate with Europe was aimed at Iran and North Korea," according to Dr. Steven Bucci, formerly Secretary Donald Rumsfeld's military assistant.[82]

The Bush 43 Administration did not have to start to build a ballistic missile defense system entirely from scratch. Due to decades of U.S. ABM Treaty-compliant research and development, it had options to continue to pursue an initial set of capabilities in various stages of research and development (for long-range ballistic missile defense systems) and deployment (for short-range and medium-range ballistic missile defense systems).

The Bush 43 Administration felt a sense of urgency regarding ballistic missile defense deployments.[83] "Secretary Rumsfeld was of the opinion that we do not have time to wait to deploy a perfect missile defense system. We needed to push out as much defensive capability as we could," according to Dr. Bucci.[84] As to where they would be deployed, "the Bush Administration evaluated which

---

[80] Author interview with the Honorable Frank Rose, Office of the Secretary of Defense, on U.S.-Czech missile defense cooperation.

[81] A government official likened the situation to a friend dating one's ex: "You just don't like it."

[82] Author interview with Steven Bucci, former military assistant to U.S. Secretary of Defense Donald Rumsfeld, 2001 to 2005, by phone, January 16, 2019.

[83] News release, "Secretary Rumsfeld Interview with Group of Reporters," U.S. Department of Defense, July 13, 2001, http://archive.defense.gov/Transcripts/Transcript.aspx?TranscriptID=1487.

[84] Author interview with Steven Bucci.

countries wanted components of a U.S. missile defense system and kept its options open as far as their placement goes," according to Ambassador J.D. Crouch, President Bush 43's first-term Assistant Secretary of Defense for International Security Policy, U.S. Ambassador to Romania in 2004 and 2005, and Assistant to the President and Deputy National Security Advisor until June 2007.[85] Congress supported efforts to deploy limited long-range ballistic missile defense systems against Iran and North Korea, unlike its continued opposition to a comprehensive ballistic missile defense against Russian long-range ballistic missiles.[86]

The Bush 43 Administration planned on deploying "ground-based interceptors, sea-based interceptors, additional Patriot (PAC-3) units, and sensors based on land, at sea, and in space" in the 2004–2005 timeframe. The President also emphasized the important role that U.S. allies and partner nations would play in U.S. missile defense plans:

> Because the threats of the 21st century also endanger our friends and allies around the world, it is essential that we work together to defend against them. The Defense Department will develop and deploy missile defenses capable of protecting not only the United States and our deployed forces, but also our friends and allies. The United States will also structure our missile defense program in a

---

[85] Author interview with Ambassador J.D. Crouch, Assistant Secretary of Defense for International Security Policy from 2001 to 2003, and Assistant to the President and Deputy National Security Advisor from March 2005 to June 2007, by phone, January 11, 2019.

[86] "President Announces Progress in Missile Defense Capabilities," December 17, 2002, https://georgewbush-whitehouse.archives.gov/news/releases/2002/12/text/20021217.html.

manner that encourages industrial participation by other nations.[87]

"The Bush Administration started informal discussions with NATO allies in July 2002," stated the Honorable Frank Rose.[88] "We wanted to demonstrate we stood with our allies as much as they stood with us," Dr. Bucci said about the initial missile defense thinking of the Bush 43 Administration.[89] The Czech Republic saw an opportunity in participating in a U.S. ballistic missile defense program. And this is where the story of official U.S.-Czech ballistic missile defense cooperation begins.

---

[87] Ibid.
[88] Author interview with the Honorable Frank Rose.
[89] Author interview with Steven Bucci.

Chapter Three
Early U.S.-Czech Ballistic Missile Defense Cooperation

The Czech Republic's strategic interests include . . . [r]educing the risk of a WMD attack (using rockets or other weapons) against the territory of the Czech Republic.

Czech *National Security Strategy*, 2003

Chapter Three familiarizes the reader with the Czech system of government to the extent that it is important to understand the case study. It outlines early U.S.-Czech ballistic missile defense cooperation. This cooperation spanned the time frame from September 2002 to January 2007, when the United States formally requested that the Czech Republic host a U.S. X-band radar on its territory.[90] During this timeframe, these efforts had varying degrees of intensity and involvement. They largely had to do with expressions of both countries' preliminary interests to cooperate on ballistic missile defense. As the United States and the Czech Republic became more involved in these informal negotiations, preliminary discussions focused on narrowing down a location for a future ballistic missile defense site on Czech territory. This chapter is organized chronologically and distinguishes among different Czech governments.

---

[90] The terms "X-band radar" and "radar" are used interchangeably in the context of the Czech Republic potentially hosting the asset.

A Brief Note on the Czech System of Governance

What does it mean that this chapter distinguishes among different Czech governments? Understanding the Czech system of governance is important for placing the case study in its proper context. U.S.-Czech ballistic missile defense cooperation was prominent on the domestic level and even contributed to the fall of one of the Czech governments. Chapter Three discusses the general way in which a Czech government functions, keeping in mind that a detailed understanding is not essential to understanding the case study.

The Czech Republic is a parliamentary democracy. It has a multi-party system, which means that several political parties compete for electoral votes. Some of these parties can be small and relatively new, popping up just in time for the next election cycle. Some of them are more established and have existed more or less since the Czech Republic was founded in 1993. Generally speaking (although not always), the more established parties are larger, more stable, and have more resources at their disposal than the "newcomers."

The legislative branch consists of the Parliament, which is divided between the Chamber of Deputies (200 members elected for a four-year term), and the Senate (81 members elected for a six-year term with a third of the Senate up for re-election every two years).[91] Political parties have to meet

---

[91] The president—whose role is otherwise largely symbolic—can dissolve the Chamber of Deputies under special circumstances outlined in the constitution. The president cannot dissolve the Senate. In the case of a dissolution of the Chamber of Deputies, preliminary elections are called.

a 5 percent electoral vote threshold to obtain a mandate in the Chamber of Deputies.[92]

A government, headed by a prime minister, is instituted when it can obtain the Chamber of Deputies' support. A political party that wins an election usually gets a first go at assembling a government, but a winning party may not be the one that ends up in the final formed government due to the nature of the multi-party system.[93] It is extremely unlikely that one political party would obtain more than 50 percent of the vote in the Chamber of Deputies (the threshold needed for a government to obtain the Chamber of Deputies' confidence), and so coalition building among parties that passed the 5 percent threshold that is necessary to be represented in the Chamber of Deputies is common.

The Chamber of Deputies can also initiate a no-confidence vote against a sitting government if it has enough mandates to proceed with the motion.[94] Should a vote of no confidence be successful, the government falls, and negotiations among political parties represented in the Chamber of Deputies to form a government begin anew.[95]

---

[92] Any party that reaches 1.5 percent of the votes has the right to be reimbursed for electoral expenses by the Czech state; this assistance is allocated based on the share of electoral votes — the more people vote for the party, the more money the party receives. Electoral coalitions of two parties must meet a 10 percent threshold, three parties must meet a 15 percent threshold, and four parties must meet a 20 percent threshold to be represented in the Chamber of Deputies.

[93] For example, if a winning party A obtains 25 percent of the electoral votes and corresponding mandates in the Chamber of Deputies, and coalition parties B, C, and D each obtain 20 percent of electoral votes and corresponding mandates, parties B, C, and D can obtain a majority vote in the Chamber of Deputies while party A will end up an opposition party. This situation happened with the May 2010 elections.

[94] The initiation of a no-confidence vote requires 50 parliamentarians in favor.

[95] This requires 101 parliamentarians in favor.

A new government that is a result of these negotiations must obtain the Chamber of Deputies' confidence.

In any election, a winning party usually obtains more than 20 percent of the vote, and the difference between the political party that wins elections with the largest number of votes and the party with the second-largest number of votes can be fairly small. Regardless of the vote breakdown, however, coalition building is a necessary feature of the Czech parliamentary system.

The executive branch, represented by the president and his office, does not have the same weight as the legislative branch. The president is largely a representative figure with very little executive power. He gets involved in international affairs largely through diplomatic relations (such as when meeting with other heads of state), and, generally speaking, does not play a major role in negotiations with other countries. The judiciary branch, represented by the courts, is not a major player in Czech foreign policy, although the Constitutional Court might be required to comment on the constitutionality of international agreements upon the request of the Parliament.

Early U.S.-Czech Ballistic Missile Defense Cooperation

There are several interesting aspects to early U.S.-Czech ballistic missile defense cooperation. First, it is surprising how little the Czechs knew about it. This is true not only for the general public, in which case a lack of interest in the technical details of a foreign defense system is understandable—but also for a large majority of Czech parliamentarians who were just as uninformed about U.S.-Czech missile defense cooperation as the rest of the country. Consequently, the understanding of how ballistic missile defense systems work was largely perfunctory among the

Czech public and its political representatives. Second, early Czech ballistic missile defense discussions with the United States were run from the Ministry of Defense, while the Ministry of Foreign Affairs took the lead later during the official part of U.S.-Czech ballistic missile defense negotiations. This was due to the technical nature of the preliminary discussions and because the Ministry of Defense administers military training areas that were considered potential locations for a future U.S. ballistic missile defense site.

One exception to the general lack of interest in a potential Czech role in the U.S. ballistic missile defense program was Jiří Payne's June 2000 letter addressed to Czech President Václav Havel. Payne, then-deputy chairman of the Foreign Affairs Committee of the Czech Chamber of Deputies and leader of the permanent Czech delegation to the NATO Parliamentary Assembly, requested that the Czech Security Council consider potential opportunities to cooperate on missile defense with the United States.[96] Payne argued that the proliferation of ballistic missiles and weapons of mass destruction threaten Czech security, and that missile defenses offer a solution to this problem.[97] Years before Americans would make a formal offer to the Czech Republic, and months before December 2001 when President Bush 43 announced a U.S. withdrawal from the Anti-Ballistic Missile (ABM) Treaty, Payne argued that it was in the Czech interest to host a U.S. missile defense radar.[98] The Czech Security Council did not take up the issue at that time, and there was no significant interest in it on the part of the Czech government as a whole.

---

[96] Jiří Payne, "Dopis presidentu Václavu Havlovi" (Letter to President Václav Havel), June 13, 2000, http://www.payne.cz/old/nmd/dopis.htm.
[97] Ibid.
[98] Ibid.

The Špidla Government: July 15, 2002–August 4, 2004

The government of Prime Minister Vladimíra Špidla, led by the Czech Social Democratic Party (ČSSD), supported technical discussions between the United States and the Czech Republic. The government did some preliminary work not only to get the United States to consider the Czech Republic as a potential missile defense host site, but also to provide information that became a basis for future missile defense cooperation discussions between the two countries. "Missile defense discussions between the United States and the Czech Republic were rather informal in the 2002–2006 timeframe. At the time, few understood potential long-term consequences that such cooperation could have," according to Karel Ulík, desk officer for Ballistic Missile Defense and Weapons of Mass Destruction Policy at the Defense Policy Department of the Czech Ministry of Defense from 2002 to 2007.[99]

The Czech media reported on the Bush 43 Administration's decision to withdraw from the ABM Treaty in 2002 but these reports generated almost no interest among the Czech general public.[100] The Honorable David Trachtenberg, Principal Deputy Assistant Secretary of Defense for International Security Policy from 2001 to 2003, visited Prague in 2002 to explain the rationale for the ABM Treaty withdrawal and stated: "The Czech Republic understood our rationale for missile defense and was supportive."[101] He also noted that "representatives of the

---

[99] Author interview with Karel Ulík, WhatsApp video conference, January 12, 2019.

[100] President Bush announced the withdrawal in December 2001 and provided the Russian Federation a six-month notice in accordance with the ABM Treaty.

[101] Author interview with the Honorable David Trachtenberg, Principal Deputy Assistant Secretary of Defense for International Security Policy

Czech government expressed a rather robust willingness to participate in U.S. missile defense plans."[102]

Despite a general agreement across the Czech political spectrum on potential ballistic missile defense cooperation with the United States as a net positive, this view was not shared universally. For example, the Czech Communist Party of Bohemia and Moravia (KSČM), a perennial of the Czech post-Cold War political scene, has historically opposed any cooperation with the United States due to its anti-Americanism and affinity for the Russian Federation.[103]

Czech Defense Minister Jaroslav Tvrdík (ČSSD) said he welcomed expert-level technical consultations about ballistic missile defense and expressed interest in Czech participation in the U.S. program during his September 2002 visit to Washington, D.C. While these discussions were merely exploratory and non-committal, Defense Minister Tvrdík seemed to indicate that other NATO states, as well as other allied countries, would benefit from ballistic missile defense capabilities.[104] These comments were controversial for some in the Czech Republic. For example, Czech Member of Parliament Vojtěch Filip (KSČM) argued that such cooperation would make the Czech Republic a target for adversaries.[105] He even asked Minister Tvrdík to resign for these comments, which Tvrdík did not do.

---

from 2001 to 2003, on U.S.-Czech missile defense cooperation, in person, January 6, 2019.

[102] Ibid.

[103] Stanislav Houdek, Zuzana Janská, and Pavel Otto, "Česko může hostit americké rakety, tvrdí v USA" (The Czech Republic Can Host U.S. Interceptors, So They Say in the United States), *Hospodářské noviny*, October 3, 2002, https://archiv.ihned.cz/c1-11601640-cesko-muze-hostit-americke-rakety-tvrdi-v-usa.

[104] "Tvrdík: V USA jsem nic nesliboval" (Tvrdík: I Did Not Promise Anything in the United States), *Hospodářské noviny*, September 20, 2002, https://archiv.ihned.cz/c1-11530250-tvrdik-v-US-jsem-nic-nesliboval.

[105] "Zahraničních politika České republiky data 9/2002" (Czech Foreign Policy Data 9/2002), Ministerstvo zahraničních věcí ČR (Czech Ministry

In October 2002, Czech Foreign Minister Cyril Svoboda of the Christian and Democratic Union-Czechoslovak People's Party (KDU-ČSL) informed the press that the government has not decided one way or another whether it would participate in a U.S. ballistic missile defense system, but that it has a "generally positive" attitude toward the project.[106] The Czech Republic also supported NATO's decision to initiate a NATO missile defense feasibility study in November 2002.[107] The study examined "options for protecting Alliance territory, forces and population centers against the full range of missile threats...consistent with the indivisibility of Allied security."[108]

The issues related to weapons of mass destruction and ballistic missile proliferation, as well as options of defending populations and installations from them, gathered more attention within the Czech government in 2003. The Czech Republic and other NATO states are within a ballistic missile range of several non-NATO countries that are perceived as (potential) adversaries. The Czech leadership indicated its concern over ballistic missile proliferation on multiple occasions, including in the Czech Republic's strategic documents. The Czech government officials discussed ballistic missile threats to the Czech Republic and to NATO publicly and privately. There was

---

of Foreign Affairs), September 2002,
https://www.mzv.cz/public/17/23/bf/991846_920825__09_2002_data.doc.

[106] Ibid. "Ujišťuji všechny, že nikdy Česká republika neřekla ústy žádného člena vlády, že jsme se rozhodli pro tu, či onu participaci (na projektu)" ("Let me assure you all that no representative of the Czech government has ever promised to participate one way or another (on the missile defense project"), and "obecně příznivý přístup" ("generally positive attitude").

[107] North Atlantic Treaty Organization, "NATO Prague Summit Declaration," November 21, 2002,
https://www.nato.int/cps/en/natohq/official_texts_19552.htm.
[108] Ibid.

no significant divergence of opinions between the United States and the Czech Republic regarding Iranian and North Korean ballistic missile threats on the official level.[109]

In March 2003, Defense Minister Tvrdík argued that the Czech Republic potentially hosting elements of a U.S. missile defense system would increase NATO's and the EU's security.[110] The Czech *National Security Strategy* from the same year noted that the government will seek out an opportunity to participate in projects or systems designed to protect Czech territory from weapons of mass destruction and the consequences of ballistic missile proliferation.[111] In the context of discussing the document, Foreign Minister Svoboda stated that he was counting on the Czech Republic's participation in U.S. missile defense plans even though the document does not specifically mention the United States in this context.[112]

North Korean and Iranian ballistic missile programs were the primary drivers of U.S. ballistic missile defense deployments to the Czech Republic and Poland, officially announced in 2007. "North Korea was our [the U.S.'s] primary concern until about 2003, then we grew more

---

[109] Nikola Hynek, "Protiraketová obrana v současném strategickém a politickém kontextu. Vztah k odstrašování a dopad třetího pilíře na dynamiku mezi relevantními aktéry" (Missile Defense in the Contemporary Strategic and Political Context. The Connection to Deterrence and the Impact of the Third Site on the Dynamics Among Relevant Actors) *Mezinárodní vztahy*, April 2008, p. 14.

[110] Ministerstvo zahraničních věcí ČR (Czech Ministry of Foreign Affairs), "Zahraničních politika České republiky dokumenty 3/2003" (Czech Foreign Policy Documents 3/2003), https://www.mzv.cz/public/7f/c0/a2/23088_14945_Dok3_2003.doc.

[111] "Bezpečnostní strategie České republiky" (National Security Strategy of the Czech Republic), 2003, p. 12.

[112] Ministerstvo zahraničních věcí ČR (Czech Ministry of Foreign Affairs), "Zahraničních politika České republiky data 7-8/2003" (Czech Foreign Policy Data 7-8/2003), https://www.mzv.cz/public/ea/3e/8b/23102_14945_Data78_2003.doc

concerned about Iran's ballistic missile threat. Predictions were that Iran would have an ICBM as early as 2015," according to Ambassador Eric Edelman, Under Secretary of Defense for Policy during the Bush 43 Administration.[113] Preliminary missile defense discussions between the United States and the Czech Republic were confined to expert levels and did not attract significant public attention. "Initial meetings were very small, quiet, and carefully crafted," stated Ambassador Crouch.[114] These discussions clarified that the Czechs agreed with the U.S. threat assessment of Iranian ballistic missiles. "A broader discussion about threats was not common, and perhaps is not common today either but we agreed with the U.S. assessment of an Iranian ballistic missile threat on the expert and official level," according to Karel Ulík, desk officer for Ballistic Missile Defense and Weapons of Mass Destruction Policy at the Defense Policy Department in the Czech Ministry of Defense from 2002 to 2007.[115]

In September 2003, the United States provided the Czech Ministry of Defense with technical requirements that a potential missile defense site in the Czech Republic would have to meet to host a U.S. base.[116] In October 2003, Foreign Minister Svoboda stated that the United States did not offer the Czech Republic an opportunity to participate in a ballistic missile defense plan but that the discussions about this issue were "serious and sensitive."[117]

---

[113] Author interview with Ambassador Eric Edelman, Undersecretary of Defense for Policy 2005–2009, by phone, January 16, 2019.

[114] Author interview with Ambassador J.D. Crouch.

[115] Author interview with Karel Ulík, by phone, January 12, 2019.

[116] Government of the Czech Republic, "Anti-Missile Defence in the Czech Republic," September 22, 2009, https://www.vlada.cz/en/media-centrum/aktualne/anti-missile-defence-in-the-czech-republic--61942/.

[117] Ministerstvo zahraničních věcí ČR (Czech Ministry of Foreign Affairs), "Zahraničních politika České republiky data 10/2003," (Czech Foreign Policy Data 10/2003),

In February 2004, the Czech government acknowledged ongoing technical discussions on missile defense and gave Defense Minister Miroslav Kostelka (not formally affiliated with any political party) a mandate to continue such discussions to include "preliminary technical and technical-organizational" information regarding a potential missile defense host site.[118] In the light of this mandate, the Czech Ministry of Defense provided the United States with information about three locations that would be most suitable for hosting a missile defense site based on technical parameters requested by the Americans in the previous rounds of discussions.[119] The three locations were the Libavá military training area in the eastern part of the country, the Brdy military training area in the south-eastern part of the country, and the Boletice military training area in the southern part of the Czech Republic. The parameters had to do with the geological structure of the surrounding ground and supporting infrastructure.[120]

Despite this progress, Foreign Minister Svoboda denied the existence of political ballistic missile defense negotiations, even as he admitted the existence of expert-level discussions.[121] The distinction between political negotiations and expert-level discussion appears to be a

---

https://www.mzv.cz/public/c9/e1/81/23110_14945_Data10_2003.doc.

[118] Government of the Czech Republic, "Usnesení vlády České Republiky č. 119" (Government Resolution No. 119), February 4, 2004, https://kormoran.vlada.cz/usneseni/usneseni_webtest.nsf/0/4C0C759480015142C12571B6006BD017.

[119] Czech Ministry of Defense, "Chronologie vývoje projektu protiraketové obrany USA" (Chronology of U.S. Missile Defense Programs), http://www.army.cz/scripts/detail.php?id=8781.

[120] Ibid.

[121] Ministerstvo zahraničních věcí ČR (Czech Ministry of Foreign Affairs), "Zahraničních politika České republiky data 7-8/2004" (Czech Foreign Policy Data 7-8/2004), August 2004, https://www.mzv.cz/public/eb/f6/65/23146_14945_Data78_2004.doc.

little blurry since it is clear that expert-level discussions would not have been conducted had they not had the blessing of the Czech political leadership.

The Gross Government: August 4, 2004–April 25, 2005

The government of Prime Minister Stanislav Gross (ČSSD) was supported by a coalition of the ČSSD, the US-DEU (Freedom Union-Democratic Union), and KDU-ČSL. The government was entangled in domestic scandals and was not particularly effective at home or internationally. There was barely any mention of ballistic missile defense cooperation with the United States in the Czech media during this time. On the other side of the "pond," the United States was conducting its own internal missile defense development and deployment review. For all intents and purposes, missile defense discussions with the United States all but stalled during this period.

The Paroubek Government: April 25, 2005–September 4, 2006

The government of Prime Minister Jiří Paroubek (ČSSD) was supported by a coalition of the ČSSD, the US-DEU, and the KDU-ČSL. The latter half of the government's tenure was a time of significant activity regarding missile defense discussions between the United States and the Czech Republic, even though Prime Minister Paroubek later marginalized these discussions and tried to distance himself from them when it became politically expedient after the ČSSD's election loss in June 2006.[122]

---

[122] "S radarem přišla vláda ČSSD, přiznal expremiér Gross" (It was the ČSSD's Idea to Participate in the Radar Project, Admitted Ex-Prime

In March 2006, the Czech press reported that the Czech Republic was one of three European candidates to host elements of a U.S. missile defense system.[123] Two months later, the Czech press reported on a U.S. plan to build a ballistic missile defense site with 10 interceptors in Europe.[124] These reports marked the beginning of public discussions about U.S. missile defense plans in Europe and about a potential role that the Czech Republic could play in them. The reports generated first interest in the issue among the Czech population. The Russian Federation's initial reaction to these reports was negative.[125]

The flurry of activity between the U.S. and Czech governments and the Czech government's perceived lack of communication to the general public regarding this topic gave rise to the No Bases Initiative.[126] The No Bases Initiative was founded as a civic movement that opposed potential U.S. missile defense deployments. It was initially comprised of about two dozen non-governmental organizations and grew as missile defense discussions and negotiations between the United States and the Czech

---

Minister Gross), iDnes.cz, August 23, 2008, https://www.idnes.cz/zpravy/domaci/s-radarem-prisla-vlada-cssd-priznal-expremier-gross.A080823_083448_domaci_adb.

[123] The other two candidates were Poland and, somewhat less seriously, the United Kingdom. Ministerstvo zahraničních věcí ČR (Czech Ministry of Foreign Affairs), "Zahraničních politika České republiky data 3/2006" (Czech Foreign Policy Data 3/2006), March 2006, https://www.mzv.cz/public/74/15/11/73274_491937_Data_mesicniku_ZP2006_03.pdf.

[124] Ministerstvo zahraničních věcí ČR (Czech Ministry of Foreign Affairs), "Zahraničních politika České republiky data 5/2006" (Czech Foreign Policy Data 5/2006), May 2006, https://www.mzv.cz/public/fb/50/60/73282_491940_Data_mesicniku_ZP2006_05.pdf.

[125] Ibid.

[126] The No Bases Initiative still exists as an anti-American and anti-NATO organization.

Republic continued. The movement's goal was to "fight against the placement of a U.S. missile defense base on the Czech territory, in a non-violent matter."[127]

Despite years of ongoing bilateral discussions, the Czech Ministry of Defense confirmed ballistic missile defense consultations with the United States on a NATO-level only at this time in the fall of 2006.[128] The government's silence likely had to do with the upcoming June 2006 elections in the Czech Republic. According to one report, the Czech Republic and the United States had an agreement to not talk about missile defense discussions publicly until after the elections.[129] Be as it may, the fact that the question was not discussed prior to the elections, neither by Czech political parties nor by their voters, caused significant problems after the elections when it was time to build a coalition that could obtain the Chamber of Deputies' approval.

In July 2006, the now-lame-duck Paroubek government hosted U.S. officials and technical experts that assessed suitability of selected locations on Czech territory for a potential U.S. missile defense site.[130] The same month,

---

[127] Author translation from Czech. "Vznik společenské iniciativy Ne základnám" (Founding of the No Bases Initiative), August 1, 2006, http://www.nezakladnam.cz/cs/106_vznik-spolecenske-iniciativy-ne-zakladnam.

[128] Ministerstvo zahraničních věcí ČR (Czech Ministry of Foreign Affairs), "Zahraničních politika České republiky data 3/2006" (Czech Foreign Policy Data 3/2006).

[129] Ivona Remundová, "Vliv mediálního obrazu na činnost občanské iniciativy Ne základnám" (The Impact of the Media's Perceived Image on the No Bases Civic Initiative's Development), Univerzita Karlova v Praze (Charles University in Prague), 2012, https://dspace.cuni.cz/bitstream/handle/20.500.11956/42091/BPTX_2 010_1__0_135018_0_98702.pdf?sequence=1.

[130] Radek Honzák, "Američané chtějí základnu v Česku už od května" (Americans Wanted the Base in the Czech Republic Since May) *Hospodářské noviny* (*Economic Newspaper*), August 8, 2006,

North Korea tested longer-range ballistic missiles that could potentially reach the western United States.[131] The Czech Ministry of Foreign Affairs stated in a response to the test that ongoing missile defense discussions are entirely appropriate in the context of Iran's and North Korea's advancing ballistic missile programs.[132] The Czech government publicly acknowledged the ongoing technical-organizational consultations regarding ballistic missile defense with the United States.[133] The government also requested that the Minister of Foreign Affairs and Minister of Defense submit a joint recommendation on how the government should respond if asked to host missile defense elements in Czech locations previously surveyed by the United States.[134]

Based on the public reporting at the time, it was not entirely clear what these elements were going to be. Some news outlets reported the United States was considering deploying a radar and interceptors on one base in the Czech Republic, others reported only on interceptors, or only on a radar. As late as fall 2006, the U.S. government's public message was that it had not yet come to a definitive decision

---

https://archiv.ihned.cz/c1-19045630-americane-chteji-zakladnu-v-cesku-uz-od-kvetna.

[131] David Ensor et al., "U.S. Officials: North Korea Tests Long-Range Missile," CNN World, July 5, 2006, http://www.cnn.com/2006/WORLD/asiapcf/07/04/korea.missile/.

[132] Ministerstvo zahraničních věcí ČR (Czech Ministry of Foreign Affairs), "Zahraničních politika České republiky dokumenty 7-8/2006," (Czech Foreign Policy Documents 7-8/2006), August 2006, https://www.mzv.cz/public/6a/fa/28/73292_492010_Dokumenty_me sicniku_ZP2006_07_08.pdf.

[133] Government of the Czech Republic, "Usnesení vlády České Republiky č. 929" (Government Resolution No. 929), July 26, 2006, https://kormoran.vlada.cz/usneseni/usneseni_webtest.nsf/WebGovR es/CBA2A2543790623DC12571CE0047EDE2?OpenDocument.

[134] Ibid.

regarding the overall missile defense architecture and deployments to Europe.[135]

In the latter part of August, the U.S. Administration reportedly decided to abandon a plan to pursue an interceptor site in the Czech Republic, but continued to consider the Czech Republic for a potential radar site.[136] This step was wise because the Czech population would be unlikely to support an interceptor deployment, of which the U.S. Administration was aware.[137] Most Czech political parties agreed that an interceptor site would require a referendum.[138] There was a fragile majority consensus in the Czech Parliament that a radar site would not require a referendum, which was important because the Czechs would likely vote against hosting a U.S. ballistic missile defense component.

In August 2006, delegations of the Czech Ministry of Foreign Affairs and Ministry of Defense led by Tomáš Pojar, then-lead negotiator of U.S.-Czech missile defense agreements who later became First Deputy Minister of Foreign Affairs, met with representatives of the U.S. Missile

---

[135] Klára Tylová, "V Česku možná bude jen radar" (There Might Only Be a Radar in the Czech Republic), *Lidové Noviny* (*People's Newspaper*), August 17, 2006, https://www.lidovky.cz/domov/v-cesku-mozna-bude-jen-radar.A060817_073036_ln_domov_znk.

[136] "USA Zřejmě Neumístí Protiraketovou Základnu v ČR" (The U.S. Probably Will Not Build a Missile Defense Interceptor Site in the Czech Republic), *Hospodářské Noviny* (*Economic Newspaper*), August 28, 2006, https://domaci.ihned.cz/c1-19176960-usa-zrejme-neumisti-protiraketovou-zakladnu-v-cr.

[137] Author interview with Petr Suchý, Head of the Department of International Relations and European Studies, Faculty of Social Studies, Masaryk University, Czech Republic, WhatsApp, November 20, 2019.

[138] "USA Zřejmě Neumístí Protiraketovou Základnu v ČR" (The U.S. Probably Will Not Build a Missile Defense Interceptor Site in the Czech Republic).

Defense Agency (MDA) in Washington, DC.[139] At the meeting, the Americans expressed sensitivity to the rising opposition to a missile defense site in the Czech Republic. The Czechs and the Americans narrowed down a selection of a potential host site to two, from three previously considered, options.[140] The Boletice military training area was deemed unsuitable as a missile defense host site.[141] The Americans also provided the Czechs with more information regarding the plan for U.S. missile defense in Europe under consideration. These fairly involved meetings are illustrative of the Paroubek government's support for U.S.-Czech ballistic missile defense cooperation, however much Paroubek tried to distance himself from these discussions later.

In hindsight, the June 2006 elections to the Czech Chamber of Deputies were a pivotal moment in the history of U.S.-Czech ballistic missile defense cooperation. More broadly, they were important for the future direction of Czech foreign policy after the end on the Cold War. The ČSSD narrowly lost these elections, and talks about forming a potential coalition between the ČSSD and the victorious Civic Democratic Party (ODS) broke down. Consequently, the ČSSD became an opposition party—and with the shift came a reassessment of the party's previous foreign and defense policy.

---

[139] "Chronologie vývoje projektu protiraketové obrany USA" (Chronology of U.S. Missile Defense Programs).

[140] Daniel Anýž, "Američané Vyřadili Ze Hry Boletice" (Americans Are Not Interested in Boletice), *Hospodářské Noviny (Economic Newspaper)*, August 18, 2006, https://archiv.ihned.cz/c1-19120060-americane-vyradili-ze-hry-boletice.

[141] "Chronologie vývoje projektu protiraketové obrany USA" (Chronology of U.S. Missile Defense Programs).

The Debate Starts I: Pros of U.S.-Czech Ballistic Missile Defense Cooperation

The Czech Republic was a straightforward choice for a potential ballistic missile defense host country for the United States due to its geography and support for such cooperation across most of the political spectrum at the time when discussions about the matter started. Czech supporters of U.S.-Czech missile defense cooperation made several arguments for why the Czech Republic should participate in U.S. missile defense plans. They argued that such cooperation is critical to strengthening the transatlantic bond between Europe and the United States with an implicit understanding that it would place the Czech Republic even more firmly in the Western military and political structures.[142] This would lead to a net increase in Czech security.

"Geopolitically, the Czech diplomacy worried about Russia, wanted to strengthen the eastern part of NATO, but also worried about balancing German influence in the region in case German behavior changes in the future," according to former First Deputy Minister Pojar.[143] Those worries were informed by the Czech historical experience of a small state wedged among larger powers and occupied for a better part of its history by the West or the East. But the Czech government representatives also understood the

---

[142] Alexandr Vondra, "Zapojení ČR do projektu protiraketové obrany" (The Czech Republic's Participation in the Missile Defense Project), Ministerstvo zahraničních věcí ČR (Ministry of Foreign Affairs), September 11, 2006, https://www.mzv.cz/jnp/cz/o_ministerstvu/archivy/clanky_a_proje vy_ministru/clanky_a_projevy_ministra_vondry_2006/zapojeni_cr_do _projektu_protiraketove.html.

[143] Author interview with Tomáš Pojar, former First Deputy Minister of Foreign Affairs and lead negotiator of U.S.-Czech missile defense agreements, by phone, January 21, 2019.

need to develop means to counter the Iranian ballistic missile threat and what such a threat could mean for NATO.

By hosting a U.S. radar site that would contribute to a NATO-wide ballistic missile defense system, the Czech Republic would become a provider of security within NATO, rather than just its consumer.[144] "The Czechs wanted to prove that they were good NATO allies since they were still relatively new to the Alliance," said the Honorable David Trachtenberg.[145] Emphasizing the multilateral benefits of the project was important in the NATO context, particularly given the fact that some NATO members were generally less enthusiastic about it than others.[146] For example, Czech diplomacy had to work very hard to alleviate the German government's dislike of U.S.-Czech missile defense plans, and ultimately Germany supported NATO missile defense efforts (and by extension U.S.-Czech ballistic missile defense cooperation).

Even though the project was envisioned as a bilateral endeavor, U.S. and Czech political representatives argued for NATO-wide cooperation as the Alliance's ballistic missile defense consensus broadened.[147] The multilateral aspect was important to counter the opponents' (completely misplaced) narrative that hosting a U.S. missile defense site

---

[144] Nikola Hynek, "Protiraketová obrana v současném strategickém a politickém kontextu. Vztah k odstrašování a dopad třetího pilíře na dynamiku mezi relevantními aktéry" (Missile Defense in the Contemporary Strategic and Political Context. The Connection to Deterrence and the Impact of the Third Site on the Dynamics among Relevant Actors), *Mezinárodní vztahy* (*International Relations*), April 2008, p. 16.

[145] Author interview with the Honorable David Trachtenberg.

[146] Alexandr Vondra, "Alexandr Vondra: Postavme Se k Základně Čelem" (Let Us Face a Missile Base), *Hospodářské Noviny* (*Economic Newspaper*), August 3, 2006, https://archiv.ihned.cz/c1-19020660-alexandr-vondra-postavme-se-k-zakladne-celem.

[147] Vondra, "Zapojení ČR do projektu protiraketové obrany" (The Czech Republic's Participation in the Missile Defense Project).

was akin to "hosting" Soviet intermediate-range ballistic missiles in the late 1980s.[148] No reasonable student of history would consider the two events to be even remotely similar. Czechoslovakia had very little say in what kinds or types of Soviet forces would be stationed on its territory during the Cold War. Nevertheless, for some reason this line of argumentation resonated with certain segments of the Czech general public, as will be discussed below.

The relative newness of the Czech Republic as a NATO member, and worries about the extent to which Article V of the North Atlantic Treaty applied to it, played a role in the Czech willingness to negotiate about participating in U.S. missile defense plans.[149] Even as late as March 2007, Czech Foreign Minister Karel Schwarzenberg suggested that the Czech Republic wanted security guarantees beyond those stemming from the 1949 North Atlantic Treaty in exchange for hosting a U.S. missile defense site.[150]

Proponents of U.S.-Czech ballistic missile defense cooperation argued that hosting a U.S. missile defense site would improve the image of the Czech Republic as a reliable ally at the forefront of technological innovation.[151] It would allow the Czech Republic to reap (generally unspecified) technological benefits stemming from

---

[148] "Jan Vidím: Potřebujeme Rakety. Proti Raketám" (We Need Rockets. Against Rockets), *Hospodářské Noviny* (*Economic Newspaper*), August 21, 2006, https://archiv.ihned.cz/c1-19131590-jan-vidim-potrebujeme-rakety-proti-raketam.

[149] The Czech Republic joined NATO in 1999.

[150] Ministerstvo zahraničních věcí ČR (Czech Ministry of Foreign Affairs), "Zahraničních politika České republiky data 3/2007" (Czech Foreign Policy Data 3/2007), March 2007, https://www.mzv.cz/public/e5/87/1/73316_491961_Data_mesicniku_ZP2007_03.pdf.

[151] Vondra, "Zapojení ČR do projektu protiraketové obrany" (The Czech Republic's Participation in the Missile Defense Project).

participating in a U.S. missile defense program.[152] Additionally, they argued that the Czech Republic would benefit from an increased pressure to professionalize its intelligence services and law enforcement in order to improve crime prevention, counter money laundering, and counter corruption.[153]

U.S.-Czech ballistic missile defense cooperation was to translate into economic benefits for the Czech Republic in general and for local economies that would be within the vicinity of a missile defense site in particular. That is because the site itself would require infrastructure updates to improve accessibility and to accommodate U.S. forces that would be stationed there. This argument was important because some of the villages in the vicinity of a presumed missile defense site were relatively poor and lacked basic infrastructure, like sewage systems or water treatment facilities.

Proponents of the system emphasized that it is purely defensive and possesses no offensive capabilities. The argument was particularly salient given the Russian Federation's opposition to the endeavor. But the system was to be optimized to counter Iran's ballistic missiles and had no appreciable capability against Russia's extensive ballistic missile arsenal.[154] Russian officials stated on numerous occasions that a U.S. ballistic missile defense system would not have any significant capability against Russia's ballistic missile force.[155]

---

[152] Ivan Gabal, "Základna USA bude spíš v Polsku. Češi ji propásli" (U.S. Base Will More Likely Be in Poland. The Czechs Missed Out), *Hospodářské noviny* (*Economic Newspaper*), August 9, 2006, https://archiv.ihned.cz/c1-19058050-ivan-gabal-zakladna-usa-bude-spis-v-polsku-cesi-ji-propasli.

[153] Ibid.

[154] Peppino DeBiasso, "Missile Defense and NATO Security," *Joint Forces Quarterly*, No. 51 (September 2008), p. 50.

[155] Mark Schneider, "Russian Lies and Hypocrisy Concerning Missile Defense," National Institute for Public Policy, April 17, 2018,

Russia is one of the most capable nuclear weapons states in the world, possesses a large number of diverse nuclear weapons, and a variety of means to deliver conventional and weapons of mass destruction payloads. The name of Russia's game was not military capabilities, at least not primarily, but concerns over whether it would be able to exercise political influence over what it perceived as its former vassal state.

The Czech Republic cannot compare to Russia in terms of raw military power. Russia is stronger by all traditional measures of power as defined by major international relations theories. Russia has a larger population and territory than the Czech Republic, more resources, and a much larger military. Granted, Russia is not a democracy and has a plethora of problems of its own, but there is no doubt that without allies, the Czech Republic could not defend itself from a Russian military attack.

Russia has continuously opposed U.S. plans to build elements of a U.S.-NATO missile defense system in Europe, despite not being particularly antagonized by the U.S. withdrawal from the ABM Treaty, as evidenced by its signing of SORT a few months after the withdrawal. But the Russian Federation's leadership expressed concerns over U.S. ballistic missile defense plans in Eastern Europe on multiple occasions and called a U.S. missile defense system a threat to its, and global, security.

The Debate Starts II: Cons of U.S.-Czech Ballistic Missile Defense Cooperation

In the Czech Republic, the main gist of objections to U.S.-Czech ballistic missile defense cooperation can be summarized as follows: "The coalition against a U.S. radar

---

https://www.nipp.org/2018/04/17/schneider-mark-russian-lies-and-hypocrisy-concerning-missile-defense/.

site on the Czech territory demanded a referendum because the public was not informed about U.S.-Czech missile defense cooperation prior to 2006 elections; was concerned over Czech sovereignty and permanent stationing of U.S. troops on the Czech territory; and disagreed with U.S. foreign policy in general, particularly war against terrorism and wars in Iraq and Afghanistan," in the words of Jan Májíček, former spokesman for the No Bases Initiative.[156]

Opponents of Czech-U.S. ballistic missile defense cooperation employed several historically incorrect analogies to frame and popularize their case. For example, they argued that hosting a U.S. ballistic missile defense site (and its military forces) would lead to the loss of Czech sovereignty. While a pro-Western trend was apparent in Czech foreign policy after the end of the Cold War, "what was surprising was its [the Czech government's] effort to permanently station a U.S. military base on Czech territory. That was a qualitative change in cooperation never tried before and likened to the Warsaw Pact by opponents of a plan to station a U.S. radar on Czech territory," according to Májíček.[157]

Opponents also argued that ballistic missile defense cooperation would make the Czech Republic more susceptible to U.S. blackmail because it would increase Czech dependence on the United States.[158] The Communist Party, a direct heir of the Communist Party of Czechoslovakia responsible for four decades of authoritarianism and for supporting the Soviet military presence on the Czechoslovak territory without any democratic oversight, equated voluntary and fairly limited cooperation between two NATO allies to the experience of

---

[156] Author interview with Jan Májíček, former spokesman for the No Bases Initiative, via WhatsApp video, January 17, 2019.

[157] Ibid.

[158] Ivan Gabal, "Základna USA bude spíš v Polsku. Češi ji propásli" (U.S. Base Will More Likely Be in Poland. The Czechs Missed Out).

the Soviet occupation of Czechoslovakia. On its face, the argument is nonsense, but it was nevertheless popular among some segments of the Czech population. After all, the Communist Party regularly obtains enough electoral votes to make it to the Parliament and was polling at about 26 percent before the June 2006 elections.

In another example of incorrectly applying historical analogies, opponents of U.S.-Czech ballistic missile defense cooperation co-opted a saying, *Opět o nás bez nás?* (which can be translated as "About us, without us, again?"), invoking the 1938 Munich Agreement between Nazi Germany, the United Kingdom, France, and Italy that led to the partition of Czechoslovakia.[159] The agreement permitted German annexation of the Czechoslovak Sudetenland, and was presented to Czechoslovakia's government as a *fait accompli*; therefore, for understandable reasons, its usage has very negative connotations in the Czech context. Opponents argued that the general public ought to be more informed about U.S.-Czech ballistic missile efforts. While there is nothing wrong with demanding transparency from one's government, likening the Munich Agreement to U.S.-Czech ballistic missile defense discussions was ludicrous. The Czech Social Democratic Party-led government kept public knowledge of initial ballistic missile defense discussions with the United States prior to 2006 to a minimum, but that was more a variable of the exploratory nature of initial discussions than a malign intent on the part of the Czech government.[160]

---

[159] "Protestní shromáždění 'Opět o nás bez nás?' v Plzni" (Protest Gathering About Us Without Us Again?), *Ne základnám* (*No Bases Initiative*), March 4, 2007, http://www.nezakladnam.cz/cs/187_protestni-shromazdeni-opet-o-nas-bez-nas-v-plzni.

[160] This is a different matter than casting a judgment on whether keeping discussions secret was desirable and helpful.

Another line of argumentation was that U.S.-Czech missile defense cooperation would make the Czech Republic a more likely target for terrorist attacks without a comparable increase in Czech security, and would therefore lead to a net decrease in Czech security.[161] The logic was that terrorists were more likely to attack targets inside the Czech Republic in retribution for its increased cooperation with the United States, or that hosting a U.S. presence on its territory would make the Czech Republic a relatively more worthy target by association. Proponents of U.S.-Czech ballistic missile defense cooperation argued that the Czech Republic was running this danger anyway since it is a NATO member state and deploys its troops to Iraq and Afghanistan.

Despite limited capabilities of a potential future U.S. missile defense system in Europe (geared toward protecting the U.S. homeland and parts of Europe from an Iranian ballistic missile attack), European U.S. missile defense sites (interceptors in Poland, and an X-band radar in the Czech Republic) were portrayed as a threat to Russia's national security. The Russian Federation understood that capabilities planned by the Bush Administration could not significantly undermine its nuclear weapons arsenal, but argued that the sites could be upgraded in the future with more capable interceptors and more capable radars. Concerns over future capabilities of potential sites formed an important basis of Russia's objections.[162]

The upgrade argument was repeated by opponents of U.S.-Czech ballistic missile defense cooperation. It was in Russia's interest to overstate the technical capabilities of the planned U.S. ballistic missile defense system. To counter the misconceptions of a U.S. threat, the United States and the

---

[161] Vidím, "Jan Vidím: Potřebujeme Rakety. Proti Raketám" (We Need Rockets. Against Rockets).

[162] Victoria Stephanova, "Missile Defense in Central Europe: The View from Moscow," *The Orator*, Vol. 3, No. 1 (2008), pp. 19-35.

Czech Republic (and other NATO states sympathetic to the idea of a missile defense system) tried to assuage Russia's concerns, but their efforts were not particularly successful. For example, U.S. Secretary of Defense Robert Gates proposed not activating a U.S. missile defense system in Europe until demonstration of proof of an Iranian ballistic missile threat, but his offer did not fall on fertile grounds in Moscow.[163]

The Czech Republic and the United States took proactive measures to ensure that a U.S. missile defense system was not a threat to other countries' populations, including Russia's.[164] For example, in October 2007, then-Prime Minister Topolánek suggested a plan to give Russian inspectors an opportunity to visit a radar site during its construction and operation (in cooperation with the Americans and contingent upon agreement from both countries).[165] But the Czech government's critics at home were not satisfied with the government's approach regardless of the steps it took to alleviate their concerns.

When the Czech government proposed measures, such as the above, to alleviate concerns regarding the project's

---

[163] "Základny aktivuje až hrozba z Íránu, navrhl Gates" (Missile Bases Will Be Activated in Concurrence with the Iranian Threat, Gates Proposed), iDnes.cz, October 23, 2007, https://www.idnes.cz/zpravy/domaci/zakladny-aktivuje-az-hrozba-z-iranu-navrhl-gates.A071023_111736_domaci_miz.

[164] The United States conducted separate discussions and negotiations and held numerous high-level meetings with the Russian representatives on the question of U.S. missile defense in Europe and in the United States. These discussions also explored potential missile defense cooperation between the two countries. Similar parallel discussions were held between NATO and the Russian Federation. This book notes them to the extent that they are relevant for its main area of concern but not beyond.

[165] "Rusové tu budou jen občas, tvrdí premiér" (The Russians Will Only Visit Sometimes, Says the Prime Minister), Lidové Noviny (People's Newspaper), October 25, 2007, https://www.lidovky.cz/domov/rusove-tu-budou-jen-obcas-tvrdi-premier.A071025_120919_ln_domov_vvr.

impact on relations with the Russian Federation, the opponents of U.S.-Czech missile defense cooperation accused the Czech government of collaborating with the Russians and compromising Czech security. When the Czech government did not demonstrate sufficient sensitivity to Russia's concerns in the eyes of missile defense cooperation opponents, it was accused of decreasing Czech and international security by destabilizing relations with Russia.

Opponents of Czech-U.S. missile defense cooperation argued that ballistic missile defenses were "destabilizing" vis-à-vis Russia and China and therefore the Czech Republic should not contribute to a potential worsening of relations between these countries. They also argued that U.S. missile defense sites in Eastern Europe would lead to an arms race and nuclear war between the United States and the Russian Federation.[166] For example, Yuri Baluyevsky, Russian Chief of the General Staff, argued that a missile defense site in the Czech Republic has the potential to cause an "arms race" and "to take away resources to solve many other problems, not only in the United States and Russia, but also in other nations."[167] The statement echoes arguments the Soviet Union made during the Cold War when it opposed U.S. military programs it did not like. Russia's extensive influence activities in the Czech Republic are highlighted in Chapter Five.

Opponents of U.S. missile defense also argued that ballistic missile defense systems do not work—how they

---

[166] Remundová, "Vliv mediálního obrazu na činnost občanské iniciativy Ne základnám" (The Impact of the Media's Perceived Image on the No Bases civic Initiative's Development).

[167] "Šéf Ruské Armády Je Proti Základně USA u Nás Či v Polsku" (Russia's Army's Boss Against a Missile Defense Base Here or in Poland), *Hospodářské Noviny* (*Economic Newspaper*), September 6, 2006, https://zahranicni.ihned.cz/c1-19242370-sef-ruske-armady-je-proti-zakladne-usa-u-nas-ci-v-polsku.

can simultaneously cause an arms race they do not explain. A version of this argument postulated that the Iranian and North Korean ballistic missile threats are not as urgent as the U.S. government and NATO presented them, and that the international community had time to reach a diplomatic solution to the problem. Discussions about arms races and destabilization in the Czech Republic did not reach the sophistication or depth of the debate in the United States, largely due to a lack of expertise on the topic among most Czech discussants. This makes sense given the relative newness of the Czech strategic community and the overall lesser importance of the topic in Czech national security discourse in the post-Cold War era.

Opponents of a U.S. radar on Czech territory portrayed the United States as an unreliable ally and an aggressive state in violation of its international commitments, particularly in the human rights field.[168] They tapped into general anti-American sentiments in Europe following the wars in Iraq and Afghanistan. In contrast, proponents of U.S.-Czech ballistic missile defense cooperation wanted to use the missile defense issue as a way to unify Europe after a difficult period post-Iraq. "The Czech Republic's primary concern was how to strengthen NATO and contribute to a healing of the transatlantic rift following a difficult period in the Alliance after the launch of the Iraq operation in 2003. A NATO ballistic missile defense system offered a great opportunity to pool and share capabilities and increase the cohesion of the Alliance," stated Petr Chalupecký, Deputy Director of the Security Policy Department in the Czech Ministry of Foreign Affairs from 2008 to 2010.[169]

---

[168] Remundová, "Vliv mediálního obrazu na činnost občanské iniciativy Ne základnám" (The impact of the Media's perceived image on the No Bases civic initiative's development).

[169] Author interview with Petr Chalupecký, Deputy Director, Security Policy Department, Czech Ministry of Foreign Affairs from 2008 to 2010, via WhatsApp video, November 13, 2019.

In addition to the arguments discussed above, two additional issues became more salient once it became clear that the missile defense component to be located on Czech territory was an X-band radar. The public and some parliamentarians raised concerns about the safety impact of the radar's beam on the Czech population and territory. The Czech media discussed the radar's potential negative consequences for an already small Czech airspace since a radar would require an establishment of a no-flight zone around it.[170] They reported that a radar beam might affect airplanes, which was a significant concern given the relatively small Czech airspace, and interfere with TV and radio signals.[171] The Czech public, especially in villages near a presumed radar site, was also concerned about the radar's potential negative health and environmental impacts. The Czech government tried to address both concerns in its public outreach efforts.

The First Topolánek Government: September 4, 2006–January 9, 2007

The ODS's first attempt to assemble a coalition government was unsuccessful because the coalition did not obtain the Czech Chamber of Deputies' approval. The provisional government under Prime Minister Miroslav Topolánek's (ODS) leadership lasted only from September 4, 2006, to January 9, 2007. On October 3, 2006, the government did not obtain consent of the Chamber of Deputies and therefore ruled with severely restricted capability to implement

---

[170] Zuzana Janečková, "Protiraketový radar USA by mohl ohrozit letadla" (U.S. Missile Defense Radar Could Endanger Airplanes), *MF Dnes*, August 29, 2006, https://zpravy.idnes.cz/protiraketovy-radar-usa-by-mohl-ohrozit-letadla-fu4-/domaci.aspx?c=A060828_213138_domaci_dp.

[171] Ibid.

policy changes until Prime Minister Topolánek assembled his second government (which obtained the Chamber of Deputies' consent on January 9, 2007). Illustrating the fragility of the post-electoral situation, this was the first time in the modern history of the Czech Republic that the Chamber of Deputies did not approve a government. The opposition parties, the Communists and the Social Democrats, had the same number of seats in the Chamber of Deputies as the coalition partners, which made Topolánek's efforts to appoint a functioning government that much harder.

Despite its limited duration, the first Topolánek government chose to continue U.S.-Czech ballistic missile defense cooperation. But the government's official position supporting this cooperation was weakened because it did not have a broad mandate that would allow it to present its position as an agreement across the political spectrum and avoid its politicization. Another challenge to U.S.-Czech ballistic missile defense cooperation arose because coalition parties after the June 2006 elections did not discuss a common position on hosting a U.S. radar on Czech territory. This slowed down formal negotiations with the Americans and cost the Czech government precious time that would have been better used to prepare its public communications campaign.[172]

The ODS was historically supportive of closer relations with the United States, and was in favor of U.S.-Czech missile defense cooperation as a way to strengthen transatlantic relations and as means to "tie" the United

---

[172] Ministerstvo zahraničních věcí ČR (Czech Ministry of Foreign Affairs), "Zahraničních politika České republiky dokumenty 3/2007" (Czech Foreign Policy Documents 3/2007),
https://www.mzv.cz/public/ef/2/cc/73318_492041_Dokumenty_mes icniku_ZP2007_03.pdf.

States closer to Europe.[173] With regard to ballistic missile defense cooperation with the United States, "Czech interests did not change over time. The basic interest was how to keep the United States in Europe and attract its attention; how to fill that power void in countries between Russia and Germany. And Czech diplomacy follows these interests up to this day," said former First Deputy Minister Pojar.[174]

Immediately following the ČSSD's election loss, the party became split on the question of continued U.S.-Czech ballistic missile defense cooperation. About a third of the ČSSD's members were reportedly in favor of the Czech Republic hosting a U.S. radar.[175] "The 2006 elections ended in a stalemate in which Paroubek, leader of the ČSSD and the previous government's Prime Minister, pursued any means to distinguish himself from Topolánek. The visible issue at the time happened to be the radar issue," stated then-Deputy Director Chalupecký.[176] Once firmly in the opposition, the Czech Social Democrats criticized the ODS-led government for continuing to pursue ballistic missile defense cooperation with the United States, the very same cooperation they oversaw for years.[177] The Civic Democrats

---

[173] Ministerstvo zahraničních věcí ČR (Czech Ministry of Foreign Affairs), "Zahraničních politika České republiky dokumenty 9/2006" (Czech Foreign Policy Documents 9/2006), September 2006, https://www.mzv.cz/public/e6/db/87/73296_492013_Dokumenty_mesicniku_ZP2006_09.pdf.

[174] Author interview with former First Deputy Minister Pojar.

[175] Viliam Buchert, "Radar v Brdech podporuje stále více voličů zelených i ČSSD" (Radar in Brdy's Support Among the Green Party and the Social Democratic Party Voters Increasing), *MF Dnes*, October 6, 2008, https://www.idnes.cz/zpravy/domaci/radar-v-brdech-podporuje-stale-vice-volicu-zelenych-i-cssd.A081006_080812_domaci_jte.

[176] Author interview with then-Deputy Director Chalupecký.

[177] There were intra-party disagreements over whether to support the plan. For example, Social Democrat Miroslav Svoboda agreed that the

criticized the ČSSD's departure from its previous support for U.S.-Czech ballistic missile defense cooperation as contrary to Czech interests, pointing out that the Czech Social Democrats had worked on advancing U.S.-Czech ballistic missile defense cooperation for years. [178]

"The radar as a military installation was not popular in public polls and so it was not damaging for Social Democrats to oppose it. It was rather tempting to use the issue in the political struggle [that followed the 2006 elections]," according to former First Deputy Minister Pojar.[179] Eventually, the ČSSD fully distanced itself from its previous support for Czech participation in a U.S. ballistic missile defense program, arguing that the "unilateral" project without a broader implementation agreement and a "clear" mission was not in the Czech Republic's interests and that the potential geopolitical and military impacts of the project were too unclear for the government to commit to a plan.[180] Having the ČSSD, the second-largest political

---

Czech Republic should host a U.S. radar site: Ministerstvo zahraničních věcí ČR (Czech Ministry of Foreign Affairs), "Zahraničních politika České republiky data 4/2007" (Czech Foreign Policy Data 4/2007), April 2007, https://www.mzv.cz/public/dc/49/79/73320_491964_Data_mesicniku_ZP2007_04.pdf.

[178] "Paroubek: ČSSD nechce základnu USA" (Paroubek: Czech Social Democratic Party Does Not Want a U.S. Missile Base), *Hospodářské noviny (Economic Newspaper)*, September 5, 2006, https://archiv.ihned.cz/c1-19225330-paroubek-cssd-nechce-zakladnu-usa.

[179] Author interview with former First Deputy Minister Pojar.

[180] Jan Červenka, "Americké protiraketové základny v ČR a Polsku z pohledu domácí veřejnosti" (U.S. Missile Defense Bases in the Czech Republic and Poland from the Perspective of the Public), *Centrum pro výzkum veřejného mínění* (Public Opinion Research Center), September 10, 2007, https://cvvm.soc.cas.cz/media/com_form2content/documents/c3/a1136/f28/%c4%8cervenka,%20Jan.%20Americk%c3%a9%20protiraketov

party at the time, in opposition to U.S.-Czech missile defense cooperation meant more legitimacy and prominence for those who opposed such cooperation. "It was advantageous that the Czech Social Democrats were in opposition to the government and therefore did not support the radar plan because it gave more legitimacy to the opposition voices," says Májíček.[181] The ČSSD's support also made it easier for the Russian Federation to exploit the issue, as will be shown in Chapter Five.

Initially, the Czech Social Democrats argued that a bilateral missile defense project between the United States and the Czech Republic would weaken the transatlantic alliance and the European Union because of the lack of a broader endorsement of ballistic missile defense systems within NATO.[182] The concern lost validity later when NATO as an institution accepted that ballistic missile defense systems contribute to the collective security of its members. The longer the ODS-led government negotiated with the Americans and then with its own coalition parliamentarians, the more the issue became politicized and the more attractive it became to use it to score domestic politics points, since a majority of the Czechs were not in favor of U.S.-Czech ballistic missile defense cooperation.

The ČSSD did not have to spend much political capital to change its stance, because when leading the government in the years prior, the government was secretive about its interactions with the Americans and severely limited the flow of information to the general public and a majority of

---

%c3%a9%20z%c3%a1kladny%20v%20%c4%8cR%20a%20Polsku%20z%20pohledu%20dom%c3%a1c%c3%ad%20ve%c5%99ejnosti.pdf, p. 4.

[181] Author interview with Májíček.

[182] Ministerstvo zahraničních věcí ČR (Czech Ministry of Foreign Affairs), "Zahraničních politika České republiky dokumenty 6/2007" (Czech Foreign Policy Documents 6/2007), https://www.mzv.cz/public/9e/e7/29/73498_492046_Dokumenty_mesicniku_ZP2007_06.pdf.

parliamentarians in both the Chamber of Deputies and the Senate.[183] Neither did the Czech Social Democrats inform Czech President Václav Klaus (who held the office from 2003 to 2013) about ongoing discussions with the United States until two months after the June 2006 elections.[184]

The ČSSD and the KSČM, along with the No Bases Initiative, argued that the Czech Republic should hold a referendum on whether to support a potential missile defense site on Czech territory. The first credible public poll about Czech attitudes to placing elements of a missile defense in the Czech Republic and Poland was conducted in September 2006 with a little over 50 percent of the respondents being "decidedly against" and "largely against" the Czech Republic hosting a U.S. ballistic missile defense base on Czech territory.[185]

The date of the poll offers yet more evidence of the lack of general awareness with which U.S.-Czech ballistic missile defense negotiations were conducted up until then. No credible public polls examining the question exist from before September 2006 because information about the United States considering the Czech Republic as a potential

---

[183] "Zápis z 8. Společné schůze zahraničního výboru, výboru pro obranu, výboru pro bezpečnost a ústavně právního výboru" (Record from the 8th Joint Session of the Committees on Foreign Affairs, Defense, Security, and Constitutional and Legal Affairs), January 31, 2007, https://www.google.com/url?sa=t&rct=j&q=&esrc=s&source=web&cd=4&ved=2ahUKEwivlZDZqcjfAhUshOAKHT8lCDQQFjADegQIBhAC&url=http%3A%2F%2Fwww.psp.cz%2Fsqw%2Ftext%2Forig2.sqw%3Fidd%3D8721&usg=AovVaw1yNiLKue_eqaMLUsnK4RF6.

[184] "Klaus podpořil referendum o radaru" (Klaus Expressed Support for a Referendum on a Radar), *Novinky.cz*, June 13, 2007, https://www.novinky.cz/domaci/116961-klaus-podporil-referendum-o-radaru.html.

[185] Červenka, "Americké protiraketové základny v ČR a Polsku z pohledu domácí veřejnosti" (U.S. Missile Defense Bases in the Czech Republic and Poland from the Perspective of the Public).

host site was simply not available.[186] Nevertheless, the idea of a referendum enjoyed broad public support, with over 70 percent of respondents being "decidedly in favor" or "largely in favor" of conducting a referendum in four polls conducted between September 2006 and May 2007.[187]

A nation-wide referendum would likely mean a death knell for future U.S.-Czech ballistic missile defense negotiations because most of the Czechs opposed hosting a U.S. military asset on their territory. This "opposition was not fundamental; it was more a case of traditional Czech soft pacifist tendencies stemming from a Czech historical experience," according to former First Deputy Minister Pojar.[188] Then-Foreign Minister Alexandr Vondra made clear that while he agreed that the matter of potential Czech hosting of a U.S. missile defense site should be a matter of broader political consensus, he warned of increased politicization of the issue.[189] The Civic Democrats, interested in continuing U.S.-Czech ballistic missile defense cooperation, opposed the idea of holding a referendum and argued that security matters were exempted from referenda by the Czech constitution, which postulates that security matters ought to be decided by the Czech Parliament with government experts' participation.[190]

---

[186] Ibid.

[187] Ibid., p. 8.

[188] Author interview with former First Deputy Minister Pojar.

[189] Vondra, "Alexandr Vondra: Postavme Se k Základně Čelem" (Let Us Face a Missile Base). Alexandr Vondra held different government positions during U.S.-Czech ballistic missile defense negotiations.

[190] "Tiskový briefing předsedy vlády ČR Mirka Topolánka po zasedání Bezpečnostní rady státu 24. Ledna 2007" (Prime Minister Mirek Topolánek's Briefing After the Meeting of the National Security Council on January 24, 2007), Czech Government, January 24, 2007, https://www.vlada.cz/cz/media-centrum/tiskove-konference/tiskovy-briefing-predsedy-vlady-cr-mirka-topolanka-po-zasedani-bezpecnostni-rady-statu-ve-stredu-24−1−2007-20882/. There is a precedent with regard to the Civic Democrats' opposition to a

Even if the previous governments' cooperative efforts were known, it is unlikely that they would play a major role in the 2006 elections. The Czech Republic enjoyed a relatively stable foreign policy consensus on the need to embed itself in Western political and military structures and on the need to strengthen relations with the United States after the end of the Cold War. This consensus was born out of the experience of the Soviet occupation and the 1989 Velvet Revolution. The radar issue was the first time since the end of the Cold War that a foreign policy issue became a significant factor in Czech domestic politics.[191] According to some, the radar episode marked the beginning of the end of that consensus shared across the political spectrum (with the exception of the Communist Party) but also within the Czech political parties.[192] Others maintain that a consensus on basic tenets of Czech foreign policy continues today and points to a continued parliamentarian support for Czech membership in NATO and the Czech military's participation in Alliance missions abroad.

The United States reportedly expressed a preference to the Czech government for a two-site ballistic missile defense option in September 2006.[193] This option was more expensive than a single site but advantageous for other reasons. For example, one missile defense site could host interceptors and another one a radar, which could involve more allied countries. Since it was clear that any Czech

---

nation-wide referendum. The Czech Republic never held a referendum on whether it should join NATO. A majority of the Czechs were in opposition to joining NATO at the time.

[191] Author interview with then-Deputy Director Chalupecký.

[192] Author interview with Petr Suchý, Head of the Department of International Relations and European Studies, Faculty of Social Studies, Masaryk University, Czech Republic.

[193] "Zápis z 8. Společné schůze zahraničního výboru, výboru pro obranu, výboru pro bezpečnost a ústavně právního výboru" (Record from the 8th Joint Session of the Committees on Foreign Affairs, Defense, Security, and Constitutional and Legal Affairs).

government would have a difficult time sustaining a political consensus on hosting an interceptor site, a two-site option opened an opportunity for the Czechs to potentially host a relatively less controversial radar. The Czech Republic also happened to be in an optimal geographic location for it. Interceptors considered for deployment at the site in Poland were a two-stage variant of the U.S. Ground-Based Midcourse Defense (GMD) interceptors being deployed to Alaska and California at the time.

The Americans decided to pursue their missile defense plans in Europe on a bilateral basis but envisioned a U.S. ballistic missile defense system in Europe being compatible with a future NATO system, and being used to defend allies if needed.[194] Some argue that conducting two separate negotiations put the United States into a stronger position vis-à-vis each of the involved countries because it did not have to respond to joint demands by the governments of Poland and the Czech Republic.[195] In reality, the governments of Poland and the Czech Republic consulted and coordinated with each other during negotiations regardless of the fact that the United States conducted two discrete sets of negotiations.[196]

---

[194] Ministerstvo zahraničních věcí ČR (Czech Ministry of Foreign Affairs), "Zahraničních politika České republiky data 11/2006" (Czech Foreign Policy Data 11/2006), November 2006, https://www.mzv.cz/public/74/3f/b/73300_491949_Data_mesicniku_ZP2006_11.pdf.

[195] Hynek, "Protiraketová obrana v současném strategickém a politickém kontextu. Vztah k odstrašování a dopad třetího pilíře na dynamiku mezi relevantními aktéry" (Missile Defense in the Contemporary Strategic and Political Context. The Connection to Deterrence and the Impact of the Third Site on the Dynamics Among Relevant Actors), April 2008.

[196] See for example "Vondra: Vysvětlíme Rusku, že systém obrany není proti němu" (We Will Explain to the Russian Federation that the Missile Defense System Is Not Aimed at It), *Rozhlas.cz*, February 20, 2007, https://www.rozhlas.cz/radio_cesko/exkluzivne/_zprava/vondra-vysvetlime-rusku-ze-system-obrany-neni-proti-nemu—321493.

In January 2008, the Czech government even stated that it would not support building a U.S. radar site on Czech territory until Poland agreed to host an interceptor site, but with delays in U.S.-Polish negotiations, this linkage was abandoned.[197] Conditioning U.S.-Czech agreements on signing agreements with Poland would mean a delay of the U.S.-Czech agreements and potentially cost the Czech government valuable time it could use to convince Czech parliamentarians and the Czech general public that these agreements were in the Czech Republic's interest.[198] In March 2008, former First Deputy Minister Pojar stated that the Czech Republic would host a U.S. radar site even if Poland did not agree to host an interceptor site.[199]

Successive Czech governments insisted on NATO-ization of U.S.-Czech ballistic missile defense cooperation. Jiří Šedivý, then-Czech Defense Minister, while supportive of U.S.-Czech ballistic missile defense cooperation, expressed the government's desire to pursue such cooperation in the context of NATO.[200] As former First

---

[197] Ministerstvo zahraničních věcí ČR (Czech Ministry of Foreign Affairs), "Zahraničních politika České republiky data 1/2008" (Czech Foreign Policy Data 1/2008), January 2008, https://www.mzv.cz/public/c5/8/76/280351_491978_Data_mesicniku_ZP2008_01.pdf.

[198] Ministerstvo zahraničních věcí ČR (Czech Ministry of Foreign Affairs), "Zahraničních Politika České Republiky Data 4/2008" (Czech Foreign Policy Data 4/2008), April 2008, https://www.mzv.cz/public/38/2/f/280359_491981_Data_mesicniku_ZP2008_04.pdf.

[199] Ministerstvo zahraničních věcí ČR (Czech Ministry of Foreign Affairs), "Zahraničních politika České republiky data 3/2008" (Czech Foreign Policy Data 3/2008), March 2008, https://www.mzv.cz/public/16/98/4/280357_491980_Data_mesicniku_ZP2008_03.pdf.

[200] "Ministr Šedivý si přeje protiraketovou základnu" (Minister Šedivý Would Like to Host a Missile Defense Base), *Hospodářské noviny* (*Economic Newspaper*), September 4, 2006, https://domaci.ihned.cz/c1-19223640-ministr-sedivy-si-preje-protiraketovou-zakladnu.

Deputy Minister Pojar explained: "The Czech insistence on the Alliance dimension of U.S.-Czech missile defense cooperation came from demands of many political representatives due to their constituencies."[201] For example, the Green Party and some Social Democrats insisted on discussing the radar with the Americans in a NATO context, which would make it more politically acceptable in the Czech Parliament and for the domestic audience.

But U.S. promises of future NATO compatibility were not enough to satisfy some coalition proponents of missile defense NATO-ization. For example, Ondřej Liška, then-Member of Parliament for the Green Party, made a point to emphasize that the missile defense project was bilateral and that there was no plan to integrate it with NATO.[202] As will be shown in Chapter Four, the issue of NATO-ization became even more important for the coalition government in the second Topolánek government.

The first Topolánek government's instability and short duration left the bilateral discussions with the United States in limbo as the United States worked through its own bureaucracy to prepare for official negotiations and waited to see how the situation in the Czech Republic evolves. For understandable reasons, "we did not want to get ahead of the Czech government," stated the Honorable Frank Rose.[203] While this approach made sense for the United States and the Czech Republic, it cost both countries valuable time when they could have been shaping a public

---

[201] Author interview with former First Deputy Minister Pojar.

[202] Ministerstvo zahraničních věcí ČR (Czech Ministry of Foreign Affairs), "Zahraničních politika České republiky dokumenty 12/2006" (Czech Foreign Policy Documents 12/2006), December 2006, https://www.mzv.cz/public/b8/8b/f4/73306_492028_Dokumenty_m esicniku_ZP2006_12.pdf.

[203] Author interview with the Honorable Frank Rose, Office of the Secretary of Defense, on U.S.-Czech missile defense cooperation.

narrative regarding the issue and be proactive rather than reactive.

In December 2006, newly sworn-in U.S. Secretary of Defense Robert Gates sent his official recommendation regarding U.S. missile defense sites in Europe to President Bush. The memo recommended that the United States deploy 10 two-stage GMD interceptors in Poland and a radar installation in the Czech Republic.[204] The recommendation drew on both political and technical considerations. "The United States wanted to make ballistic missile defense an integral part of U.S. defense planning and didn't want 'fortress' America," according to Ambassador Edelman.[205] In response, Russian General Baluyevsky said that placing elements of a U.S. missile defense system near Russian borders was an adversarial step.[206]

The Bush Administration decided on deploying an X-band radar to the Czech Republic. It would not be a completely new radar system; the radar was at the time located on the Kwajalein atoll in the Marshall Islands in the Pacific Ocean and would be upgraded before being deployed to the Czech Republic.[207] The radar would allow the United States to detect incoming ballistic missiles

---

[204] Robert Gates, *Duty: Memoirs of a Secretary at War* (New York: Vintage, 2015), p. 159.

[205] Author interview with Eric Edelman, Under Secretary of Defense for Policy 2005–2009.

[206] "Klaus jede do Moskvy. Radil se s Topolánkem o radaru" (Klaus Is Going to Moscow. He Talked with Topolánek about the Radar), *Aktuálně.cz*, April 13, 2007, https://zpravy.aktualne.cz/domaci/politika/80bama-jede-do-moskvy-radil-se-s-topolankem-o-radaru/r~i:article:397864/. To clarify: The Czech Republic does not share borders with the Russian Federation. Poland shares borders with Kaliningrad Oblast, a Russian exclave that does not share a direct border with the Russian Federation. Aside from that, Poland does not share borders with the Russian Federation.

[207] The radar is still deployed there as of the writing of this book.

primarily from Iran, and give the GMD system a better chance to intercept adversarial ballistic missiles before they got closer to their target, either in the United States or in Europe.[208] "A third [ballistic missile defense] site in Europe would give us look-shoot-look capability for interceptors deployed in Alaska and California. But they would also solve the issue of decoupling U.S. and European security," Ambassador Edelman explained.[209] In addition to protecting the U.S. homeland, GMD interceptors in Poland would provide limited protection from the Iranian intermediate-range ballistic missiles.[210]

President Bush 43 approved the recommendation "a few weeks later" even as Russia protested U.S. actions.[211] The Administration was aware of difficulties that the issue might cause for Czech politicians: "We were aware of considerable resistance from Czech citizens and also of Russia's major public relations effort in the Czech Republic," said Dr. Bucci.[212] "From the beginning, the Americans were aware of the disconnection between the political and the general population level. We understood there was a strong popular opposition to a U.S. radar on the

---

[208] Ministerstvo zahraničních věcí ČR (Czech Ministry of Foreign Affairs), "Zahraničních politika České republiky data 1/2007" (Czech Foreign Policy Data 1/2007), January 2007, https://www.mzv.cz/public/fd/f7/5e/73308_491959_Data_mesicniku_ZP2007_01.pdf.

[209] Author interview with Eric Edelman, Under Secretary of Defense for Policy 2005–2009.

[210] Congressional Budget Office, "Options for Deploying Missile Defenses in Europe," February 2009, https://www.cbo.gov/sites/default/files/111th-congress-2009-2010/reports/02-27-missiledefense.pdf.

[211] Gates, *Duty: Memoirs of a Secretary at War*, p. 163.

[212] Author interview with Dr. Steven Bucci, Military Assistant to U.S. Secretary of Defense Donald Rumsfeld 2001–2005.

Czech territory," the Honorable Frank Rose agreed.[213] The Americans were also aware that their motivations for ballistic missile defense cooperation were distinct from those of their Czech counterparts. The Czech political goals "had everything to do with Russia" and "the U.S. deployments on their [Czech and Polish] soil would be a concrete manifestation of U.S. security guarantees against Russia beyond our commitments under the NATO treaty," according to former Secretary Gates.[214] This is accurate, although incomplete. The Czechs also just wanted to be seen as good allies. U.S. goals were primarily military having to do with an Iranian ballistic missile threat.[215]

Despite hopes to the contrary, the debate about a radar site in the Czech Republic proved no less controversial than the debate about an interceptor site. To make matters worse, the Czech debate was not particularly well informed, both in terms of the public debate but also with respect to Czech decision-makers. As will be shown in Chapter Five, this made the situation ripe for a Russian disinformation campaign.

---

[213] Author interview with the Honorable Frank Rose, Office of the Secretary of Defense, on U.S.-Czech missile defense cooperation.

[214] Gates, *Duty: Memoirs of a Secretary at War*, p. 403.

[215] Ibid., p. 404.

Chapter Four
The Rise and Fall of U.S.-Czech Ballistic Missile Defense Cooperation

It was the end of a dream of one generation of Czech transatlanticists.

A Czech citizen's observation of President Obama's decision to cancel the planned radar site in the Czech Republic, 2019

Chapter Four chronicles official U.S.-Czech ballistic missile defense negotiations between January 19, 2007 (when the United States publicly announced its interest in the Czech Republic as a potential radar site host location) and September 16, 2009 (when the Obama Administration decided to cancel plans to place an X-band radar on Czech territory). U.S.-Czech negotiations coincided with the Civic Democratic Party–led (ODS-led) coalition's second attempt to assemble a government that obtained a vote of confidence in the Chamber of Deputies on January 19, 2007.

The Second Topolánek Government: January 9, 2007–May 8, 2009

The ODS coalition with the Christian and Democratic Union-Czechoslovak People's Party (KDU-ČSL), the Green Party, and Independents lasted from January 9, 2007, to May 8, 2009, when the government fell after a successful no-confidence vote in the Czech Chamber of Deputies. The government of Prime Minister Miroslav Topolánek was fragile from the beginning and relied on support of two renegade parliamentarians from the ČSSD, to ČSSD leader

Jiří Paroubek's immense personal consternation. While these parliamentarians said they would tacitly tolerate Prime Minister Topolánek's government, they did not commit to vote for its legislative proposals, thereby weakening the government's ability to implement its program.

Even though Prime Minister Topolánek's second attempt at assembling a government was more successful than the first, quickly changing circumstances, internal instability, and political turmoil made it difficult for the United States to read the political situation in the Czech Republic, particularly in the context of a large number of Czech citizens being opposed to hosting a U.S. missile defense site.[216]

On January 19, 2007, the United States announced its interest to start negotiations on Czech involvement in U.S. ballistic missile defense plans.[217] The announcement marked a formal beginning of missile defense negotiations between the two countries. Discussions before then were technical, conducted generally out of sight of the general public, and ambiguous as to which missile defense components the Czech Republic might host. But the period before the official start of negotiations was also marked by a close coordination and increased frequency of contacts on both political and expert levels, increased attention to the issue on the part of other states inside and outside NATO (particularly the Russian Federation), and the beginning of intense public discussions and protests against a potential U.S. military presence in the Czech Republic.

---

[216] Daniel Anýž, "Raketová základna USA v Evropě je nejistá" (U.S. Missile Base in the Czech Republic Uncertain), *Hospodářské noviny* (*Economic Newspaper*), October 23, 2006, https://archiv.ihned.cz/c1-19586430-raketova-zakladna-usa-v-evrope-je-nejista.

[217] "Chronologie vývoje projektu protiraketové obrany USA" (Chronology of U.S. Ballistic Missile Defense Programs).

In response to a U.S. announcement, the Czech National Security Council (NSC) took up the issue at one of its meetings. On January 24, 2007, the Czech NSC requested that the Ministers of Defense and of Foreign Affairs establish a joint expert team that would prepare the Czech government's negotiating positions regarding ballistic missile defense cooperation with the United States.[218] The team consisted of about 10 people from the Ministries of Foreign Affairs and Defense and was led by Tomáš Pojar, who later became First Deputy Minister of Foreign Affairs.[219]

The Czech government also decided to establish a support team of about 12 people from the Ministries of Foreign Affairs, Defense, the Interior, and Finance, as well as the intelligence services, to monitor and make recommendations regarding related domestic and international aspects of the issue.[220] The Czech government mandated that the Ministers of Defense and Foreign Affairs begin consultations with local governments and both chambers of the Czech Parliament.[221] Lastly, the Minister of the Interior and Information Technologies, and the Minister of Defense, in cooperation with Czech intelligence services, were tasked to prepare an assessment of risks and threats in

---

[218] Government of the Czech Republic, "Usnesení Bezpečnostní rady státu č. 7" (Resolution of the National Security Council No. 7), January 24, 2007, http://portal.chmi.cz/files/portal/docs/katastrofy/15zasedani/bezradst.pdf.

[219] "Zápis z 8. Společné schůze zahraničního výboru, výboru pro obranu, výboru pro bezpečnost a ústavně právního výboru" (Record from the 8th Joint Session of the Committees on Foreign Affairs, Defense, Security, and Constitutional and Legal Affairs).

[220] Ibid.

[221] "Usnesení Bezpečnostní rady státu č. 7" (Resolution of the National Security Council No. 7).

relation to the potential location of a U.S. radar site on Czech territory.[222]

In a press conference following the Czech NSC meeting, Prime Minister Topolánek emphasized that negotiations with the United States were just beginning and that a decision to host a radar site was not pre-determined, a position that President Klaus emphasized, too.[223] Prime Minister Topolánek highlighted that any decision to host a "foreign military presence" would require an agreement in both the Czech Senate and Chamber of Deputies as well as a presidential signature, and that a U.S. military site would not be exempt from Czech jurisdiction.[224] He highlighted the security benefits of a U.S. ballistic missile defense system in Europe to the Czech Republic and to other NATO allies, and dismissed concerns over a radar site worsening relations with Russia and potentially China.[225] Lastly, Prime Minister Topolánek emphasized that the process of negotiating necessary agreements with the United States would take months, if not years.[226]

Questions raised by Czech journalists previewed issues that would be discussed among the public after the government's announcement. They asked about the potential of the site to worsen relations with the Russian Federation, whether the government should hold a referendum on the issue, whether the government should link negotiations about a radar site with its potential participation in the U.S. Visa Waiver Program (VWP), and

---

[222] Ibid.

[223] "Tiskový briefing předsedy vlády ČR Mirka Topolánka po zasedání Bezpečnostní rady státu 24. Ledna 2007" (Prime Minister Mirek Topolánek's Briefing after the Meeting of the National Security Council on January 24, 2007).

[224] Ibid.

[225] Ibid.

[226] Ibid.

what the communication strategies for the site on both the local and international level will be.[227]

The United States delivered an official note requesting that the Czech Republic host an X-band radar on its territory on January 25, 2007.[228] The official note ended eight months of speculation about what it is that the United States intends to do in Europe.[229] The Czech Chamber of Deputies Committee on Foreign Affairs acknowledged the U.S. official note and stated that it did not have enough information to take a position on the matter. It requested that the Czech government continue to regularly inform members of the committee on the issue.[230]

The Russian Federation's reaction to the official request was swift. Andrei Kokoshin, Chairman of the State Duma Committee on the Commonwealth of Independent States and Relations with Expatriates, said that there will be (unspecified, but certainly unpleasant) consequences if the Czech Republic decides to host a U.S. missile defense system.[231] During the same timeframe, General Yuri Baluyevsky issued another pre-emptive threat when he said that elements of a U.S. missile defense system would be just another set of targets that Russia would destroy first in the

---

[227] Ibid.

[228] The official note also specified that the United States was interested in Poland hosting GMD interceptors.

[229] "Chronologie vývoje projektu protiraketové obrany USA" (Chronology of U.S. Ballistic Missile Defense Programs), and "Zápis z 8. Společné schůze zahraničního výboru, výboru pro obranu, výboru pro bezpečnost a ústavně právního výboru" (Record from the 8th Joint Session of Committees Foreign Affairs, Defense, Security, and Constitutional and Legal Affairs).

[230] Ibid., p. 9.

[231] Ministerstvo zahraničních věcí ČR (Czech Ministry of Foreign Affairs), "Zahraničních politika České republiky data 1/2007" (Czech Foreign Policy Data 1/2007), January 10, 2019, https://www.mzv.cz/public/fd/f7/5e/73308_491959_Data_mesicniku_ZP2007_01.pdf.

case of a conflict.[232] Vladimir Popovkin, General Director of the Russian Federal Space Agency, called an X-band radar on Czech territory an "apparent" threat to Russia's security.[233] Russian security expert Leonid Ivashov argued that Czech security would be damaged if the Czech Republic decided to host a U.S. radar site.[234] Russia's narratives found their way into the Czech public discourse and were often uncritically parroted by opponents of U.S.-Czech ballistic missile defense cooperation.

The Czech government's official responses to Russia's threats echoed arguments that the United States was making to Russia: that the system is defensive, is not aimed at Russia, and does not have capabilities against its nuclear arsenal.[235] The Czech government had to be cautious regarding how it communicated its ballistic missile defense cooperation efforts to the Russian government because of other NATO states' sensitivity to Russia's concerns (particularly Germany's and France's) and due to the Czech government's awareness of the U.S. Administration's desire to not portray its ballistic missile defense system as destabilizing relations with Russia in the U.S. domestic context. Austria, the Czech Republic's neighbor to the south (not a NATO member) perceived U.S.-Czech ballistic missile defense cooperation negatively, too. General Baluyevsky softened his rhetoric somewhat after bilateral

---

[232] Ibid.

[233] "Rusko: Americká základna v ČR je 'jasná hrozba'" (Russia: U.S. Base in the Czech Republic Is a "Clear Threat"), *Hospodářské noviny*, January 22, 2007, https://zahranicni.ihned.cz/c1-20236130-rusko-americka-zakladna-v-cr-je-jasna-hrozba.

[234] "Americká základna prý poškodí bezpečnost ČR" (U.S. Base Is Argued to Be Damaging to the Czech Republic's Security), *Týden*, February 6, 2007, https://www.tyden.cz/rubriky/domaci/americka-zakladna-pry-poskodi-bezpecnost-cr_2700.html?showTab=nejctenejsi-7.

[235] Ministerstvo zahraničních věcí ČR (Czech Ministry of Foreign Affairs), "Zahraničních politika České republiky data 1/2007" (Czech Foreign Policy Data 1/2007).

meetings on the issue with the Czechs in April 2007, but Russia's animosity toward the project persisted.[236]

The Czech government began its somewhat limited communications and outreach efforts in concurrence with the official announcement of the beginning of U.S.-Czech negotiations. These efforts were insufficient and were criticized on multiple levels. "The [Czech] government's information campaign started too late due to post-2006 electoral instability and was decidedly one-sided and biased in favor of radar," according to Májíček. The opposition to a U.S. radar placement on Czech territory was better organized and put the Czech and U.S. governments on defense.

From the beginning, it was clear that the government would have a difficult task communicating the issue effectively to Czech parliamentarians and the Czech public because of low information levels among both groups. Before the issue could be discussed on its merits, some general level of education was required. For example, a Czech parliamentarian incorrectly noted that he heard that a radar site would require an underground nuclear power reactor to meet its energy demands at the government's first briefing about a U.S. request to place a radar site on Czech territory in January 2007.[237] This was not only wrong, but also easily verifiable. Another parliamentarian mentioned that the site in Poland would host about "300 antirockets" (meaning interceptors) instead of the planned 10.[238]

---

[236] Ministerstvo zahraničních věcí ČR (Czech Ministry of Foreign Affairs), "Zahraničních politika České republiky data 4/2007" (Czech Foreign Policy Data 4/2007).

[237] Ministerstvo zahraničních věcí ČR (Czech Ministry of Foreign Affairs), "Zápis z 8. Společné schůze zahraničního výboru, výboru pro obranu, výboru pro bezpečnost a ústavně právního výboru" (Record from the 8th Joint Session of the Committees on Foreign Affairs, Defense, Security, and Constitutional and Legal Affairs), p. 13.

[238] Ibid.

"Politicians were largely ignorant of the issue and were not interested in the issue," said Petr Suchý, Head of the Department of International Relations and European Studies at Masaryk University.[239] The public debate was not much better informed. For example, some argued that an X-band radar in the Czech Republic could be used to track Russian submarines at sea, which is complete nonsense.[240] The Czech government did not even have a chance to officially respond to a U.S. request before mayors from villages in the vicinity of a presumed radar site complained about the government's lack of information about the project and called for a referendum on it.[241]

On January 31, 2007, three committees of the Chamber of Deputies (the Foreign Affairs Committee, the Constitutional and Legal Affairs Committee, and the Security Committee) jointly met to inform the parliamentarians about a U.S. request to begin negotiations on whether the Czech Republic will host a U.S. radar on its territory.[242] After the briefing, Prime Minister Topolánek echoed themes of the press conference that he gave after acknowledging a U.S. request earlier, but this time placed

---

[239] Author interview with Petr Suchý, Head of the Department of International Relations and European Studies, Faculty of Social Studies, Masaryk University, Czech Republic.

[240] "'Smyslem toho projektu je nikdy ho nepoužít,' říká o americké protiraketové obraně velvyslanec v USA Petr Kolář" ("The Point of This Project Is to Never Have to Use It," Says Czech Ambassador to the United States Petr Kolář About the U.S. Missile Defense System), Česká televize (Czech television), August 30, 2007, https://ct24.ceskatelevize.cz/archiv/1464663-smyslem-toho-projektu-je-nikdy-ho-nepouzit-rika-o-americke-protiraketove-obrane.

[241] Ministerstvo zahraničních věcí ČR (Czech Ministry of Foreign Affairs), "Zahraničních politika České republiky data 3/2007" (Czech Foreign Policy Data 3/2007).

[242] "Zápis z 8. Společné schůze zahraničního výboru, výboru pro obranu, výboru pro bezpečnost a ústavně právního výboru" (Record from the 8th Joint Session of the Committees on Foreign Affairs, Defense, Security, and Constitutional and Legal Affairs).

more emphasis on the NATO dimension of the project. Topolánek pledged to provide "relevant and correct" information about the matter.[243] Both Minister of Defense Vlasta Parkanová and Minister of Foreign Affairs Karel Schwarzenberg emphasized that the U.S. ballistic missile defense system was proven, technologically feasible, and does not constitute a threat to the Russian Federation or to China.[244] The committee meetings came amid reports on U.S. preliminary talks on missile defense with the United Kingdom in February 2007.[245] These talks, however, did not advance significantly.

The North Atlantic Treaty and the 2000 Status of Forces Agreement (SOFA) between the Czech Republic and other NATO countries constituted departure points for negotiations on a legal framework that would guide the U.S. military presence on Czech territory. The existing legal framework was inadequate for the type of cooperation that a U.S. radar site would require. The Czech government had to negotiate two new legally binding agreements that required approvals of both chambers of the Czech Parliament and a presidential signature. These two agreements were the Ballistic Missile Defense Agreement (BMDA) with the United States and a bilateral SOFA with the United States. In order for the Czech Republic to host a U.S. radar, the Czech government would also have to implement additional local agreements and update a law on the protection of secret information.[246]

---

[243] Ibid.

[244] Ibid.

[245] "USA jednají s Brity o základně" (The U.S. Is Negotiating with Britain Over a Base), *Lidové Noviny* (*People's Newspaper*), February 24, 2007, https://www.lidovky.cz/svet/usa-jednaji-s-brity-o-zakladne.A070224_124044_ln_zahranici_svo.

[246] "Zápis z 8. Společné schůze zahraničního výboru, výboru pro obranu, výboru pro bezpečnost a ústavně právního výboru" (Record

Over time, Russia's aggressive rhetoric and influence operations on Czech territory permitted the Czech government to speak more openly about its concerns about Russia's desire to project its political influence on Czech territory. In February 2007, Nikolay Solovtsov, Commander of Russia's Strategic Missile Troops, threatened to aim Russia's missiles at U.S. missile defense targets in the Czech Republic and Poland.[247] In response, Czech Foreign Minister Schwarzenberg stated tongue-in-cheek that Russia's threats are more likely to improve polling regarding Czech participation in U.S. missile defense plans.[248] But Russia's threats did not seem to significantly sway the Czechs' views regarding U.S. ballistic missile defense plans on Czech territory.

Two months later, on March 28, 2007, the Czech government responded favorably to a U.S. request to begin negotiations with the United States.[249] In its response, the Czech government recognized and acknowledged ballistic missile threats and emphasized the need to incorporate a potential U.S. radar site in the Czech Republic into a NATO missile defense architecture in the future. The Czech government specified types of preliminary technical surveys and activities, such as environmental cleanup, that the Americans were allowed to conduct in narrowing down

---

from the 8th Joint Session of the Committees on Foreign Affairs, Defense, Security, and Constitutional and Legal Affairs).

[247] Ministerstvo zahraničních věcí ČR (Czech Ministry of Foreign Affairs), "Zahraničních politika České republiky data 2/2007" (Czech Foreign Policy Data 2/2007),
https://www.mzv.cz/public/c1/76/a7/73312_491960_Data_mesicnik u_ZP2007_02.pdf.

[248] Ibid.

[249] Government of the Czech Republic, "Usnesení vlády České Republiky č. 322" (Government Resolution No. 322), March 28, 2007, https://kormoran.vlada.cz/usneseni/usneseni_webtest.nsf/WebGovR es/94CB4DE9F5D32F4FC12572AC0043D2E5?OpenDocument.

a potential future radar location in the Czech Republic.[250] The Czech government's response outlined political boundaries within which the negotiations would be conducted and highlighted issues that were of particular importance to different political parties in the ruling coalition. The United States and the Czech Republic were hopeful that negotiations were going to be concluded by the end of 2007.[251] The estimate proved to be too optimistic as negotiations continued well into 2008.

The issue of a radar's potential impact on the environment was politically important to keep the Green Party's support of the government.[252] The Green Party ran on a platform of ecological sustainability and environmental issues in the June 2006 elections.[253] These issues resonated with the Czech public, particularly because of the damage to the environment caused by the Warsaw Pact armies during the Cold War when they contaminated military training areas with munitions, mines, and toxic chemicals. Environmental cleanup in those areas has been an ongoing issue for successive Czech governments since the dissolution of the Warsaw Pact in 1991.

---

[250] Government of the Czech Republic, "Tisková konference předsedy vlády ČR Mirka Topolánka po zasedání vlády ČR 28. 3. 2007" (Prime Minister Mirek Topolánek's Press Conference After the Czech Government's Meeting on March 28, 2007), March 28, 3007, https://www.vlada.cz/cz/media-centrum/tiskove-konference/tiskova-konference-predsedy-vlady-cr-mirka-topolanka-po-zasedani-vlady-cr-ve-stredu-28—3—2007-21953/.

[251] Ministerstvo zahraničních věcí ČR (Czech Ministry of Foreign Affairs), "Zahraničních politika České republiky data 3/2007" (Czech Foreign Policy Data 3/2007).

[252] "Tisková konference předsedy vlády ČR Mirka Topolánka po zasedání vlády ČR 28. 3. 2007" (Prime Minister Mirek Topolánek's Press Conference after the Czech Government's Meeting on March 28, 2007).

[253] Eva Kneblová, "Volební strategie Strany zelených ve volbách do Poslanecké sněmovny v roce 2006" (The Green Party's 2006 Election Strategy to the Chamber of Deputies), *Central European Political Studies Review*, Vol. XI, Nos. 2–3 (2009), pp. 181–209.

To an outside observer, it may be puzzling why the environmental impact of military activities in a relatively remote forested area was such a salient issue in the Czech Republic. The reason is mushroom gathering—one of the Czechs' favorite pastime activities. Military training areas often look like pristine nature preserves and are undisturbed by city noise—perfect for mushrooming. Even though people are not allowed to enter military areas on a regular basis, many do so, especially those who live nearby.[254] Some people also utilize these military areas for hunting, although hunting is not nearly as popular as mushrooming.[255]

To demonstrate that the radar's effects on the environment and human health would be minimal, the Americans hosted several visits to the Marshall Islands and to the United States beginning in 2007. The purpose of these visits was twofold: one, to inform Czech policymakers and decision-makers about how a U.S. missile defense system works up close; and two, to demonstrate that a radar would have no negative health effects on Czech citizens and the environment by showing the Czech visitors a similar radar that is deployed on Kwajalein Atoll in the Marshall Islands near local population centers.

Representatives of the Czech Ministry of Foreign Affairs and Ministry of Defense visited the Missile Defense Agency's (MDA's) Missile Defense Integration and Operations Center and the North American Air Defense

---

[254] Karel Ferschmann, "Starostové chtěli informace o radaru aneb jak to skutečně bylo" (Mayors Wanted Information About the Radar and What Really Happened), *Obec Němčovice* (*The Village of Němčovice*) blog, September 23, 2007, https://www.nemcovice.cz/starostove-chteli-informace-o-radaru-aneb-jak-to-skutecne-bylo/.

[255] A testament to its natural beauty, Brdy became a Protected Landscape Area in 2016.

Command in Colorado Springs, in April 2007.[256] Six Czech parliamentarians (three Social Democrats and three Civic Democrats) and a delegation from the Czech Ministry of Foreign Affairs and the Ministry of Defense visited the Marshall Islands to see the same X-band radar that was to be dismantled and rebuilt in the Czech Republic the same month. They had an opportunity to talk with operators of the system as well as inhabitants of the Marshall Islands, and got an insight into how the X-band radar affects their everyday lives.[257] One Communist, and one member of the KDU-ČSL Party, did not obtain a U.S. visa to be able to participate, reportedly due to their failure to submit the required paperwork to the U.S. embassy in Prague on time.[258] At least one Social Democrat, Miroslav Svoboda, said he was supportive of a U.S. radar deployment to the Czech Republic after the visit.[259] The other two Social Democrats that participated in the trip, Miroslav Svoboda and Antonín Seďa, also stopped voicing concerns about the radar after their trip.[260]

Prime Minister Topolánek and Minister of Defense Parkanová visited Czech villages near a presumed location for the U.S. radar in April 2007, about three months after the

---

[256] "Chronologie vývoje projektu protiraketové obrany USA" (Chronology of U.S. Ballistic Missile Defense Programs).

[257] "O radaru na Marshallových ostrovech" (About the Radar on Marshall Islands), http://www.army.cz/scripts/detail.php?id=9069.

[258] Ministerstvo zahraničních věcí ČR (Czech Ministry of Foreign Affairs) "Zahraničních politika České republiky data 4/2007" (Czech Foreign Policy Data 4/2007).

[259] "Poslanec ČSSD viděl radar USA. Jsem pro, vzkázal" (ČSSD Parliamentarian Saw Radar in the USA. I'm For it, He Said), *MF Dnes*, April 19, 2007, https://www.idnes.cz/zpravy/zahranicni/poslanec-cssd-videl-radar-usa-jsem-pro-vzkazal.A070419_155621_domaci_ost.

[260] "Americká kampaň za radar začíná masírovat Čechy" (American Campaign for Radar Starting to "Massage" the Czechs), *MF Dnes*, April 23, 2007, https://www.idnes.cz/zpravy/domaci/americka-kampan-za-radar-zacina-masirovat-cechy.A070423_081538_mfdnes_cen.

U.S. official request.²⁶¹ The discussions with the local population were "passionate" and covered both health and security aspects of the issue.²⁶² But they hardly changed the locals' hearts and minds about the radar.

At the same time, Russia's opposition to a U.S. ballistic missile defense site on Czech (and Polish) territory was increasing, despite the Czech government's efforts to counter it. In April 2007, President Putin equated placing components of a U.S. missile defense system in Poland and the Czech Republic to U.S. efforts to place Pershing intermediate-range ballistic missiles in Europe during the Cold War.²⁶³ Equating the two is nonsensical: While Pershing missiles were offensive systems, ballistic missile defense systems are, well, defensive. Besides, U.S. Pershing deployments demonstrated NATO's unity in the face of Soviet threats, which was one of significant contributors to the Soviet Union's demise. Putin considers the fall of the Soviet Union one of the greatest geopolitical disasters of the 20th century, so it is no wonder that Pershing deployments constitute such a powerful imagery in his mind. Countries that have joined NATO since the end of the Cold War would unlikely judge Pershing deployments so harshly. Putin's disgust with the idea of a U.S. radar in the Czech Republic also hinted at another commonality between Pershing deployments and U.S.-Czech ballistic missile cooperation: Russia's active measures campaign against a U.S. radar on Czech territory drew from tactics and methods that Russian

---

²⁶¹ Ministerstvo zahraničních věcí ČR (Czech Ministry of Foreign Affairs), "Zahraničních politika České republiky data 5/2007" (Czech Foreign Policy Data 5/2007), May 2007, https://www.mzv.cz/public/9f/6/80/73324_491966_Data_mesicniku_ZP2007_05.pdf.

²⁶² Ibid.

²⁶³ Ministerstvo zahraničních věcí ČR (Czech Ministry of Foreign Affairs), "Zahraničních politika České republiky data 4/2007" Czech Foreign Policy Data 4/2007).

intelligence services used to manipulate the so-called peace movement in West Germany against U.S. Pershing deployments in the 1980s, as is further discussed in the following chapter.[264]

To help to alleviate Russia's and Allied concerns, Secretary of Defense Robert Gates and Secretary of State Condoleezza Rice wrote in April 2007:

> The system we have in mind is limited, and the missiles have no warhead at all. It is oriented against a potential enemy with a small arsenal, attempting to blackmail our people, sow chaos, and sap our collective will. Development of such a limited system is realistic. Critics of this approach should also be realistic: This system is of no use against a huge nuclear and ballistic missile arsenal, such as that possessed by Russia. Talk of a new "arms race" with Russia is anachronistic and not grounded in reality: America and Russia under the Treaty of Moscow are reducing our strategic nuclear warheads to levels not seen in decades.[265]

Secretary Gates's efforts to move relations with Russia in a more positive direction, at times caused considerable concerns in the Czech Republic, for example when he stated in October 2007 that the Russians might be permitted to maintain a presence at the radar site without prior coordination with the Czech representatives.

---

[264] For the Czech intelligence services' role in the Pershing deployments, see Vladimír Černý and Petr Suchý, "Spies and Peaceniks: Czechoslovak Intelligence Attempts to Thwart NATO's Dual-Track Decision," *Cold War History*, March 1, 2020, pp. 1–19, https://doi.org/10.1080/14682745.2020.1724963.

[265] Robert Gates and Condoleezza Rice, "Commentary: The West Needs a Defense System That Works," American Forces Press Service, April 26, 2007, http://archive.defense.gov/news/newsarticle.aspx?id=32960.

In May 2007, a high-level U.S. delegation visited Prague to negotiate the BMDA and the SOFA agreements. The Czech Foreign Ministry was responsible for negotiating the BMDA and the Defense Ministry was the lead for negotiating the SOFA.[266] The agenda for the meeting and contents of draft agreements were coordinated between the two governments in advance. This was a "zero round" (also called exploratory round) of negotiations.

In preparation for the negotiations with the Americans, Czech negotiators "studied U.S. missile defense cooperation with countries like South Korea, Israel, or Canada," according to Ambassador Kuchyňová-Šmigolová, then-member of the Czech negotiation team for the potential missile defense site in the Czech Republic.[267] For the Americans, Czech familiarity with SOFAs between the United States and other countries sometimes led to confusion and delay in negotiations because the Czechs wanted a similar "deal" as other nations. From an American perspective, such demands were unwarranted because original reasons for why certain provisions were in other countries' SOFAs were not applicable to the Czech case.

On the domestic level, the Czech government responded to Russia's influence activities on Czech territory by being more vocal about Russia's political threats to Czech interests. Prime Minister Topolánek stated that the Czech Republic does not want to belong to a Russian sphere

---

[266] Ondřej Ditrych, "Spojené státy americké v české zahraniční politice" (The United States of America in Czech Foreign Policy), in *Česká zahraniční politika v roce 2007: Analýza ÚMV* (*Czech Foreign Policy in 2007: IIR Analysis*) Prague, Czech Republic: Institute of International Relations, 2008, pp. 185–200, http://www.dokumenty-iir.cz/Knihy/CZP07.pdf.

[267] Author interview with Veronika Kuchyňová-Šmigolová, via Skype, January 22, 2019.

of influence "again."[268] He also highlighted a symbolic continuity between the Czech Republic's accession to NATO and a (hoped for) U.S.-Czech missile defense agreement ratification as the conclusion of a process of regaining the Czech Republic's freedom, and considered U.S.-Czech missile defense cooperation an expression of responsibility for this freedom.[269] He emphasized what he called a moral component of the U.S. ballistic missile defense program—and equated Europe's willingness to host it with Europe's willingness to survive.[270]

Prime Minister Topolánek underscored that the backbone of Czech foreign policy is the transatlantic relationship, that "our" responsibility was to prevent a return of the Czech Republic to the Russian geopolitical influence, and that prevention of such is the real utility of the U.S. radar site on Czech territory.[271] This was one of the few more direct articulations of Czech geopolitical interests in the context of Russia's geopolitical challenge. Prime Minister Topolánek echoed a similar theme in his May 2007 remarks at a conference on "U.S. Missile Defence in Europe:

---

[268] Ministerstvo zahraničních věcí ČR (Czech Ministry of Foreign Affairs), "Zahraničních politika České republiky data 5/2007" (Czech Foreign Policy Data 5/2007).

[269] Ibid.

[270] Ministerstvo zahraničních věcí ČR (Czech Ministry of Foreign Affairs), "Zahraničních politika České republiky data 5/2007" (Czech Foreign Policy Data 5/2007).

[271] Miroslav Topolánek, "Projev Předsedy Vlády ČR Mirka Topolánka Na U.S. Konané Na MZV 31.5.2007" (Conference on U.S. Missile Defence in Europe: Consequences for the Transatlantic Relationship, Prague, Czech Republic, May 31, 2007), https://www.vlada.cz/cz/clenove-vlady/premier/vyznamne-projevy/projev-predsedy-vlady-cr-mirka-topolanka-na-u-s—missile-defence-in-europe-consequences-for-the-transatlantic-relations-konane-na-mzv-31-5-2007-23163/. The Czech original: "Nedopustit oslabení naší vůle k obraně. Nedopustit, abychom se opět plíživě sunuli do sféry geopolitického vlivu Ruska. To je ten pravý důvod, proč u nás má stát radarová základna. Už jenom proto stojí za to udržet tuto vládu."

Consequences for the Transatlantic Relations" at the Czech Ministry of Foreign Affairs in Prague. The majority of his talk focused on the need to defend one's freedom in the face of Russia's newfound geopolitical ambitions. Prime Minister Topolánek did not mention Iranian or North Korean ballistic missiles until the end of his talk, and even then the mention was brief and relatively insignificant.[272]

The Czech Ministry of Defense that led initial (and fairly extensive) missile defense meetings between the U.S. and Czech governments (and that had institutional memory on the issue), did not want to assume a more active role in the government's communications efforts because it wanted to avoid an impression of undue military interference with the civilian execution of the state's international policy. "The Czech Ministry of Defense's role was that of implementation. The Ministry recognized that it was primarily the role of the Ministry of Foreign Affairs to participate in political debates about the radar site," stated Jakub Čimoradský, then Deputy Head of the International Law Section of the Czech Ministry of Defense.[273]

To help to unify the government's messaging strategy, the government appointed Tomáš Klvaňa to be the Special Government Envoy for Communications of the Missile Defense Program between May 25, 2007 and March 2008.[274]

---

[272] Ibid.

[273] Author interview with Jakub Čimoradský, Deputy Head of the International Law Section of the Czech Ministry of Defense, WhatsApp video, January 15, 2019.

[274] Petr Zlatohlávek and natoaktual.cz, "Bývalý Klausův mluvčí bude český 'pan Radar'" (Klaus's Former Spokesperson Will Be a Czech "Mr. Radar"), *MF Dnes*, May 28, 2007, https://www.idnes.cz/zpravy/nato/byvaly-klausuv-mluvci-bude-cesky-pan-radar.A070528_073206_zpr_nato_pal, and Barbora Němcová and ČTK, "Klvaňa skončil jako zmocněnec pro radar" (Klvaňa Ends His Role as Special Envoy for Radar), *MF Dnes*, March 31, 2008, https://www.idnes.cz/zpravy/domaci/klvana-skoncil-jako-zmocnenec-pro-radar.A080331_150018_domaci_ban.

He was faced with a difficult task—explaining a technical issue to a public not versed or interested in the peculiarities of a U.S. ballistic missile defense system, further made difficult by the Czech government's own lack of clarity on the issue. "It was impossible to simplify the expert debate on missile defense for Czech politicians and so sometimes we ended up with a cacophony of voices," stated former First Deputy Minister Pojar.[275]

Special Government Envoy Klvaňa underscored the Czech government's intent to better inform Czech citizens about U.S. missile defense plans during his June 2007 visit to Washington, DC.[276] But in the Czech Republic, he found himself in hot water almost instantly. The communications campaign devised under his supervision was ineffective and amateurish by many participants' accounts of these events. For example, President Václav Klaus directly criticized Special Government Envoy Klvaňa's communications efforts as trivializing and simplifying the issue. Klaus labeled the government's efforts to explain threats and risks as nonexistent.[277]

Others argued that this characterization was unfair and that Special Government Envoy Klvaňa was made a scapegoat for the government's admittedly overall poor performance on the communications front. On balance, it is not clear that the government *could* devise a public relations campaign that would have convinced the Czechs to support

---

[275] Author interview with former First Deputy Minister Pojar.

[276] Ministerstvo zahraničních věcí ČR (Czech Ministry of Foreign Affairs), "Zahraničních politika České republiky data 6/2007" (Czech Foreign Policy Data 6/2007), https://www.mzv.cz/public/93/12/38/73490_491969_Data_mesicnik u_ZP2007_06.pdf.

[277] Ministerstvo zahraničních věcí ČR (Czech Ministry of Foreign Affairs), "Zahraničních politika České republiky data 7-8/2007" (Czech Foreign Policy Data 7-8/2007), August 2007, https://www.mzv.cz/public/f4/c4/6e/73492_491975_Data_mesicniku _ZP2007_07_08.pdf.

a U.S. radar on their territory, but the government made several unwise steps that made such convincing more difficult. For example, hiring Klvaňa was a questionable decision on its own, not because of his lack of formal qualifications, but due to his general inability to connect with Czech citizens, which made him an ineffective communicator. A second complicating factor was that at the time of his hiring, he worked as Area Head of Communication for the British American Tobacco company in the Czech Republic, making it all too easy to portray him in a negative light — and, by extension, the U.S.-radar issue. His sophisticated style was unsuited to connecting with locals near a potential future radar site.[278] The Americans, naturally, did not want to get involved in Czech domestic political debates. But they were aware of domestic difficulties the Czech government was facing, and of increasing controversy associated with the issue.

On June 3, 2007, the Czech government announced that, conditional on the BMDA and SOFA being approved by the Parliament, a future U.S. radar would be built in the Brdy military training area. Selecting a site in Brdy was beneficial from the perspective of domestic politics because the location was one of the three locations considered by the previous Czech Social Democrats-led government.[279] The main criteria for the selection of this location was a balance of military, security, technical, and environmental factors.

---

[278] Robert Čásenský, "Zpověď zoufalého příznivce radaru" (Confession of a Desperate Radar Supporter), *MF Dnes*, September 8, 2007, https://www.idnes.cz/zpravy/domaci/zpoved-zoufaleho-priznivce-radaru.A070907_191544_nazory_ost.

[279] Government of the Czech Republic, "Tiskový briefing předsedy vlády ČR Mirka Topolánka po zasedání Bezpečnostní rady státu 3. Června 2007" (Prime Minister Mirek Topolánek's Briefing after the Meeting of the National Security Council on 3 June, 2007), June 3, 2007, https://www.vlada.cz/scripts/detail.php?id=23827.

The selection was final pending a favorable conclusion of more involved (and expensive) U.S. technical surveys.[280]

A few days after the announcement, President Bush visited Prague and met with Czech government representatives. His visit was marked by protests against the radar site. In one of the Czech government's public relations mishaps, Minister of Defense Parkanová and Czech singer Jan Vyčítala released a song "Welcome Radar," a CD of which Minister Parkanová gave to President Bush. The song was set to the tune of the Soviet propaganda song "Good Day, Major Gagarin." The optics of the whole endeavor were rather poor, and opponents of U.S.-Czech radar cooperation made analogies between the Czech government courting the Soviet Union in the 1960s and the United States in the 2000s, however inapplicable the analogy was given the different circumstances at each of the times.

On June 28, 2007, 35 mayors of villages potentially affected by a U.S. radar site founded the League of Mayors (*Liga starostů*) with the intent of opposing the U.S. radar in Brdy.[281] The initiative did not steer the Czech government away from the plan. In concurrence with a final site selection within the Brdy military training area in July 2007, the ODS officially announced that while it supported the radar, it would not support a referendum on whether the Czech Republic should host it.[282] The ODS's decision was criticized by the opposition parties and by some coalition

---

[280] Ibid.

[281] Jan Neoral, "Starosta píše dopis" (The Mayor Writes a Letter), *Plzeňský Deník* (*Pilsen Journal*), September 25, 2007, https://plzensky.denik.cz/zpravy_region/starosta_pise_dopis_20070925.html.

[282] Ministerstvo zahraničních věcí ČR (Czech Ministry of Foreign Affairs), "Zahraničních politika České republiky dokumenty 7-8/2007" (Czech Foreign Policy Data 7-8/2007), August 2007, https://www.mzv.cz/public/36/53/2/73500_492053_Dokumenty_mesicniku_ZP2007_07_08.pdf.

partners as being undemocratic, but it was necessary if there was to be a radar in the Czech Republic at all.

The Czech and U.S. governments faced an additional challenge as a result of selecting a location that used to be a Warsaw Pact military operating area. By virtue of this fact, the concentration of inhabitants with anti-American views within the vicinity of the Brdy military training area was likely higher than in other parts of the Czech Republic. This is because many people in the region stayed there after they finished their service in the pro-Soviet Czechoslovak Army during the Cold War, which meant they spent their professional lives focused on fighting the "bad" capitalists led by the United States.[283] The pre-existing links made this segment of the population a perfect target for exploitation by the Russian Federation.

Once the Czech government announced a final site selection, the American partners moved fast. A team of specialists from the MDA surveyed the selected site from August 13 to 16, 2007.[284] The follow-up work clarified that a radar site would require a destruction of between 10 hectares and 30 hectares of forested area.[285] This news was received negatively by the Czech public and by the local population that used the area for recreational activities (especially mushroom picking). The need to destroy forests also created a public relations problem for the coalition Green Party, as the party ran on a platform of protecting the environment.

---

[283] Ferschmann, "Starostové chtěli informace o radaru aneb jak to skutečně bylo" (Mayors Wanted Information About the Radar and What Really Happened).

[284] "Chronologie vývoje projektu protiraketové obrany USA," (Chronology of U.S. Ballistic Missile Defense Programs).

[285] "Kvůli radaru padne les o rozloze až sedmi Václaváků" (A Forested Area the Size of Seven Wenceslas Squares Will Be Destroyed Because of the Radar), *Aktuálně.cz*, January 19, 2008, https://zpravy.aktualne.cz/domaci/kvuli-radaru-padne-les-o-rozloze-az-sedmi-vaclavaku/r~i:article:518932/.

In August 2007, the Czech Ministry of Defense released a preliminary technical study that concluded that an X-band radar has no potential to expose Czech citizens or the environment to harmful radiation levels.[286] The purpose of the study was to alleviate the local population's growing concerns about the radar's potential health effects. The Czech Ministry of Defense's study analyzed the potential impact of the radar on each of the 378 nearby villages, many of them with fewer than a hundred people.[287] The number of examined villages gives a sense of the communications challenge on the local level, in addition to the need for the government to win over a majority of fellow Czech citizens not living in the vicinity of a potential radar site, but being sympathetic to those who did.

The study did not indicate any potential significant health impacts stemming from a radar deployment, but it was not accepted as credible by the opponents of the project. Experts agreed that a radar could cause psychosomatic illnesses, such as sleeplessness or anxiety, and highlighted the need for the government to properly communicate with the local communities in order to ease anxieties caused by a potential deployment.[288] Other technical experts challenged conclusions of the Czech Ministry of Defense's preliminary version of the study on the grounds of its lack of precise

---

[286] Czech Ministry of Defense, "Předběžné posouzení vlivu radiolokační stanice EBR (European Based Radar) na zdravotní stav populace v okolí vojenského újezdu Brdy" (Preliminary Assessment of the Impact of the EBR (European Based Radar) on Population's Health Within the Brdy Military Training Area), August 2007,
http://data.idnes.cz/soubory/zpr_nato/A070817_MAD_CELKOVA_Z PRAVA_K_RADARU.PDF.

[287] Ibid.

[288] "Radar zdraví nepoškodí. Ale může vyvolat syndrom" (Radar Does Not Harm Health. But it Can Cause Psychosomatic Syndrome), *Aktuálně.cz*, August 17, 2007,
https://zpravy.aktualne.cz/domaci/radar-zdravi-neposkodi-ale-muze-vyvolat-syndrom/r~i:article:488181/.

data that made it impossible for third parties to verify the study's conclusions. As if in response to these criticisms, the Czech government prepared another study with more granular data in November 2007, confirming the conclusions of the previous study.[289]

Some local mayors considered the 2007 study results untrustworthy, and were by default hostile to any U.S. presence near "their" villages for reasons highlighted earlier.[290] Many mayors complained about a "catastrophically bad level of communication by governmental politicians toward the general public," general misinformation, and a lack of communication on the part of the Czech government in a letter they sent to the Czech Prime Minister, Ministers, Parliamentarians, and Senators on September 25, 2007.[291] The letter, based on misinformed opinions rather than facts, is illustrative of a lack of knowledge about the issue among mayors—who ought to be informed better and with whom the Czech government should have communicated first.

The letter stated that the mayors were united against the "lies" of some politicians and that their opposition to a U.S. radar was not a result of "anti-Americanism, leftism, or communism."[292] The mayors argued that the government did not have the electoral mandate to commit the Czech Republic to such a project, that the radar was fracturing European unity and militarizing space, and that it would

---

[289] "Vědci poprvé zpochybnili studii o radaru. Je povrchní" (Scientists Question the Radar Study for the First Time. It is Perfunctory), *Aktuálně.cz*, November 9, 2007, https://zpravy.aktualne.cz/domaci/vedci-poprve-zpochybnili-studii-o-radaru-je-povrchni/r~i:article:513528/.

[290] "Radar zdraví nepoškodí. Ale může vyvolat syndrom" (Radar Does Not Harm Health. But it Can cause Psychosomatic Syndrome), *Aktuálně.cz*.

[291] Neoral, "Starosta píše dopis" (The Mayor Writes a Letter).

[292] Ibid.

have negative consequences for the environment and people living within its vicinity.[293] The mayors noted that the U.S. House of Representatives cut funding for the project. They also argued that the United States was trying to move intercept points from its territory to Europe, so that Europe, not the United States, would be affected by debris from a real-life missile intercept. The statement is ridiculous on its face. Illustrating just how nonsensical the mayors' opposition became, they also noted that "the fact that Europe, and not the United States, will be polluted by radioactivity [from an intercept] does not seem to bother the Bush Administration."[294]

At the end of September and through early October 2007, a team led by Czech Principal Health Officer and Deputy Minister of Health Michael Vít visited the Marshall Islands to conduct on-site surveys to conclusively confirm that an X-band radar would meet all Czech public safety and health requirements.[295] The team confirmed basic conclusions of the August 2007 study that there would be no harmful consequences to the public in the vicinity of a U.S. X-band radar in the Czech Republic.[296] In early September 2007, Czech and U.S. negotiators met in Prague to discuss the BMDA. The American delegation had provided its draft agreement earlier in April 2007 in

---

[293] Ibid.

[294] Ibid.

[295] Czech Ministry of Defense, "Výsledky cesty expertů na Marshallovy ostrovy" (Results of the Experts' Trip to the Marshall Islands), October 9, 2007,
https://www.google.com/url?sa=t&rct=j&q=&esrc=s&source=web&cd=1&ved=2ahUKEwjUzeDmrc_fAhXvs1kKHcoQBGoQFjAAegQIARAC&url=http%3A%2F%2Fwww.army.cz%2Fimages%2Fid_8001_9000%2F8446%2F174.doc&usg=AovVaw0I1oYU3SdQHU1gpWZaeX69.

[296] Ibid.

preparation for the meeting, and the Czechs countered with their version in August 2007.[297]

In October 2007, representatives from the Ministry of Defense, the Office of the Government,[298] the AMI Communications agency (a private company in charge of coordinating the government's communications), and the War Veterans Association met to discuss the missile defense issue.[299] Meeting participants agreed that the Czech government must improve its information outreach to the Czech population. Secretary Gates's visit to Prague the same month, however, made matters worse for the Czech government when Secretary Gates went off script and mentioned that the Russians could potentially maintain a permanent military presence at a radar site in the Czech Republic.[300]

This was a particularly tone-deaf comment that was perceived negatively by large segments of the Czech population, opponents and supporters alike. Even the Civic Democrats, the most vocal supporters of a radar deployment to the Czech Republic, said they would not

---

[297] Ministerstvo zahraničních věcí ČR (Czech Ministry of Foreign Affairs) "Zahraničních politika České republiky data 9/2007" (Czech Foreign Policy Data 9/2007), September 2007, https://www.mzv.cz/public/7e/6c/e4/73494_491976_Data_mesicniku_ZP2007_09.pdf.

[298] The Office of the Government is the central body of state administration and performs supportive bureaucratic tasks for the Czech government.

[299] Ministerstvo zahraničních věcí ČR (Czech Ministry of Foreign Affairs), "Zahraničních politika České republiky data 10/2007" (Czech Foreign Policy Data 10/2007), October 2007, https://www.mzv.cz/public/1a/6a/b7/73496_491972_Data_mesicniku_ZP2007_10.pdf.

[300] "Američané se omlouvají za výroky o Rusech v Brdech" (Americans Apologized for Their Statements about the Russians in Brdy), iDnes.cz, November 17, 2007, https://zpravy.idnes.cz/americane-se-omlouvaji-za-vyroky-o-rusech-v-brdech-fsk-/zpr_nato.aspx?c=A071117_123637_zpr_nato_inc.

support the project should Russia maintain a permanent presence at the U.S. radar site on Czech territory.[301] Then-U.S. Undersecretary of Defense for Policy Eric Edelman was sent to Prague on an unplanned trip a day after Secretary Gates's departure to smooth out Secretary Gates's comments.

Despite these hiccups, hosting a U.S. radar remained the Czech government's foreign policy priority. Vondra, who then became Czech Deputy Prime Minister, argued that "countries in Central and Eastern Europe are especially motivated to contribute to its [a U.S. missile defense system] creation. History gave us a bitter lesson in the area of defense and it is unquestionable reality that for these countries, maintaining a U.S. presence on their territory will always be a priority of a first order."[302]

In November 2007, U.S. airmen and MDA personnel visited the Brdy military training area to assess its infrastructure needs.[303] With most technical surveys

---

[301] Ministerstvo zahraničních věcí ČR (Czech Ministry of Foreign Affairs), "Zahraničních politika České republiky data 10/2007" (Czech Foreign Policy Data 10/2007).

[302] Ministerstvo zahraničních věcí ČR (Czech Ministry of Foreign Affairs), "Zahraničních politika České republiky dokumenty 10/2007" (Czech Foreign Policy Documents 10/2007), https://www.mzv.cz/public/d3/62/46/73504_492048_Dokumenty_mesicniku_ZP2007_10.pdf. In the Czech original: "země střední a východní Evropy jsou však zvláště motivovány k tomu, aby přispěly k jeho vytvoření. Historie nám dala hořkou lekci v oblasti bezpečnosti a je nezpochybnitelnou realitou, že udržení americké přítomnosti na evropském území bude pro tyto země vždy prvořadou prioritou." Some government officials expressed a similar idea in pointing out a difference between what may be loosely translated as countries where an American soldier set foot and those where a Soviet soldier set foot.

[303] Ministerstvo zahraničních věcí ČR (Czech Ministry of Foreign Affairs), "Zahraničních politika České republiky data 11/2007" (Czech Foreign Policy Data 11/2007), https://www.mzv.cz/public/47/42/b7/279831_491973_Data_mesicniku_ZP2007_11.pdf.

confirming that the location was, indeed, appropriate for a U.S. radar, political negotiations regarding the BMDA and SOFA between the Czech Republic and the United States picked up speed. A U.S. delegation visited Prague in November 2007, and while some progress was made, it was increasingly clear that the governments would not be able to conclude an agreement before the end of the year as originally planned.[304] That caused concern in some circles, as U.S. presidential elections were growing near, and the Topolánek government was becoming weaker and internally more divided. The longer it took to negotiate the agreement, the more difficult it became to obtain a parliamentary consent to the agreement.

Paroubek, now leader of the opposition ČSSD, called the existence of an Iranian ballistic missile threat a "virtual reality," and, during his November 2007 visit to Washington, DC, argued that the position of his party toward the U.S. plan to place an X-band radar in the Czech Republic would change once Iran had such missiles. This was a marked change of opinion from a year earlier when he was Prime Minister and when his Foreign Ministry labeled ballistic missile defense discussions between the two countries appropriate in a context of North Korea's July 2006 ballistic missile test.[305]

Then, in December 2007, the U.S. government published an intelligence assessment that Iran's nuclear weapons program halted in 2003.[306] The publication contributed to the Czech public's skepticism about whether a missile defense system is a necessary and timely response to the

---

[304] Ibid.

[305] Ibid.

[306] Mark Mazzetti, "U.S. Report Says Iran Halted Nuclear Weapons Program in 2003," *The New York Times*, December 3, 2007, https://www.nytimes.com/2007/12/03/world/americas/03iht-cia.5.8573960.html?mtrref=www.google.com&gwh=340AF68633DE07E99B967DDEE31EBE81&gwt=pay.

Iranian threat.³⁰⁷ The same month, Mykhail Kamynin, spokesperson of Russia's Ministry of Foreign Affairs, threatened "retaliatory steps" if the United States placed elements of its missile defense system in Poland and the Czech Republic.³⁰⁸ This would be Russia's last significant threat against the Czech Republic until June 2008. Russia also suspended its participation in the Conventional Forces in Europe Treaty that limits and restricts the conventional weaponry of states that are party to it in December 2007.³⁰⁹

The Czechs had an inkling that a future U.S. Administration might change the Bush Administration's missile defense plans, and that such a change would be more likely under a Democratic Administration. In March 2008, Prime Minister Topolánek stated that a successful John McCain presidential candidacy would guarantee continuity for the Bush Administration's missile defense plan, but that he didn't expect significant changes on this issue should Barack Obama be elected.³¹⁰ The Czech politicians repeatedly expressed the belief that the general U.S. interest in placing a radar on Czech territory would not

---

³⁰⁷ The public discourse did not quite make a distinction between a nuclear and a ballistic missile threat.

³⁰⁸ Ministerstvo zahraničních věcí ČR (Czech Ministry of Foreign Affairs), "Zahraničních politika České republiky data 12/2007" (Czech Foreign Policy Data 12/2007), https://www.mzv.cz/public/f3/1c/91/280349_491974_Data_mesicniku_ZP2007_12.pdf.

³⁰⁹ "Russia Suspends Participation in CFE Treaty," Radio Free Europe/Radio Liberty, December 12, 2007, https://www.rferl.org/a/1079256.html.

³¹⁰ Ministerstvo zahraničních věcí ČR (Czech Ministry of Foreign Affairs), "Zahraničních politika České republiky data 3/2008" (Czech Foreign Policy Data 3/2008).

change, regardless of whether the next U.S. Administration was Democratic or Republican.[311]

The Czech government faced increasing pressure at home from opponents of the radar site. The amount of political capital that the government representatives spent on promoting the plan made it very difficult for Czech radar-site proponents to believe that the United States would "leave them hanging" by cancelling the plan altogether. After all, they were the best allies the United States had in the Czech Republic—and other countries in Europe, particularly in Eastern Europe, were monitoring the situation and making judgments about U.S. credibility and reliability. Because the Czech government was still in the process of convincing its own coalition partners of the desirability of U.S. radar deployments, any hint of doubt on its part would make these already difficult discussions even harder.

The Czech government proceeded on the assumption that there would be no changes in U.S. missile defense plans. In January 2008, Foreign Minister Schwarzenberg caused a stir when he indicated that a U.S. X-band radar on Czech territory could be used to track Russia's systems. He said that how a radar will be used is a matter to be negotiated in the agreement, and that agreements may be revised.[312] He went on to say that he didn't mind if the radar "looked" into Russian territory, especially since the Russian

---

[311] Ministerstvo zahraničních věcí ČR (Czech Ministry of Foreign Affairs), "Zahraničních politika České republiky data 1/2008" (Czech Foreign Policy Data 1/2008).

[312] "Rozhovor redaktorky Terezy Nosálkové s ministrem Schwarzenbergem v Hospodářských novinách z 17.12.2007" (Tereza Nosálková's Interview with Minister Schwarzenberg in *Economic Newspaper* 12/11/2007), *Hospodářské noviny (Economic Newspaper)*, December 17, 2007,
https://www.mzv.cz/jnp/cz/o_ministerstvu/archivy/clanky_a_proje vy_ministru/clanky_a_projevy_ministra_schwarzenberga/karel_schwa rzenberg_radar_zamereny_na.html.

radars presumably "look" into Czech territory.³¹³ His comments to some extent went against the narrative that the radar would not have any impact on Russia. The same month, the Czech government hosted the "Czech Republic –U.S. Ballistic Missile Defense Industry, Research, and Business Seminar" exploring the possibility of Czech companies participating in U.S. ballistic missile technology research and development.³¹⁴ The seminar included all major U.S. defense contractors involved in U.S. ballistic missile defense efforts. General Henry Obering, then director of the MDA, stated that Czech companies could be eligible to gain about $100 million worth of contracts.³¹⁵

Even as BMDA and SOFA negotiations picked up speed, the Czech government's communications continued to be generally ineffective and reactive. A year after the United States sent an official note asking whether the Czech Republic would be open to hosting a U.S. radar, the Czech government stated that it was not interested in spending taxpayers' money on a public relations campaign aimed at convincing the Czech population to support the plan to host elements of a U.S. missile defense system.³¹⁶ The No Bases Initiative managed to take advantage of a lack of the Czech government's commitment to a proactive public campaign and framed the issue in ways that put the government on

---

313 Ibid.

314 Ministerstvo zahraničních věcí ČR (Czech Ministry of Foreign Affairs), "Zahraničních politika České republiky data 1/2008" (Czech Foreign Policy Data 1/2008).

315 "Denní souhrn zpráv" (Daily News Summary), Rádio Praha (Radio Prague), June 16, 2009, https://www.radio.cz/cz/rubrika/bulletin/zpravy−1917.

316 Ministerstvo zahraničních věcí ČR (Czech Ministry of Foreign Affairs), "Zahraničních politika České republiky data 1/2008" (Czech Foreign Policy 1/2008). The official reason was that such an effort is not appropriate given the fact that agreements with the United States were not completed yet.

the defensive.[317] Its representatives labeled even limited government communications efforts as spending taxpayers' resources on a lobbying campaign in favor of a radar.

The Czech government countered with an argument that it was presenting Czech citizens with facts based on which they ought to make their decision, not misleading them about the radar's capabilities and U.S. intent. The environment was ripe for misinformation and disinformation, which opened opportunities for the Russian Federation to exploit the situation to its advantage. "Russia's opposition to U.S.-Czech missile defense cooperation was stronger than we [the Czech government] expected," stated Ambassador Kuchyňová-Šmigolová, then-member of the Czech negotiation team for the potential missile defense site in the Czech Republic.[318] Russia's influence operations in the Czech Republic are an example of Russia's first successful "active measures" campaign on the territory a new NATO member state since the end of the Cold War, which is why this book devotes a separate chapter to them.

The BMDA and the SOFA rounds of negotiations were conducted separately.[319] In concurrence with the negotiations, technical and preparatory visits related to the selected radar site continued. A U.S. delegation visited Prague in February 2008. This round of negotiations brought the two countries very close to a conclusion of the BMDA. Prime Minister Topolánek stated that he

---

[317] Remundová, "Vliv mediálního obrazu na činnost občanské iniciativy Ne základnám" (The Impact of the Media's Perceived Image on the No Bases Civic Initiative's Development).

[318] Kuchyňová-Šmigolová, Interview on U.S.-Czech Missile Defense Cooperation.

[319] "Chronologie vývoje projektu protiraketové obrany USA" (Chronology of U.S. Ballistic Missile Defense Programs).

anticipated that the agreement would be signed at NATO's Bucharest Summit in April 2008.[320]

As the conclusion of radar negotiations between the Czech Republic and the United States neared, the publicity of the No Bases Initiative continued to rise, including on the international scene. In March 2008, Jan Tamáš, the initiative's spokesman, traveled to the United States to meet with members of Congress and speak at several conferences with a broader objective to start a movement against a U.S. radar in the Czech Republic in the United States—and to strengthen general tendencies against ballistic missile defense within some U.S. policy and decision-making circles.[321] His efforts resonated with some parts of the arms control community traditionally opposed to U.S. ballistic missile defense efforts. They had extremely limited or no impact on Congress, which largely considered the issue within the purview of the executive branch (with the exception of appropriations and authorizations) and was being informed about the status of negotiations as they unfolded by the executive branch.[322]

In May 2008, the Czech government published another report on potential health and environmental impacts of a U.S. radar in a planned location near the village of Míšov in Brdy.[323] The report, which relied on measurements and data

---

[320] Ministerstvo zahraničních věcí ČR (Czech Ministry of Foreign Affairs), "Zahraničních politika České republiky data 2/2008" (Czech Foreign Policy Data 2/2008), https://www.mzv.cz/public/e9/19/d0/280355_491979_Data_mesicniku_ZP2008_02.pdf.

[321] Ministerstvo zahraničních věcí ČR (Czech Ministry of Foreign Affairs), "Zahraničních politika České republiky data 3/2008" (Czech Foreign Policy Data 3/2008).

[322] Author interview with Thomas Moore, former staff member, U.S. Senate, by phone, November 21, 2019.

[323] Government of the Czech Republic, "Vláda vzala na vědomí zprávu o zhodnocení zdravotních rizik z provozu radaru EBR, projednala také transportéry" (The Government Recognized a Report on Assessing

from an on-site visit of Czech representatives to the Marshall Islands, concluded that the U.S. radar did not have the potential to generate electromagnetic fields of strength that would be harmful to local populations and the environment.[324] The report had little impact on the opponents of a U.S. radar deployment because they were already too distrustful of any information that did not support their preconceived ideas.

The U.S. Radar, the Czech Republic, and NATO

The Czech Republic and the United States announced the conclusion of negotiations on the placement of a U.S. radar in the Czech Republic at the NATO Bucharest Summit in April 2008.[325] The joint announcement confirmed that a U.S.

Health Risks Stemming from the Operation of the European Radar, and also Discussed a Transporter Issue), March 5, 2008, https://www.vlada.cz/cz/media-centrum/aktualne/vlada-vzala-na-vedomi-zpravu-o-zhodnoceni-zdravotnich-rizik-z-provozu-radaru-ebr—projednala-take-transportery-32330/.

[324] Lukáš Jelínek, "Zhodnocení možných zdravotních rizik vyvolaných elektromagnetickým zářením radiolokátoru EBR v případě, že bude umístěn ve vojenském újezdu Brdy na kótě 718 u obce Míšov" (An Assessment of the Potential Risks Stemming from Electromagnetic Fields Caused by a Radar in the Case of its Placement in the Brdy Military Training Area Near Míšov Village), (Prague, Czech Republic, Národní referenční laboratoř pro neionizující elektromagnetická pole a záření, 2008) (National Reference Laboratory for Non-Ionizing Electromagnetic Fields and Radiation), https://www.google.com/url?sa=t&rct=j&q=&esrc=s&source=web&cd=2&ved=2ahUKEwjD4Za18-3fAhWKTN8KheMyD4QQFjABegQICBAC&url=https%3A%2F%2Flegacy.blisty.cz%2Ffiles%2F2008%2F07%2F27%2Fradar-mzd.doc&usg=AovVaw1ZX6WvXOCQD0red9TxO5yz.

[325] "Česko se dohodlo s USA na radaru, smlouvu podepíše za měsíc" (The Czech Republic and the United States Agreed on a Radar, the Agreement Will Be Signed in a Month), Natoaktual.cz, April 3, 2008, http://www.natoaktual.cz/cesko-se-dohodlo-s-usa-na-radaru-

radar on Czech territory would be connected to other elements of a missile defense system in the United States and Europe and that U.S.-Czech security cooperation was an important contribution to NATO's collective security.[326] Emphasizing the security contributions of U.S.-Czech missile defense cooperation to NATO as a whole, and getting NATO to acknowledge it as such, was an important achievement of the Czech and U.S. government's diplomatic efforts (in cooperation with other states sympathetic to the idea of a missile defense system).[327]

Russian President Putin surprisingly refrained from mentioning the missile defense issue immediately after the Czech-U.S. announcement of the conclusion of BMDA

---

smlouvu-podepise-za-mesic-pm7-/na_zpravy.aspx?c=A080403_155553_na_cr_m02.

[326] Ibid.

[327] Hynek, "Protiraketová obrana v současném strategickém a politickém kontextu. Vztah k odstrašování a dopad třetího pilíře na dynamiku mezi relevantními aktéry" (Missile Defense in the Contemporary Strategic and Political Context. The Connection to Deterrence and the Impact of the Third Site on the Dynamics among Relevant Actors), p. 17. The full text of the joint statement reads: "The United States and the Czech Republic are pleased to announce the completion of negotiations on a missile defense agreement. We plan to sign the agreement in the near future. This agreement is an important step in our efforts to protect our nations and our NATO Allies from the growing threat posed by the proliferation of ballistic missiles and weapons of mass destruction. This agreement calls for the stationing of a U.S. radar in the Czech Republic to track ballistic missiles. The radar will be linked to other U.S. missile defense facilities in Europe and the United States. In addition to deepening our bilateral strategic relationship, we strongly believe that our cooperation in this area will make a substantial contribution to NATO's collective capability to counter existing and future threats in the 21st century, and will be an integral part of any future NATO-wide missile defense architecture." Ministerstvo zahraničních věcí ČR (Czech Ministry of Foreign Affairs), "Zahraničních politika České republiky dokumenty 4/2008" (Czech Foreign Policy Documents 4/2008), https://www.mzv.cz/public/88/9b/6e/280371_492061_Dokumenty_mesicniku_ZP2008_04.pdf.

negotiations.[328] Czech political representatives even mentioned positive developments regarding Russia's objections against a U.S. radar site in the Czech Republic during this timeframe.[329] Perhaps Russia was motivated by not wanting to attract unwelcome attention given its plans to invade Georgia (the invasion took place in August 2008).

Announcing the conclusion of negotiations at the Bucharest Summit was a logical (and symbolic) next step in a NATO-ization of U.S.-Czech ballistic missile defense cooperation, a process that begun in the Czech Republic very early on. Framing U.S.-Czech missile defense cooperation as an Alliance matter underscored the continuity of Czech foreign policy since the end of the Cold War. "Several elements contributed to NATO-ization of the issue: NATO is a guarantor of Czech security, and so its support for a U.S. missile defense project was critical to preserve indivisibility of the north Atlantic security; once allies agree within NATO, the divisive potential of a U.S. missile defense plan in Europe was diminished. The Czech domestic angle was: NATO made a U.S. radar site in the Czech Republic more domestically acceptable," according to Karel Ulík, desk officer for Ballistic Missile Defense and Weapons of Mass Destruction Policy at the Defense Policy Department of the Czech Ministry of Defense from 2002 to 2007.[330] If the Czech Republic and other like-minded nations succeeded in framing U.S. European ballistic missile defense deployments as a NATO contribution, other

---

[328] "Překvapení: Putin o radaru nemluvil" (Surprise: Putin Did Not Discuss the Radar), *Lidové Noviny* (*People's Newspaper*), April 4, 2008, https://www.lidovky.cz/svet/prekvapeni-putin-o-radaru-nemluvil.A080404_123546_ln_zahranici_bat.

[329] Ministerstvo zahraničních věcí ČR (Czech Ministry of Foreign Affairs), "Zahraničních politika České republiky dokumenty 4/2008" (Czech Foreign Policy Documents 4/2008).

[330] Author interview with Karel Ulík, Desk Officer, Ballistic Missile Defense and Weapons of Mass Destruction Policy, Defense Policy Department, Czech Ministry of Defense 2002-2007.

Alliance member states were less likely to object to U.S.-Czech bilateral cooperation on missile defense. Additionally, while "most of NATO's security infrastructure is in the West; a legacy of the Cold War, U.S. assets in Eastern Europe, would balance that to some degree," according to Petr Chalupecký, Deputy Director of the Security Policy Department at the Czech Ministry of Foreign Affairs from 2008 to 2010.[331]

There was the matter of Czech parliamentary mathematics too. The Czech government was motivated by the insistence of the Green Party, one of the coalition parties, to link Czech-U.S. missile defense cooperation to Alliance politics as closely as possible.[332] The Green Party conditioned its continued participation in the government coalition on the United States stating that its missile defense system will be a part of NATO in the future and that nations in the Council of Europe and the North Atlantic Council (NAC) would not be fundamentally opposed to the project.[333] Because the Czech government could not afford to lose any votes in the Chamber of Deputies, it had to meet the Green Party's demands.

The Czech government would likely promote an Alliance dimension of its cooperation with the United States even had it not been for domestic concerns over a fragile coalition government. For one, NATO has been a pillar of Czech security since its accession in 1999. Additionally, many diplomats and professionals involved in missile

---

[331] Author interview with then-Deputy Director Chalupecký.

[332] Hynek, "Protiraketová obrana v současném strategickém a politickém kontextu. Vztah k odstrašování a dopad třetího pilíře na dynamiku mezi relevantními aktéry" (Missile Defense in the Contemporary Strategic and Political Context. The Connection to Deterrence and the Impact of the Third Site on the Dynamics among Relevant Actors), p. 17.

[333] Ministerstvo zahraničních věcí ČR (Czech Ministry of Foreign Affairs), "Zahraničních politika České republiky dokumenty 3/2007" (Czech Foreign Policy Documents 3/2007).

defense negotiations with the United States had experience working on NATO-related issues. Joining NATO, the goal of Czech diplomacy after the fall of the Soviet Union, was a relatively fresh experience when the United States withdrew from the ABM Treaty and informal discussions about missile defense between the two countries started.

Czech diplomacy was aware of the importance of a strong transatlantic link to the Czech Republic's (and Europe's, in a broader context) security. Its goal was for U.S. ballistic missile defense in Europe not to become yet another source of division between the United States and other NATO member states. It wanted to see this issue as a contributor to the healing of a rift between the two sides of the Atlantic after controversies and differences of opinion on the wars in Iraq and Afghanistan.

The Czech government had another pragmatic reason to support NATO-ization of the missile defense issue. The Czech public's support for NATO was much higher than the Czech public's support for a U.S. radar site on Czech territory, with over half of the Czech population in favor of Czech membership in NATO, as Figure 4 shows.[334] The government hoped that by linking the two, some of NATO's popularity would rub off on the radar project. In early 2009, when the public debate about missile defense was at its most visible, the satisfaction with Czech membership of NATO was at its all-time high between 2002 and 2012.[335] The Czech public's opposition to a radar on Czech territory

---

[334] Matouš Pilnáček, "Občané o členství České republiky v NATO–leden 2017" (Citizens on the Czech Republic's Membership in NATO–January 2017), Centrum pro výzkum veřejného mínění (Public Opinion Research Center), February 16, 2017,
https://cvvm.soc.cas.cz/media/com_form2content/documents/c2/a2 162/f9/pm170216a.pdf.

[335] Had there been a referendum on a Czech accession to NATO prior to 1999, it is likely that the Czechs would have voted against joining NATO, as proponents of missile defense did not fail to point out when they were asked about their general lack of support for a referendum.

decreased from 70 percent in December 2007 to 65 percent in January 2009.[336] Another public poll showed that when the radar issue was linked to NATO explicitly, the opposition to the radar decreased to 55 percent.[337]

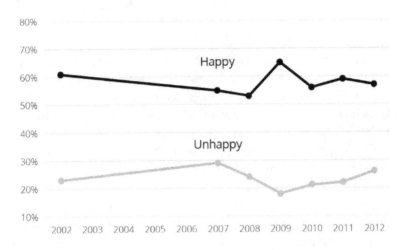

Fig. 4. **Poll on Happiness with Czech Membership in NATO**

Source: Centrum pro výzkum veřejného mínění (Public Opinion Research Centre).

Czech and other like-minded states' diplomatic efforts to get NATO to endorse missile defense were successful.

---

[336] Jan Červenka, "Jak občané hodnotí rozhodnutí vlády USA odstoupit od plánu na vybudování protiraketové radarové základny v ČR?" (How Do Czech Citizens Assess the Cancellation of the U.S. Decision to Build a Radar in the Czech Republic?), Public Opinion Research Centre, November 30, 2009, https://cvvm.soc.cas.cz/media/com_form2content/documents/c2/a655/f9/100971s_pm91130a.pdf.

[337] "Radar nechceme, řekli v referendu Mirošovští" (We Don't Want a Radar, the Citizens of Mirošov Village Said in a Referendum), *Lidové Noviny* (*People's Newspaper*), June 24, 2007, https://www.lidovky.cz/domov/radar-nechceme-rekli-v-referendu-mirosovsti.A070624_125226_ln_domov_fho.

NATO grew more supportive of a U.S. missile defense project over time. In July 2005, the Alliance concluded a ballistic missile defense feasibility study commissioned in 2002. The study was acknowledged by heads of state and governments at the Riga Summit in November 2006.[338] The study concluded that U.S. missile defense plans, including potentially placing a radar site in the Czech Republic, were compatible with a wider NATO missile defense project and that technical fusion between different elements of the system was technologically plausible.[339]

For the Czech government, there was a cost to framing ballistic missile defense cooperation with the United States as a NATO project on the domestic level. Overlapping U.S.-Czech bilateral negotiations on missile defense with a NATO framework led to miscommunication and the Czech public's general confusion about the radar's role in the overall NATO missile defense architecture. The Czech public and some parliamentarians, uninformed about defense and foreign policy issues to begin with, were now required to make sense not only of U.S.-Czech ballistic missile defense cooperation, but also of how it contributes to NATO's security and how it fits within the NATO command and control structure. This inevitably led to difficult questions regarding ballistic missile defense in NATO command and control arrangements, specifics of which were being negotiated at NATO in parallel to U.S.-Czech ballistic missile defense discussions. Some thought that because the radar and missile defense system in Europe would eventually be a part of NATO, the NAC would have final say on whether an incoming missile would be

---

[338] DeBiasso, "Missile Defense and NATO Security," September 2008, p. 50.

[339] "Zápis z 8. Společné schůze zahraničního výboru, výboru pro obranu, výboru pro bezpečnost a ústavně právního výboru" (Record from the 8th Joint Session of the Committees on Foreign Affairs, Defense, Security, and Constitutional and Legal Affairs), p. 5.

intercepted. That would be, of course, impossible due to the short missile flight times, and even shorter time to make a decision to intercept. NATO itself would not declare an "interim" ballistic missile defense capability until 2012.[340]

As early as August 1, 2007, Jiří Šedivý, then-Czech Assistant Deputy Prime Minister for European Affairs, confirmed that NATO would not have a final command and control authority over U.S. radar sites in Poland and the Czech Republic.[341] While that statement should not have surprised anyone with basic knowledge of the issues involved, the focus from some parts of the political spectrum was on a desire for even larger connectivity between NATO and a U.S. radar in the Czech Republic, even to the point of giving the NAC a vote on whether an incoming missile should be intercepted, which would have been unacceptable to the Americans because that would have meant giving up too much U.S. decision-making control.[342] Adding to the confusion on this issue, Prime Minister Topolánek stated in February 2008 that a U.S. missile defense system in Europe, was from the beginning, built as an Alliance system.[343] Statements like this made the government needlessly vulnerable to charges of being dishonest with the voters when they realized that the

---

[340] Paul Dodge and Michael Ziemke, "NATO Ballistic Missile Defense," in Yonah Alexander and Richard Prosen, eds., *NATO: From Regional to Global Security Provider* (Lanham, MD: Lexington Books, 2017), pp. 155-69.

[341] Ministerstvo zahraničních věcí ČR (Czech Ministry of Foreign Affairs), "Zahraničních politika České republiky dokumenty 7-8/2007" (Czech Foreign Policy Documents 7-8/2007).

[342] "Šéfvyjednavač Rood: Radar nebude řídit NATO" (Chief Negotiator Rood: NATO Won't Have a Radar Command and Control), *Aktuálně.cz*, May 5, 2008, https://zpravy.aktualne.cz/zahranici/sefvyjednavac-rood-radar-nebude-ridit-nato/r~i:article:604317/.

[343] Ministerstvo zahraničních věcí ČR (Czech Ministry of Foreign Affairs), "Zahraničních politika České republiky data 2/2008" (Czech Foreign Policy Data 2/2008).

Americans were going to keep unilateral command and control of U.S. missile defense assets in Europe.

Opponents of U.S.-Czech ballistic missile defense cooperation argued that the Czech Republic should wait until negotiations at NATO were concluded and then discuss a U.S. radar placement. They also argued that U.S. retention of command and control authority over its radar meant that it would not contribute to NATO members' security. Proponents were quite correctly arguing that NATO cannot come to a decision on missile defense specifics until details of a U.S.-Czech bilateral ballistic missile defense agreement are known.

The confusion made it yet more difficult for the Czech government to counter negative public images, disinformation, and misinformation about a U.S. radar. In general, the situation illustrates difficulties that democratic governments face when they publicly discuss issues that are of technical nature but usually not prominent in a public discourse until an outside impetus makes them more interesting to the general public. In this case, the outside impetus was created by the virtue of the issue being one of the most significant Czech foreign and defense policy developments after the end of the Cold War, and politization that had to do with a unique post-2006 electoral constellation. To the extent that NATO-zation of the issue increased support for a U.S. radar site in the Czech Republic, it was more effective internationally than domestically.

Despite these difficulties, announcing the BMDA conclusion at the Bucharest Summit underscored the Czech government's emphasis on the multilateral dimension of the project; optics more acceptable to the general population than a perception that a project is solely bilateral between the United States and the Czech Republic. The Bucharest Summit declaration itself expressed a preference for complementarity of U.S. and NATO missile defense systems and endorsed U.S. missile defense plans in Europe as a contribution to Allied security.[344]

Following the announcement about a conclusion of negotiations on the BMDA between the two countries, a group of U.S. experts on defense, logistics, public health, and the environment conducted more elaborate and expensive surveys on a Czech location for a radar site between June 16 and 20, 2008.[345] Exploratory geological work continued through the latter half of 2008 and the beginning of 2009, and resulted in some damage to local communications and trees, as well as increased noise levels. These negative impacts were noted with concern in villages in the vicinity of a future presumed radar site, particularly

---

[344] North Atlantic Treaty Organization, "Bucharest Summit Declaration," April 3, 2008, https://www.nato.int/cps/us/natohq/official_texts_8443.htm. The relevant part of the Bucharest Summit declaration reads: "Ballistic missile proliferation poses an increasing threat to Allies' forces, territory and populations. Missile defence forms part of a broader response to counter this threat. We therefore recognise the substantial contribution to the protection of Allies from long-range ballistic missiles to be provided by the planned deployment of European-based United States missile defence assets. We are exploring ways to link this capability with current NATO missile defence efforts as a way to ensure that it would be an integral part of any future NATO-wide missile defence architecture. Bearing in mind the principle of the indivisibility of Allied security as well as NATO solidarity, we task the Council in Permanent Session to develop options for a comprehensive missile defence architecture to extend coverage to all Allied territory and populations not otherwise covered by the United States system for review at our 2009 Summit, to inform any future political decision."

[345] Vladimír Lukovský, "Pobyt amerických expertů na protiraketovou obranu v ČR" (U.S. Missile Defense Experts' Stay in the Czech Republic), *Department of Defense*, June 17, 2008, https://www.vlada.cz/scripts/modules/fs/icv.vlada.cz/cz/media-centrum/aktualne/pobyt-americkych-expertu-na-protiraketovou-obranu-v-cr-36539/.

since the government had argued that the impact on the local environment would be minimal.[346]

Agreements Signed...at Last

On July 8, 2008, U.S. Secretary of State Condoleezza Rice and Czech Foreign Minister Karel Schwarzenberg signed the final text of the BMDA in Prague.[347] In a public show of disagreement with the event, the Czech Social Democrats hosted Russian General Baluyevsky—who had previously threatened NATO members with nuclear attacks in retaliation for hosting components of a U.S. ballistic missile defense system—at their headquarters in Prague the same day.[348] The Social Democrats' action is illustrative of various Czech politicians legitimizing, and opening the way for, Russia's influence in the Czech Republic, a trend that started in the late 1990s.

Russia issued a strong statement condemning the BMDA signing between the Czech Republic and the United States, and cancelled its own ballistic missile defense

---

[346] "Geologický průzkum u kóty ničí cesty i stromy" (Geological Survey Is Destroying Roads and Trees), *Rokycanský Deník* (*Rokycany Journal*), December 5, 2008,
https://rokycansky.denik.cz/zpravy_region/geologicky-pruzkum-u-koty-podle-lidi-nici-cesty-i-.html.

[347] "Česko a USA podepsaly hlavní smlouvu o radaru" (The Czech Republic and the United States Signed a Main Missile Defense Agreement), a *iDnes.cz*, June 8, 2008,
https://www.idnes.cz/zpravy/domaci/cesko-a-usa-podepsaly-hlavni-smlouvu-o-radaru.A080708_143558_domaci_jw.

[348] Václav Dolejší, "Schwarzenberg: I v ČSSD budou pro radar. Ale až po volbách" (Schwarzenberg: Social Democrats will support the radar. But after elections.), *iDnes.cz*, July 9, 2008,
https://www.idnes.cz/zpravy/domaci/schwarzenberg-i-v-cssd-budou-pro-radar-ale-az-po-volbach.A080708_215554_domaci_abr.

discussions with the United States.[349] Within days of the BMDA signing, Russia cut oil supplies to the Czech Republic by almost half, prompting an official protest from the Czech government.[350] This was one of Russia's first modern uses of oil as an energy weapon. Even though Russia did not explicitly say that the cut was because of the BMDA, the political message was clear. It was further underscored when President Putin ordered the supplies to be restored a few days later, instead of claiming that the disruption was caused by malfunctioning equipment or another legitimate (non-hostile) reason.[351] Russia's action illustrates the connection between the Russian government and its business sector; it would be incorrect to think about them as separate the way one tends to think about business and the government in the United States and other democratic countries.

The Czech and U.S. governments were aware that getting the Czech Parliament to give its consent to the agreement was going to be difficult.[352] In an effort to increase the chances of its passing, Prime Minister Topolánek's government made a brief attempt to link the

---

[349] "Rusové zostřili rétoriku, pohrozili kvůli podpisu radaru" (The Russians Toughened Their Talk Because of the Signing of the Radar Agreement), *iDnes.cz*, July 8, 2008, https://www.idnes.cz/zpravy/zahranicni/rusove-zostrili-retoriku-pohrozili-kvuli-podpisu-radaru.A080708_161058_domaci_ban.

[350] Harry de Quetteville, "Russian Oil Supplies to Czech Republic Cut after Missile Defence Deal with US," *The Telegraph*, July 14, 2008, https://www.telegraph.co.uk/news/worldnews/europe/russia/2403798/Russian-oil-supplies-to-Czech-Republic-cut-after-missile-defence-deal-with-US.html. At the time, the Czech Republic imported about 70 percent of its oil from Russia.

[351] "Putin zavelel: obnovte dodávky ropy do Česka" (Putin Gave a Command: Restore Oil Supplies to the Czech Republic), *Novinky.cz*, July 21, 2008, https://www.novinky.cz/ekonomika/145430-putin-zavelel-obnovte-dodavky-ropy-do-ceska.html.

[352] There was no equivalent congressional process required from the Americans.

potential ratification of the agreement with a ratification of the Lisbon Treaty being debated in the European Union member countries during this timeframe—and which did not have broad popular support in the Czech Republic. Prime Minister Topolánek indicated that his government would support the Lisbon Treaty if the opposition supported the BMDA.[353] This proposed trade was criticized by the opposition parties as "reckless," and the effort was eventually abandoned.[354]

In the BMDA, the United States and the Czech Republic emphasized the agreement's contributions to transatlantic security. For example, Article III of the agreement stated that, "The United States fully intends for the United States ballistic missile defense system to be an interoperable and integral part of evolving NATO missile defense capabilities."[355] The agreement, article by article, specified terms of construction of the radar site; personnel matters; use of the radar site; its construction and operation; property ownership; radar site management communications; ballistic missile defense command and control; financial responsibilities; procedures related to handling controlled unclassified information; procedures related to handling classified information; radar site security; protection of the environment; claims; procedures

---

[353] This proposal has to be understood in the context of the ODS's traditional anti-EU stance.

[354] "My schválíme Lisabonskou smlouvu, vy radar, handlují politici" (We Will Approve the Lisbon Treaty, You Will Support the Radar, Politicians Trade), *iDnes.cz*, June 1, 2008, https://www.idnes.cz/zpravy/domaci/my-schvalime-lisabonskou-smlouvu-vy-radar-handluji-politici.A080601_134205_domaci_adb.

[355] Embassy of the United States in the Czech Republic, "Agreement Between the Czech Republic and the United States of America on Establishing a United States Ballistic Missile Defense Radar Site in the Czech Republic," July 8, 2008, http://www.aic.cz/cms/Agreement_EN.pdf.

for implementation and disputes; and information about entry into force, amendment, and duration procedures.[356]

The United States agreed to make the BMDA public just a few weeks after negotiations concluded. The step was intended to help the Czech government to demonstrate its commitment to transparency, a significant distinguishing feature from previous discussions conducted under the Social Democrats' supervision. The opposition used this transparency to criticize the agreement and the Czech government without giving the government due credit for getting the United States to agree to the disclosure so soon after the negotiations concluded.

There were several domestically politically contentious issues for the Czech government in the agreement. The fact that the United States was to retain command and control authority over its missile defense system was misused by opponents of the radar site as evidence that the Czech government was not being truthful about the radar's NATO contribution.[357] The agreement also specifically exempted the United States from responsibility for "the release, or its effects, of any pre-existing contamination, hazardous wastes, hazardous materials, or non-hazardous wastes," and specified that "prior to leaving the radar site, the United States shall provide timely removal and disposal of all known hazardous wastes, hazardous materials, and non-hazardous wastes introduced at the radar site."[358] This was

---

[356] The full text of the agreement is available at ibid.

[357] "Schwarzenberg přiznal, že antiraketu odpálí Američané" (Schwarzenberg Admitted that Interceptors Will Be Fired by the Americans), *Novinky.cz* (*Newspaper.cz*), October 7, 2007, https://www.novinky.cz/domaci/124088-schwarzenberg-priznal-ze-antiraketu-odpali-americane.html.

[358] Embassy of the United States in the Czech Republic, "Agreement Between the Czech Republic and the United States of America on Establishing a United States Ballistic Missile Defense Radar Site in the Czech Republic."

interpreted as evidence that the Czech government did not care about the environment enough.

This practice is consistent with U.S. policy worldwide and in concrete terms meant that the Czech Republic would be responsible for remediation of any contamination that originated from times before the U.S. radar site construction started, even if it was uncovered during the construction (including a disposition of unexploded ordnance). The provision made sense given the Warsaw Pact armies' notorious disregard for the environment and given U.S. concerns over being held liable for mitigating Soviet-era contamination. U.S. on-site surveys assessed the level of contamination to provide a baseline to which the environment was to return should a radar in the Czech Republic no longer be necessary or should the Czech Republic withdraw its agreement to host it, in which case the United States would be forced to dismantle its radar, abandon the site, and return it to an agreed upon status.

The Czech government's charm offensive against the Czech population who opposed the U.S. radar continued with some help from the United States. In an effort to help to dissuade concerns of the Czechs who lived near the radar site, General Obering and Richard Graber, then-U.S. Ambassador to the Czech Republic, met with local mayors in July 2008.[359] Topics included the radar's impact on health and wellbeing of citizens that would live near the site, as well as the radar's role in the overall U.S. missile defense architecture. The meeting illustrated that local opposition to a U.S. radar deployment was not uniform. In general, members of the municipal councils were inclined to treat a potential radar deployment more favorably than the

---

[359] Karel Hutr, "Radar bude v provozu dvě hodiny" (The Radar Will Be Operational for Two Hours), *Příbramský deník* (*Příbram Journal*), July 11, 2008, https://pribramsky.denik.cz/galerie/radarbrdy.html?mm=544931&back=2833746097-2109-47&photo=2.

mayors, particularly in the context of the Czech government's promises to improve the local infrastructure network.[360]

Some members of municipal councils were also aware that the recurring U.S. investments associated with a radar deployment would benefit local economies in otherwise relatively poor areas. In October 2008, 12 representatives of villages in the vicinity of a presumed future radar site visited U.S. Air Force Base at Ramstein in Germany, and the Polygone Electronic Warfare Tactic Range in Germany, to meet with local German representatives and members of the public to learn about their experience of cooperating with the United States first-hand.[361] The Czechs' visit underscored their divisions with regard to a potential U.S. presence on Czech territory, with some arguing that the project is necessary, and with others saying it would just cause economic dependence on the Americans and make ballistic missile attacks on the Czech Republic more likely.[362]

The SOFA negotiations continued after the BMDA signature. These negotiations were more difficult from a U.S. perspective than the BMDA negotiations because they had to do with conduct of U.S. personnel on foreign territory, a politically sensitive issue for both governments. The Czech government approved the SOFA on September 10, 2008.[363] The SOFA was signed by Secretary Gates and

---

[360] Ibid.

[361] Pavel Eichler, "Starostové z Brd viděli dvě americké základny. Ale bez radaru" (Mayors from Brdy Saw Two U.S. Bases. But Without the Radar), *MF Dnes*, October 14, 2008,
https://www.idnes.cz/zpravy/zahranicni/starostove-z-brd-videli-dve-americke-zakladny-ale-bez-radaru.A081013_170237_zahranicni_pei.

[362] Ibid.

[363] "Vláda schválila smlouvu SOFA, radar i půda pod ním zůstane Česku" (The Government Approved the SOFA, Radar, and the Soil Underneath Will Remain Czech), iDnes.cz, September 10, 2008,

Minister Parkanová on September 19, 2008, in London.[364] The SOFA provided "for the status of United States forces, its personnel and dependents who are present in the territory of the Czech Republic in connection with the radar site" and "for the status of United States contractors and United States contractor employees present in the territory of the Czech Republic in connection with construction and operation of the radar site."[365]

The Czech Republic retained sovereignty over the site of the future U.S. radar and mandated that the United States follow Czech regulations during the site construction.[366] The Czech Republic agreed to provide external security and protection for the site. Among contentious negotiation issues between the two governments was the fact that the SOFA was relatively narrow and specific to building and operating the U.S. radar site. The United States was interested in a broader agreement, so it would not have to negotiate another agreement if it decided on an additional military presence at some point in the future (with the Czech government's consent, of course). The Czech government wanted a narrow agreement to make it more acceptable domestically and increase the agreement's chances of passing in both chambers of Parliament, which the Americans eventually accepted.

---

https://www.idnes.cz/zpravy/domaci/vlada-schvalila-smlouvu-sofa-radar-i-puda-pod-nim-zustane-cesku.A080910_142601_domaci_klu.

[364] "Parkanová podepsala smlouvu o pobytu amerických vojáků v ČR" (Parkanová Signed an Agreement Regulating U.S. Troops' Stay in the Czech Republic), *iDnes.cz*, September 19, 2008,
https://www.novinky.cz/domaci/150035-parkanova-podepsala-smlouvu-o-pobytu-amerických-vojaku-v-cr.html.

[365] Embassy of the United States in the Czech Republic, "Agreement between the United States of America and the Czech Republic on the Status of United States Forces Present in the Territory of the Czech Republic."

[366] Ibid.

Matters related to jurisdiction over U.S. personnel operating a radar, and their dependents, and whether U.S. personnel would be allowed to carry arms, as well as how taxation would be handled were among other contentious issues.[367] As a matter of U.S. policy, the United States does not pay taxes related to stationing its forces or building its sites to other countries. Additionally, the SOFA specified criminal liabilities; taxation obligations and exemptions for U.S. personnel and civilians operating the site; criminal jurisdiction and cooperation on such matters between the two countries; claims procedures; U.S. military postal system, banking system, and currency exchange activities; logistics support; utilities and communications; environmental and health and safety issues; and labor force hiring and salary procedures; and contained a section on the agreement's implementation and dispute resolution procedures.[368] Both the SOFA and the BMDA were signed as agreements of unlimited duration.

As negotiations concluded and the Czech government approved both the BMDA and SOFA, domestic political support for the treaties continued to suffer. The radar issue was discussed among political parties as they competed for senatorial and regional elections in October 2008. In these elections, the Czech Social Democrats soundly and decisively defeated the Civic Democrats. The Czech Social Democrats gained 16 seats in the Czech Senate where agreements with the United States would have to be approved. While the coalition parties retained a majority, the margins narrowed, indicating potential trouble for the

---

[367] "Parkanová podepsala smlouvu o pobytu amerických vojáků v ČR" (Parkanová Signed an Agreement Regulating U.S. Troops' Stay in the Czech Republic).

[368] Full text of the agreement at: Embassy of the United States in the Czech Republic, "Agreement Between the United States of America and the Czech Republic on the Status of United States Forces Present in the Territory of the Czech Republic."

already weak Topolánek government. The de facto defeat indicated a power shift from the ruling coalition to the Czech Social Democrats.

The ODS's support for a U.S. radar site and the government's lack of an effective communication strategy with the general public were cited as the two most significant reasons for the party's defeat, especially by opponents of U.S.-Czech ballistic missile defense cooperation, who generally erred of the side of inflating the role of the radar issue in Czech elections.[369] U.S.-Czech missile defense cooperation was not the only reason, and it probably wasn't the main reason, for why the ruling coalition lost its power. That did not stop the Russian Federation from touting the election results as definitive proof of the Czech Republic's rejection of the radar site, and of Czech foreign policy's pro-Western orientation in general.[370] Russia's view was narrow and propagandistic, but there is no denying that the radar issue contributed to the Czech government coalition parties' losses. According to a poll commissioned by the Czech Ministry of Foreign Affairs, the radar issue was an election consideration for only about a fifth of the voters in the fall 2008 elections.[371] A more important electoral factor was the government's

---

[369] Josef Mlejnek, "Politolog: ODS utržila K.O. a leží bezvládně v ringu" (Political Scientist: Civic Democrats Are Knocked Out and Laying Helplessly in the Ring), *iDnes.cz*, October 19, 2008, https://www.idnes.cz/zpravy/domaci/politolog-ods-utrzila-k-o-a-lezi-bezvladne-v-ringu.A081018_205844_nazory_ton.

[370] "Ruský tisk o volbách: radar prohrál" (Russian Press on Elections: Radar Lost), *Lidové Noviny* (*People's Newspaper*), October 27, 2008, https://www.lidovky.cz/svet/rusky-tisk-o-volbach-radar-prohral.A081027_093749_ln_zahranici_nev.

[371] Viliam Buchert, "Radar v Brdech podporuje stále více voličů zelených i ČSSD" (More Green Party and Social Democratic Party Voters Support Radar in Brdy), *MF Dnes*, October 6, 2008, https://www.idnes.cz/zpravy/domaci/radar-v-brdech-podporuje-stale-vice-volicu-zelenych-i-cssd.A081006_080812_domaci_jte."

support of other unpopular steps, such as increasing health care fees and cutting some of the state's welfare programs, which certainly did not resonate with a majority of the Czech voters.

Emboldened by the election results, the Czech Social Democrats and the Communists continued to challenge the government's support for the U.S. radar site. They argued that the public debate about the BMDA required more time—with the goal of delaying the vote until the change of government in the Czech Republic, or of the presidential administration in the United States. They knew that the government's communication campaign was ineffective and that the issue continued to suffer from a great degree of negative publicity. Additionally, the opposition parties pursued an option of submitting the agreement for a review to the Czech Constitutional Court.[372] If the Constitutional Court took up the issue, voting in Parliament would have to be delayed until the Constitutional Court provided its opinion on the constitutionality of the agreement and whether it required a three-fifths vote in Parliament (rather than a simple majority vote).[373]

The gist of the opposition's objections to the agreement was that the Czech constitution did not envision a situation in which there would be a permanent military presence on Czech territory and therefore required an opinion of the Constitutional Court. The Topolánek government would not be able to get three-fifths of members in the Chamber of

---

[372] "ČSSD navrhne Sněmovně předložit radar Ústavnímu soudu" (Social Democrats to Propose that the Radar Agreement Be Sent to the Constitutional Court), *Novinky.cz*, November 7, 2008, https://www.novinky.cz/domaci/153869-cssd-navrhne-snemovne-predlozit-radar-ustavnimu-soudu.html.

[373] "ČSSD zvažuje, že dá americký radar k Ústavnímu soudu" (The Social Democratic Party Is Considering the Constitutional Court's Review for the Radar Agreement), *iDnes.cz*, November 1, 2008, https://www.idnes.cz/zpravy/domaci/cssd-zvazuje-ze-da-americky-radar-k-ustavnimu-soudu.A081101_155058_domaci_cen.

Deputies to agree to the BMDA; a simple majority of present members was a high enough hurdle already. Fortunately for the Czech government, the opposition was not able to get enough votes in the Senate to refer the treaty to the Constitutional Court.

On October 31, 2008, the Czech Republic and the United States signed an agreement on technical missile defense cooperation.[374] The agreement provided Czech companies and research institutions with opportunities to participate in research and development of advanced technologies, including those of a more general character and not related to missile defense. The Czech Republic is one of the few countries in the world that has signed such an agreement with the United States.[375] It is an example of another transcending legacy of U.S.-Czech ballistic missile defense cooperation.

In the public domain, the discussion about the Czechs hosting a U.S. missile defense site was sometimes linked to the question about whether Czech citizens will continue to need a visa to travel to the United States. Czech politicians were in favor of de-linking the issues, likely because they understood the difficulties of getting the agreements through the House of Deputies and did not want the potential rejection to hurt the Czech Republic's chances of

---

[374] Ministerstvo obrany (Ministry of Defense), "Podpis Rámcové dohody mezi ČR a USA" (Signing of the Framework Agreement Between the Czech Republic and the United States), N/A, http://www.army.cz/scripts/detail.php?id=12315.

[375] Nikola Hynek, "Protiraketová obrana v současném strategickém a politickém kontextu. Vztah k odstrašování a dopad třetího pilíře na dynamiku mezi relevantními aktéry" (Missile Defense in the Contemporary Strategic and Political Context. The Connection to Deterrence and the Impact of the Third Site on the Dynamics among Relevant Actors), p. 15.

joining the United States' Visa Waiver Program (VWP).³⁷⁶ But the issues were connected, since joining the VWP would take away one of U.S. ballistic missile defense cooperation opponents' arguments, namely the claim that the Americans treated the Czechs like a second-class allies.³⁷⁷ But on November 17, 2008, the Czech Republic joined the VWP, and Czech tourists no longer have to obtain a rather expensive visa to visit the United States.³⁷⁸ This was a significant achievement for Czech diplomacy and another one that transcends U.S.-Czech ballistic missile defense cooperation.³⁷⁹

The Czech Senate gave its consent to the ratification of the BMDA and the SOFA on November 27, 2008, with 49 Senators voting in favor of, and 32 against, the agreement.³⁸⁰ The timing of the vote signaled to the Americans the Czech

---

³⁷⁶ Ministerstvo zahraničních věcí ČR (Czech Ministry of Foreign Affairs), "Zahraničních politika České republiky data 3/2007" (Czech Foreign Policy Data 3/2007).

³⁷⁷ Author interview with Petr Suchý, Head of the Department of International Relations and European Studies, Faculty of Social Studies, Masaryk University, Czech Republic.

³⁷⁸ News release, "President Bush Announces Visa Waiver Program Expansion—VWP Travel Begins November 17," U.S. Department of State, November 17, 2008,
https://travel.state.gov/content/travel/en/us-visas/visa-information-resources/visas-news-archive/20081117_president-bush-announces-visa-waiver-program-expansion---vwp-tra.html.

³⁷⁹ For example, the United States did not accept Poland into the Visa Waiver Program until 2019.

³⁸⁰ Senát (Senate), "Vládní návrh, kterým se předkládá Parlamentu České republiky k vyslovení souhlasu s ratifikací Dohoda mezi Českou republikou a Spojenými státy americkými o zřízení radarové stanice protiraketové obrany Spojených států v České republice, podepsaná dne 8. Července 2008 v Praze" (Government Proposal for the Parliament of the Cech Republic to Consent to Ratification of the Agreement Between the Czech Republic and the United States on Building a U.S. Radar Station in the Czech Republic, Signed on 8 July, 2008, in Prague), November 27, 2008,
.senat.cz/xqw/xervlet/pssenat/hlasy?G=9432&O=7.

government's hope that the Obama Administration, which was to take office in January 2009, would not cancel the plan, even though "reservations about the Missile Defense Project [meaning the Bush Administration's third site plan] were visible in some of candidate Obama's speeches," stated Barbora Ešnerová of the Permanent Delegation of the Czech Republic to NATO.[381] Candidate Obama announced during his campaign: "I will cut tens of billions of dollars in wasteful spending. I will cut investments in unproven missile defense systems. I will not weaponize space."[382]

Prime Minister Topolánek decided to delay the final vote on the agreements in the Chamber of Deputies until after President Obama took office. The government did not have enough political support in the Chamber of Deputies to ratify the agreement, which undoubtedly played a role in his decision.[383] Meanwhile, the delay just provided fuel to the fire for the opponents of U.S.-Czech ballistic missile defense cooperation. "The opposition said that President Obama was going to cancel the radar project, which made it hard to defend the project in the Czech Parliament," Ešnerová remarked.[384] Meanwhile, Russia's increasingly assertive foreign policy, especially after its invasion of Georgia in August 2008, made Czech radar supporters'

---

[381] Author interview with Barbora Ešnerová, Head of Political Unit, Permanent Delegation of the Czech Republic to NATO, and previously Political Counselor from the Czech Ministry of Foreign Affairs to the Czech Embassy in the United States, by phone, January 18, 2019.

[382] Angie Drobnic Holan, "Obama Wants to Reduce Stockpiles, Not Disarm," *Politifact*, July 15, 2008, https://www.politifact.com/truth-o-meter/statements/2008/jul/15/chain-email/obama-wants-to-reduce-stockpiles-not-disarm/.

[383] Ministerstvo zahraničních věcí ČR (Czech Ministry of Foreign Affairs), "Zahraničních politika České republiky data 11/2008" (Czech Foreign Policy Data 11/2008), https://www.mzv.cz/public/bb/3f/b4/1124291_1058485_Data_mesic niku_ZP_11_08.doc.

[384] Author interview with Barbora Ešnerová.

geopolitical rationale for participating in a U.S. ballistic missile defense program more acute.[385] But the Czech government was unable to capitalize on the Czech public's sentiment after Russia's invasion of Georgia to strengthen its case for a radar as a geopolitical hedge against Russia's influence. The Czech public's opposition to a U.S. radar site remained at about 67 percent in September 2008.[386]

The situation in concurrence with the U.S. presidential transition made the continuation of work on placing a U.S. radar on Czech territory even more challenging. The possibility of the U.S. missile defense plans being re-evaluated by the new U.S. administration was perceived as real in the Czech Republic, particularly since the U.S. Congress mandated that the new administration conduct a comprehensive review of U.S. ballistic missile defense policy. While the Czech government's public statements indicate that, while it expected some level of change regarding U.S. missile defense policy, many government officials did not expect the Obama Administration to cancel the radar site on Czech territory altogether.[387] As Ešnerová explained: "We were never told openly [that a radar would be cancelled] and so, naturally, we continued in the negotiation and later on in the dialogue with the new U.S.

---

[385] Ministerstvo zahraničních věcí ČR (Czech Ministry of Foreign Affairs), "Zahraničních politika České republiky dokumenty 11/2008" (Czech Foreign Policy Documents 11/2008), https://www.mzv.cz/public/2a/2d/c5/1124293_1058486_Dokumenty_mesicniku_ZP_11_08.doc.

[386] Dan Prokop, "Ruský vpád do Gruzie podporu radaru nepřinesl, ukázal průzkum" (Russia's Invasion of Georgia Did Not Increase Radar's Support), *MF Dnes*, October 3, 2008, https://www.idnes.cz/zpravy/domaci/rusky-vpad-do-gruzie-podporu-radaru-neprinesl-ukazal-pruzkum.A081003_175630_domaci_dp.

[387] Ministerstvo zahraničních věcí ČR (Czech Ministry of Foreign Affairs), "Zahraničních politika České republiky dokumenty 11/2008."

administration and in getting our Parliamentarians on board [in support of the radar site]."[388]

The Czechs were also at times assured by the Bush Administration that a radar in the Czech Republic would be necessary and contribute to a U.S. missile defense architecture even without interceptors in Poland, giving them additional grounds for optimism.[389] Perhaps U.S. statements like that were aimed at increasing pressure on Poland, as negotiations with Poland reportedly stalled due to Polish demands for U.S. assistance with modernizing the Polish military in the spring 2008 timeframe.[390] Similarly, reports that the United States retained an option to build missile defense sites elsewhere in Europe should the negotiations with the Czech Republic or Poland prove unproductive were perhaps meant to increase pressure on the Czech and Polish Parliaments to ratify the agreement.[391]

The Topolánek government's continued efforts to get the agreements with the United States ratified were ultimately unsuccessful. Just how increasingly precarious the government's situation had become, was on full display on March 17, 2009. The BMDA and SOFA almost got voted down in the Czech Chamber of Deputies after the opposition took advantage of absences of some coalition parliamentarians and attempted to schedule a vote on them.[392] The embarrassed government coalition had to

---

[388] Author interview with Barbora Ešnerová.

[389] "USA: Radar v Česku chceme, i když Poláci řeknou ne" (USA: We Want a Radar in the Czech Republic Even if the Poles Say No), *Aktuálně.cz*, April 2, 2008, https://zpravy.aktualne.cz/zahranici/usa-radar-v-cesku-chceme-i-kdyz-polaci-reknou-ne/r~i:article:601295/.

[390] Ibid.

[391] "USA mají plán B pro základnu" (The USA Has a Plan B for a Base), *Lidové Noviny (People's Newspaper)*, January 27, 2009, https://www.pressreader.com/czech-republic/lidove-noviny/20070127/281775624685033.

[392] "Vláda nechce riskovat zamítnutí radaru, ze Sněmovny ho nečekaně stáhla" (The Government Does Not Want to Risk a Rejection of the

withdraw both agreements from consideration to avoid a last-minute defeat.[393]

On March 25, 2009, the Topolánek government faced its fifth vote of no-confidence in the Czech Chamber of Deputies—which was successful this time around. The Topolánek government was toppled due to corruption scandals, supporting unpopular steps like lowering government support for families with children, increasing out-of-pocket health care fees, and supporting the radar.[394] In practical terms, it meant that "the Czech government influence on the U.S. decision-making process once the administrations changed was limited because it was very much weakened by the domestic politics and the public did not support a U.S. missile defense radar on the Czech territory," according to Čimoradský.[395]

The fall of the Topolánek government illustrated the significant role that egos and personal ambitions played in the whole U.S.-Czech ballistic missile defense debate. The no-confidence vote in the Chamber of Deputies was orchestrated by the opposition parties, led by the ČSSD's Paroubek. The government's loss of confidence was a domestic embarrassment to Prime Minister Topolánek personally and to the Czech Republic internationally because the country chaired the European Union at that

---

Radar in the Chamber of Deputies, It Withdrew the Agreement Unexpectedly), *iDnes.cz*, March 17, 2009,
https://www.idnes.cz/zpravy/domaci/vlada-nechce-riskovat-zamitnuti-radaru-ze-snemovny-ho-necekane-stahla.A090317_162522_domaci_jw.

[393] Ibid.

[394] "Koaliční vláda padla kvůli aférám, krizi a radaru" (The Coalition Government Fell Due to Crises and the Radar), *Deník.cz*, March 25, 2009, https://www.denik.cz/z_domova/vlada-pad-neduvera-afery-krize-radar20090325.html.

[395] Author interview with Jakub Čimoradský, Deputy Head of the International Law Section of the Czech Ministry of Defense.

time.[396] The government's fall was also a public relations gift to opponents of U.S.-Czech ballistic missile defense cooperation—and to the Russian Federation.

The Fischer Government: May 8, 2009–July 13, 2010

After the Topolánek government fell, negotiations started among the political parties to form a new government. Political parties eventually agreed to nominate and support Jan Fischer, Director of the Czech Statistical Office at the time, as Prime Minister.[397] The "caretaker" government was supposed to rule only until the preliminary elections notionally scheduled for fall 2009, but ended up serving the remainder of the regular electoral term until the October 2010 elections.[398]

Upon taking office, Prime Minister Fischer decided that the government would not take up a SOFA and BMDA ratification in the Czech Chamber of Deputies, because he felt he did not have a mandate to solve such a controversial

---

[396] Martin Komárek, "Jak moc poškodil pád vlády dobré jméno Česka" (How Damaging the Fall of the Government Was to the Czech Republic's Good Reputation), *iDnes.cz*, April 21, 2009, https://www.idnes.cz/zpravy/archiv/jak-moc-poskodil-pad-vlady-dobre-jmeno-ceska.A090420_171229_kavarna_bos.

[397] "Premiérem má být šéf ČSÚ Fischer, dohodla koalice s ČSSD" (The Social-Democratic-Led Coalition Agreed that the New Prime Minister Will Be Director of the Czech Statistical Office Fischer), *Novinky.cz*, April 5, 2009, https://www.novinky.cz/domaci/165694-premierem-ma-byt-sef-csu-fischer-dohodla-koalice-s-cssd.html.

[398] "Úřednická vláda pod vedením Jana Fischera končí" (The Bureaucratic Cabinet Under the Leadership of Jan Fischer Ends), *iRozhlas*, July 12, 2010, https://www.irozhlas.cz/zpravy-domov/urednicka-vlada-pod-vedenim-jana-fischera-konci-_201007121648_mkopp.

issue.[399] New Defense Minister Martin Barták ordered the Ministry of Defense to destroy the fence around the presumed future radar site, a symbolic step underscoring the government's unwillingness to engage with the issue and welcomed by local citizens and opponents of a U.S. radar on Czech soil.[400] But Barták also expressed regrets that the Czech Chamber of Deputies did not approve the agreements negotiated with the United States because if it had, the Czech Republic would have "at least some assurances" that the project would move forward in a new administration.[401]

The Obama Administration's silence on the future of a U.S. radar in the Czech Republic was a telltale sign that the project was in a danger of cancellation. Then in February 2009, the administration stopped all practical preparations for the construction of a site in the Czech Republic.

Statesmen from Central and Eastern European countries attempted to remind the Obama Administration of the symbolic importance of ballistic missile defense cooperation with the Czech Republic and Poland in an open letter published in the *Gazeta Wyborcza* on July 16, 2009. A part of the letter relevant to missile defense efforts read:

---

[399] "Fischer: O vládě budu mít jasno ve čtvrtek" (Fischer: I Will Be Clear About the Government on Thursday), *Česká televize* (Czech Television), April 25, 2009, https://ct24.ceskatelevize.cz/domaci/1410558-fischer-o-vlade-budu-mit-jasno-ve-ctvrtek.

[400] "Plot kolem místa pro americký radar zmizí, rozhodl ministr Barták" (Minister Barták Decided to Do Away with a Fence Around the Future U.S. Radar Site), iDnes.cz, May 15, 2009, https://www.idnes.cz/zpravy/domaci/plot-kolem-mista-pro-americky-radar-zmizi-rozhodl-ministr-bartak.A090515_191326_domaci_ban.

[401] "Denní souhrn zpráv" (Daily News Compilation). Full quotation in Czech: "Já si myslím, že byla velká chyba, že jsme neschválili ve sněmovně ty radarové smlouvy, protože jsme mohli mít alespoň nějakou jistotu."

> [T]he issue [ballistic missile defense cooperation with the United States] has nevertheless also become—at least in some countries—a symbol of America's credibility and commitment to the region. How it is handled could have a significant impact on their future transatlantic orientation. The small number of missiles [meaning interceptors] involved cannot be a threat to Russia's strategic capabilities, and the Kremlin knows this. We should decide the future of the program as allies and based on the strategic plusses and minuses of the different technical and political configurations. The Alliance should not allow the issue to be determined by unfounded Russian opposition. Abandoning the program entirely or involving Russia too deeply in it without consulting Poland or the Czech Republic can undermine the credibility of the United States across the whole region.[402]

The letter made little difference to the Obama Administration, intent on pursuing a "reset" policy with the Russian Federation—even after Russia's August 2008 invasion of Georgia, and knowing about Russia's aggressive influence operations against U.S. and Czech interests in the Czech Republic. Meanwhile, ČSSD leader Paroubek met with Putin in Moscow in July 2009 in a curious meeting unaccompanied by Czech diplomats. Paroubek reportedly promised to Putin that he would make the radar issue an upcoming election topic.[403] The Czech

---

[402] Valdas Adamkus et al., "An Open Letter to the Obama Administration from Central And Eastern Europe," Radio Free Europe/Radio Liberty, July 16, 2009, https://www.rferl.org/a/An_Open_Letter_To_The_Obama_Administration_From_Central_And_Eastern_Europe/1778449.html.

[403] Adam Bartoš, "Udělám z radaru téma kampaně, oznámil Paroubek Putinovi" (Paroubek Told Putin He Will Make the Radar a Campaign Issue), *MF Dnes*, July 9, 2009,

Republic continued to be in a contact with the Obama Administration's officials but had very limited means to affect the outcome of the U.S. policy process, even as it became clearer that the Administration was going to change the plan. It would be difficult to affect the U.S. policy process under the best of circumstances, but the provisional nature of the Fischer government made it nearly impossible.

In September 2009, the Obama Administration announced its decision to abandon the Bush 43 plan to build a radar site in the Czech Republic and place interceptors in Poland. The timing of the announcement was poor. The administration announced its decision on the 70th anniversary of the Soviet occupation of Poland.[404] Even worse, President Barack Obama phoned Prime Minister Fischer to inform him of the decision just after midnight, giving the Czech government almost no time to organize itself for a response in the morning media cycle.

Whether the Bush Administration's missile defense plan for Europe was a casualty of President Obama's "reset" policy with Russia is a matter of a dispute, but the Russian government certainly felt that its influence operations were successful, and this perception likely emboldened it to continue its aggressive foreign policy. The Obama Administration denied that the cancellation had "anything to do with Russia."[405]

The Obama Administration pursued its own missile defense plan for Europe on the grounds of technology

---

https://www.idnes.cz/zpravy/domaci/udelam-z-radaru-tema-kampane-oznamil-paroubek-putinovi.A090709_175545_domaci_adb.

[404] Ken Dilanian, "Obama Scraps Bush Missile-Defense Plan," ABC News, N/A, https://abcnews.go.com/Politics/obama-scraps-bush-missile-defense-plan/story?id=8604357.

[405] Jordan Fabian, "McCain: Missile Shield Cancellation a 'Victory for Putin,'" *The Hill*, September 17, 2009, https://thehill.com/blogs/blog-briefing-room/news/59203-mccain-missile-shield-cancellation-a-victory-for-putin.

maturation and intermediate-range threat maturation: "The Obama Administration decision not to deploy the radar was driven primarily by the need to deploy a sensor in Southeastern Europe to more effectively address the Iranian short- and medium- ballistic missile threat. On top of that, there was serious concern that the Czech Parliament would never approve the basing agreement. Indeed, Secretary of Defense Gates made this point in his memoirs," said the Honorable Frank Rose.[406] The European Phased Adaptive Approach (EPAA), as the plan was called, called for a deployment of sea- and land-based versions of Standard Missile-3 interceptors and accompanying advanced sensors.[407] If executed as planned, the EPAA would provide more capability against intermediate-range, and even long-range, ballistic missiles than the Bush 43 Administration's ballistic missile defense plan (albeit on a longer timeframe). In reality, the Obama Administration and Congress underfunded, and in 2013 cancelled, the SM-3 IIB interceptor that would have capabilities against intercontinental-range ballistic missiles and that was to be deployed in 2022.

Poland agreed to host a missile defense site under the Obama Administration's missile defense architecture in October 2009.[408] Romania agreed to host a second missile defense site in 2010.[409] Russia undoubtedly re-focused its

---

[406] Author interview with the Honorable Frank Rose, Office of the Secretary of Defense, on U.S.-Czech missile defense cooperation.

[407] Jesse Lee, "Stronger, Smarter, and Swifter Defenses," The White House, September 17, 2009, https://obamawhitehouse.archives.gov/blog/2009/09/17/stronger-smarter-and-swifter-defenses.

[408] "Poland Agrees to Host Part of New U.S. Missile Defense Plan," CNN World, October 21, 2009, http://edition.cnn.com/2009/WORLD/europe/10/21/poland.missiles/index.html.

[409] Kristen Chick, "Romania Agrees to Host US Missile Interceptors," *The Christian Science Monitor*, February 5, 2010,

influence operations on these two countries. Why Russia has been successful in the Czech Republic but not in Poland and Romania deserves a further detailed study that is beyond the framework of this book. Reasons likely have to do with the Czech Republic's unlucky timing of a U.S.-Czech radar cooperation and with differences in strategic cultures and their respective views of Russia itself. The Obama Administration's announcement of the decision made the pro-Atlanticists' position in the Czech Republic that much weaker—and the Russian Federation very happy.

According to the polls, a vast majority of the Czech general public welcomed the Obama Administration's decision, even including most supporters of the radar plan, perhaps because they were tired of all the controversy the radar had caused.[410] The Czech Social Democrats welcomed the decision as a sensible step given Iran's short- and medium-range ballistic missile program; so did the Communists and members of the No Bases Initiative.[411] "Opponents of the radar site plan were happy when the Obama Administration changed its missile defense policy. They were arguing that superpowers do not take smaller states' interests into account and treat their allies with

---

https://www.csmonitor.com/World/terrorism-security/2010/0205/Romania-agrees-to-host-US-missile-interceptors.

[410] Jan Červenka, "Jak občané hodnotí rozhodnutí vlády USA odstoupit od plánu na vybudování protiraketové radarové základny v ČR?" (How Do Czech Citizens Assess the Cancellation of the U.S. Decision to Build a Radar in the Czech Republic?), Public Opinion Research Centre, November 30, 2009, https://cvvm.soc.cas.cz/media/com_form2content/documents/c2/a6 55/f9/100971s_pm91130a.pdf.

[411] "Obama je zbabělec, řekl v reakci na rozhodnutí o radaru Jan Vidím" (Obama Is a Coward, Said Jan Vidím in Response to Radar Decision), *Lidové Noviny* (*People's Newspaper*), September 17, 2009, https://www.lidovky.cz/domov/obama-je-zbabelec-rekl-v-reakci-na-rozhodnuti-o-radaru-jan-vidim.A090917_103443_ln_domov_pks.

cynicism. They saw the announcement as a confirmation of their beliefs and as a victory of popular resistance," according to Májíček.[412]

For proponents of U.S.-Czech ballistic missile defense cooperation in the Czech Republic, the Obama Administration's announcement was a tragedy, sometimes at a personal level. Former Prime Minister Topolánek argued that the missile defense plan change meant a loss of U.S. interest in Central Europe.[413] Other members of his party went as far as to call President Obama's decision a betrayal.[414] Secretary of Defense Gates mentions in his memoirs that "the Polish and Czech governments were probably relieved that they could avoid a showdown with their parliaments; the plan would have lost for sure in Prague."[415] The statement misses the point. While historical "what ifs" are always hard to play, it is plausible that a successive Czech government with a more secure majority in the Chamber of Deputies would have led to the approval of the BMDA and SOFA. The Obama Administration's statement, announced in the way it was, undermined U.S. credibility among its staunchest supporters in the region.

The Obama Administration tried to find face-saving ways for the Czech Republic to continue diminished missile defense cooperation. Secretary Gates emphasized that the United States had told both the Czech and Polish governments that the United States wanted them to be involved in missile defense in Europe regardless of the U.S. decision to cancel the radar site in the Czech Republic.[416] In

---

[412] Author interview with Jan Májíček, former spokesperson of the No Bases Initiative.

[413] "Obama je zbabělec, řekl v reakci na rozhodnutí o radaru Jan Vidím" (Obama Is a Coward, Said Jan Vidím in Response to Radar Decision).

[414] Ibid.

[415] Robert Gates, *Duty: Memoirs of a Secretary at War* (New York: Vintage, 2015), p. 403.

[416] Ibid.

the case of the Czech Republic, that involvement was to take the shape of a regional missile defense command and control center, reported in the Czech news in October 2009.[417] Earlier Obama Administration officials' statements that the Czech Republic was an ideal candidate to host interceptors under the new U.S. missile defense plan did not seem to lead to substantive discussions between the two governments regarding this matter.[418]

October and November 2009 marked what the Czech media dubbed a U.S. "diplomatic offense" in the Czech Republic.[419] In October 2009, U.S. Vice President Joe Biden visited the Czech Republic and welcomed the fact that the Czech Republic was standing by to participate in the Obama Administration's missile defense plan.[420] An expert group visited the Czech Republic in November 2009 to discuss missile defense issues. The U.S. offered the Czech Republic

---

[417] "V Česku by mohlo být velitelství nového protiraketového systému" (The New Missile Defense Command and Control Center Could Be in the Czech Republic), *iDnes.cz*, October 8, 2009, https://www.idnes.cz/zpravy/zahranicni/v-cesku-by-mohlo-byt-velitelstvi-noveho-protiraketoveho-systemu.A091008_124210_zahranicni_ipl.

[418] Petr Štefan and ČTK, "Střely nového štítu budou v Evropě za šest let, Česko je hlavním kandidátem" (Interceptors of the New Defense Shield Will Be in Europe in Six Years, the Czech Republic Is One of the Main Candidates), *MF Dnes*, September 18, 2009, https://www.idnes.cz/zpravy/zahranicni/strely-noveho-stitu-budou-v-evrope-za-sest-let-cesko-je-hlavnim-kandidatem.A090918_184600_zahranicni_stf.

[419] "Američané posílají do Česka tři delegace kvůli protiraketové obraně" (Americans Send Three Delegations to the Czech Republic Because of Missile Defense), *iDnes.cz*, November 4, 2009, https://www.idnes.cz/zpravy/domaci/americane-posilaji-do-ceska-tri-delegace-kvuli-protiraketove-obrane.A091104_115248_domaci_jw.

[420] "Biden: USA a Česko budou jednat o raketách v listopadu" (Biden: The United States and the Czech Republic Will Negotiate Rockets in November), *Aktuálně.cz*, October 23, 2009, https://zpravy.aktualne.cz/zahranici/biden-usa-a-cesko-budou-jednat-o-raketach-v-listopadu/r~i:article:650969/.

an opportunity to embed its representative within the U.S. MDA.[421] The expert-level visit was followed by a visit from Ellen Tauscher, U.S. Under Secretary of State for Arms Control and International Security Affairs in September 2009.[422] The United States made the formal offer to the Czech government to host a U.S. early warning data center in November 2009.[423] Opponents of U.S.-Czech ballistic missile defense cooperation argued that a U.S. command and control center would be even more dangerous to Czech (and European) security than a radar site, and that the Fischer government did not have a mandate to negotiate a command and control center for "cosmic wars."[424] This was nonsense. The center would actually make very few contributions to NATO or U.S. missile defense efforts, which is why the Czech government eventually declined the Czech Republic's participation in the project.

In concurrence with the radar cancellation, the Obama Administration conducted its own, roughly year-long, congressionally mandated missile defense policy review. Results of this review were published in the 2010 Ballistic

---

[421] "Česko bude mít zástupce mezi tvůrci americké protiraketové obrany" (The Czech Republic Will Have a Representative Among the Creators of U.S. Missile Defense), *iDnes.cz*, November 6, 2009, https://www.idnes.cz/zpravy/domaci/cesko-bude-mit-zastupce-mezi-tvurci-americke-protiraketove-obrany.A091106_154342_domaci_jw.

[422] "Američané posílají do Česka tři delegace kvůli protiraketové obraně" (Americans Send Three Delegations to the Czech Republic Because of Missile Defense).

[423] Judy Dempsey and Dan Bilefsky, "Czechs, Disliking Role, Pull Out of U.S. Missile Defense Project," *New York Times*, June 15, 2011, https://www.nytimes.com/2011/06/16/world/europe/16shield.html. In the Czech original: "velitelství kosmických válek."

[424] "Žádné rakety USA ani velitelství kosmických válek na území ČR!" (No U.S. Missiles and No Space Warfare Command Center on Czech Territory!), Ne základnám (No Bases), October 20, 2009, http://www.nezakladnam.cz/cs/1727_zadne-rakety-usa-ani-velitelstvi-kosmickych-valek-na-uzemi-cr-.

Missile Defense Review (BMDR). In the BMDR, the administration focused on "regional deterrence architectures" and argued that technological developments afforded the United States new technical opportunities in the field of sensor technology (thereby obviating the need to deploy the radar to the Czech Republic).[425] The BMDR stated that the long-range Iranian ballistic missile threat was not as urgent and advanced as the Bush Administration had believed, and that focusing on regional ballistic missile defense architecture was more appropriate for addressing emerging ballistic missile challenges to U.S. forward deployed forces and allies.[426]

For some Czechs, the policy change was not unexpected. "President Obama's missile defense architecture was not a surprise. We didn't lobby to change the decision and were not in a position to do so, given the fact that we did not ratify the agreements in the Czech Parliament," according to former First Deputy Minister Pojar.[427]

The Czech government's inability to get the Parliament to approve the agreements between the two countries in a timelier manner likely cost the Czech Republic the opportunity to host a the U.S. radar site. Had the construction of the site been more advanced when the Obama Administration started to reconsider its plans, it would have been more difficult to cancel the site.

The Fischer government continued consultations with the Obama Administration on potential joint cooperative missile defense actions, particularly related to defense

---

[425] U.S. Department of Defense, "Ballistic Missile Defense Review Report," February 2010, https://dod.defense.gov/Portals/1/features/defenseReviews/BMDR/BMDR_as_of_26JAN10_0630_for_web.pdf.

[426] Ibid.

[427] Author interview with former First Deputy Minister Pojar.

research and development.[428] It managed to accomplish several of them. For example, in February 2010, the United States opened a branch of the Office of Naval Research in Prague.[429] The branch, still operating as of this writing, focuses on promoting science and technology collaboration between researchers from the United States and Central and Eastern Europe through the Collaborative Science Program and the Visiting Scientist Program, and provides research grants.[430]

In June 2010, the Czech government approved a previous government's agreement between the Czech Republic and United States that opened up opportunities for Czech scientists to participate in U.S. high-tech military research and development activities.[431] The United States has this type of agreement with only a few allies in the world. While the Czech government denied the notion that this agreement was compensation for the cancellation of the radar plan, the thought that these efforts may have been

---

[428] Jan Fisher, "Premiér Fischer odpověděl Iniciativě Ne základnám" (Prime Minister Fischer Responds to the No Bases Initiative), Ne Základnám (No Bases), January 20, 2010, http://www.nezakladnam.cz/cs/1772_premier-fischer-odpovedel-iniciative-ne-zakladnam.

[429] "Američané v Praze otevřeli vývojové zázemí pro námořní pěchotu" (Americans Opened a Branch of the Office of Naval Research in Prague), *iDnes.cz*, February 26, 2010, https://www.idnes.cz/zpravy/zahranicni/video-americane-v-praze-otevreli-vyvojove-zazemi-pro-namorni-pechotu.A100225_123407_vedatech_jw.

[430] U.S. Navy, "Office of Naval Research, Prague, Czech Republic," https://www.onr.navy.mil/en/Science-Technology/ONR-Global/Locations-Global/Prague-ONR-Global.

[431] "České hlavy míří do exkluzivního klubu, vláda schválila smlouvu s USA" (Czech Experts to Become Part of an Exclusive Club, the Government Approved an Agreement with the United States), *iDnes.cz*, April 27, 2010, https://www.idnes.cz/zpravy/domaci/ceske-hlavy-miri-do-exkluzivniho-klubu-vlada-schvalila-smlouvu-s-usa.A100427_124731_domaci_klu.

connected on some level is inescapable.⁴³² The agreement did not require the Czech Parliament's consent, which was advantageous given the fiasco over the BMDA and SOFA.

The May 2010 parliamentary elections brought a narrow victory for the Social Democrats at 22.09 percent of the vote, followed by the Civic Democrats at 20.22 percent of the vote.⁴³³ But the Social Democratic Party was not able to assemble a coalition government that would obtain the Chamber of Deputies' approval, and so the party remained in the opposition. The Civil Democrats, led by new Prime Minister Petr Nečas, ended up assembling the next government coalition.

The Nečas Government: July 13, 2010–July 10, 2013

The Nečas government updated the Czech national security strategy in 2011.⁴³⁴ The strategy stated that in concurrence with NATO's 2010 Strategic Concept and steps to strengthen Article V of the North Atlantic Treaty, the Czech Republic actively supported the development and deployment of NATO missile defense architecture and explored opportunities to participate in it.⁴³⁵ The issue, listed as "priority" number 50 out of a total of 96 priorities

---

⁴³² Ibid.

⁴³³ "Volby Do Poslanecké Sněmovny Parlamentu České Republiky 2010" (Elections to the Czech Chamber of Deputies 2010), *iDnes.cz*, May 29, 2010, https://www.idnes.cz/volby/parlamentni/2010.

⁴³⁴ Government of the Czech Republic, "Bezpečnostní strategie České republiky" (National Security Strategy of the Czech Republic), 2011, https://www.dataplan.info/img_upload/7bdb1584e3b8a53d337518d988763f8d/bezpecnostni_strategie_cr_2011.pdf.

⁴³⁵ Ibid. In the Czech original "aktivně podporuje rozvoj a budování územní protiraketové obrany NATO a zkoumá možnosti konkrétního zapojení do tohoto systému."

clearly lost significance for the Czech government after President Obama's radar cancellation.

The Nečas government continued ballistic missile defense discussions with the United States about a potential early warning missile defense site in the Czech Republic.[436] The center was to "consist of two offices with computers and other technical equipment that would gather data on potential incoming missiles, on their targets and the possible affected areas. These data would then be passed on to radars and other parts of the missile shield."[437] An early warning data center would not require an international agreement with the United States and did not involve a permanent U.S. presence on Czech territory, saving the government the trouble of another society-wide debate.[438]

Alexandr Vondra, Czech Minister of Defense at the time, initially called the plan a "valuable consolation."[439] But his enthusiasm was short-lived as it became clear that the center would make no real contribution to a U.S. (or NATO) ballistic missile defense system and that it would cost the Czech Republic resources to obtain data that it could obtain through NATO anyway. In June 2011, the Czech Republic rejected the U.S. offer to host an early

---

[436] Jan Richter, "Czech Republic to Host Part of New Missile Defence Shield," Radio Praha, July 30, 2010,
https://www.radio.cz/en/section/curraffrs/czech-republic-to-host-part-of-new-missile-defence-shield.

[437] Ibid.

[438] Ministerstvo zahraničních věcí ČR (Ministry of Foreign Affairs of the Czech Republic), "Zahraničních politika České republiky dokumenty 7-8/2010" (Czech Foreign Policy Documents 7-8/2010),
https://www.mzv.cz/public/e1/44/d1/991028_920007_Dokumenty_mesicniku_ZP2010_07_08.doc.

[439] Tom Jones, "Czechs Won't Host AMD Early Warning Center," Česká pozice, June 15, 2011, http://ceskapozice.lidovky.cz/czechs-won-t-host-amd-early-warning-center-fij-/tema.aspx?c=A110615_111924_pozice_19164.

warning data center.[440] Defense Minister Vondra said about the decision that: "Our ideas about the future cooperation are more colorful than just a room or two with some screens there."[441] There were some differences of opinion within Czech defense and foreign policy circles on the utility of having at least some U.S. assets on Czech territory with the losing side of the argument stating that *some* U.S. assets were better than *no* U.S. assets.

Overall, "[t]he offer to host the radar site on Czech territory and the subsequent negotiations had substantially increased the scope and the depth of the U.S.-Czech relations, leading, for instance, to the establishment of the U.S.-Czech Strategic Dialogue and of the so-called High Level Defense Group with Pentagon officials. When the radar plan got cancelled, we had to find new themes for the U.S.-Czech relations," explained Ešnerová.[442] The Czech government envisioned cooperation with the United States on the radar issue as the beginning of a broader strategic effort. After the cancellation, the strategic dialogue between the two countries never again reached the intensity and the depth it had at the peak of U.S.-Czech ballistic missile defense cooperation during the 2007–2008 timeframe.

Figure 1 shows the varying levels of cooperation between the United States and the Czech Republic from 2002 to 2011. There was no significant ballistic missile defense cooperation in 2005 because the Czech government was entangled in a domestic scandal, and the U.S. government was in the process of analyzing its own ballistic missile defense options. Similarly, there were no notable ballistic missile defense activities between the two countries

---

[440] Dempsey and Bilefsky, "Czechs, Disliking Role, Pull Out of U.S. Missile Defense Project."

[441] Ibid.

[442] Author interview with Barbora Ešnerová, Head of Political Unit, Permanent Delegation of the Czech Republic to NATO.

after the Czech rejection to host a U.S. early warning center in June 2011.

Fig. 1. **Levels of Czech Republic Cooperation with U.S. on Ballistic Missile Defense**

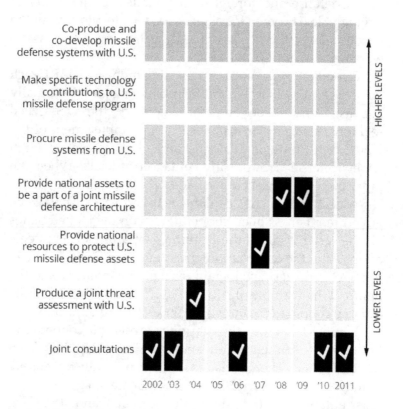

Source: Author's analysis.

Conclusion

This chapter provided a chronological overview of the successive Czech governments' activities as they related to a broader question of U.S.-Czech ballistic missile defense cooperation. Both countries started preliminary technical discussions as early as 2002, and these discussions ultimately resulted in official negotiations between 2007 and 2008 on the conditions under which the Czech Republic would host a U.S. X-band radar on its territory.

In 2009, the Obama Administration decided to proceed with a different missile defense plan for Europe and cancelled the Bush 43 Administration's plan to place an X-band radar in the Czech Republic. Discussions and negotiations between two countries continued until June 2011, when the Czech Republic decided to reject a U.S. offer to host an early warning data center on its territory due to a lack of the center's substantive national security contributions.

The chronological approach allowed the uncovering themes that were particularly salient in the Czech public discourse on both the national and international level as the topic of U.S.-Czech missile defense cooperation became more known and visible among the general public. Among them were issues related to the importance of the project for the Czech Republic's security; the emerging role of Russian influence operations in the Czech Republic; and the importance that some Czech political parties ascribed to the project as a way to contribute to the security of all NATO allies and increase the Czech Republic's prestige by becoming a provider of security, rather than a consumer.

The discussion between the two countries also revolved around issues related to potential economic benefits that the Czech Republic could obtain from closer U.S.-Czech missile defense cooperation. Lastly, Chapter Four highlighted the importance of electoral politics and knowledge of individual politicians' personalities in both the United States and the Czech Republic, and their impact on negotiations between the two countries.

Chapter Five
Russia's Influence Operations on Czech Territory During the Radar Debate

> [T]he operations of the Russian [intelligence]services aimed at the Czech Republic and its allies may be part of a broader and prolonged campaign designed to undermine EU and NATO integrity, isolate the United States (or encourage isolationist moods in the USA), and regain control over the security of the once-Soviet-ruled territories in Europe, regardless of the results of the anti-missile radar negotiations.
>
> Czech Security Information Service
2006 Annual Report

Russia's influence operations on Czech territory are a largely untold aspect of U.S.-Czech ballistic missile defense discussions and negotiations between 2002 and 2011. There are several reasons why few people, whether Czech or American, know about Russia's influence operations during this timeframe.

First, being public about Russia's influence activities on Czech territory has been extremely politically sensitive due to a continued involvement of some Czech politicians with the Russian Federation on both local and national levels. Second, Russia's disinformation campaign has been aimed at delegitimizing any suggestions that Russia meddles in Czech politics. Russia has managed to penetrate the Czech media and public discussions, giving the Russian government the opportunity to spread propaganda in ways that are not easily traceable, making its disinformation more believable to the Czech public—which generally sees Russia as a malign actor. Third, it is extremely difficult to trace sources of funding of anti-radar movements and activities in the Czech Republic back to the Russian Federation, even though these movements were evidently well funded and organized from the beginning of the more visible part of U.S.-Czech ballistic missile defense discussions, which started in summer 2006. This is because the Czech Republic is the travel destination of choice for many Russians, making it easy to bring cash for nefarious purposes. Fourth, the Czech Republic's joining of the Schengen Area on December 21, 2007, made it more difficult for the Czech intelligence services to trace the movement of suspicious people in and out of the Czech Republic.[443] Fifth, Russia spent more than a decade building a comprehensive network consisting of agents and pro-Russian Czechs, ready to conduct intelligence and influence operations at the command of Russia's leadership. According to the Czech Security Information Service's reports cited below, this infrastructure was activated during U.S.-Czech ballistic missile defense negotiations and discussions. In building that infrastructure, Russia often made use of relationships that existed since before the fall of the Berlin Wall, and was able to draw on its familiarity with the environment in the Czech Republic.

Now, over a decade later, it is possible to sketch out a picture of Russia's activities and the general approaches the Russian Federation used to influence the Czech public and political elites. In bits and pieces, a majority of this information is available in the Czech Security Information Service's annual reports, including in their English translations.[444] This chapter relies on reports in the original

---

[443] The Schengen Area is a border-free area within which the citizens of 26 European countries may travel freely without passports.

[444] These reports are available in English on the Czech Security Information Service's web site: https://www.bis.cz/annual-reports/. This chapter draws on reports in Czech, the original language in which they were written.

language of their writing, Czech. Translations are by this author.

Understanding Russia's methods and tactics is important because its operations against the U.S. radar in the Czech Republic can be considered successful, which makes it more likely that the Russian Federation will use and has been using similar tactics in other states, including in other NATO member states. It is reasonable to assume that Russia ran a similar campaign to discredit U.S.-Czech ballistic missile defense cooperation in the United States, but whether and to which extent this operation was successful is beyond the scope of this book, however interesting that question is for U.S. allies. Understanding Russia's methods, tactics, and causal mechanisms that made its anti-radar success possible is a prerequisite for countering Russia's future influence operations and increasing society's resilience to their influence. It is important to keep in mind, however, that details of Russia's activities and names of personalities involved are still not widely known.

Building Russia's Networks on Czech Territory

Czech intelligence services have been concerned about Russia's activities on Czech territory since the end of the Cold War.[445] While Russia's intelligence activities focused

---

[445] During the Cold War, Czech intelligence services collaborated closely with those of the Soviet Union against those Czechs who presented a potential problem for the Soviet regime, leaving the institution with a need to rebuild its credibility and public trust in a democratic state. In an October 2019 poll, 47 percent of respondents trusts the Czech Security Information Service, its best result in modern history. Only 17 percent of respondents trusted the institution in February 1995. Jan Červenka, "Tisková zpráva: Důvěra vybraným institucím – říjen a listopad 2019" (Press Release: Public Trust and Selected Institutions –

on organized crime and were not particularly well coordinated from within the Russian Federation in the early 1990s, the late 1990s brought concerns over the Russian Federation's "efforts to regain its superpower status and influence in Central Europe; an effort that is not justified by references to ideologies like during the Cold War but to power politics."[446] Vladimir Putin's ascendancy to power resulted in Russia's intelligence services' increase in importance and funding, and an increase in their activities. Due to Putin's patronage, Russia's intelligence services were eventually able to penetrate large parts of the Russian economy and state, making it virtually impossible to distinguish between state and private business activities.[447] A key data point to remember here is that in Russia (and by extension, its activities abroad), intelligence activities are not strictly separated from business or diplomatic activities like in the United States or other democratic societies.

Russia's activities in the late 1990s focused on fomenting a resurgence of left-wing radicalism on Czech territory. Russia reportedly utilized left-wing movements to try to shape Czech public opinion and obtain its support for Russia's political and power interests in the Central

---

October and November 2019), Český statistický úřad (Czech Statistical Office), December 10, 2019,
https://cvvm.soc.cas.cz/media/com_form2content/documents/c2/a5063/f9/pi191210.pdf.

[446] Czech Security Information Service, "Bezpečnostní informační služba: Zpráva o činnosti za rok 1998 a 1999" (Annual Report of the Security Information Service for 1998 and 1999), 1999,
https://www.bis.cz/public/site/bis.cz/content/vyrocni-zpravy/zprava-o-cinnosti-za-rok-1998-a-1999.pdf.

[447] Czech Security Information Service, "Bezpečnostní informační služba: Zpráva o činnosti za rok 2008" (Annual Report of the Security Information Service for 2008), 2009,
https://www.bis.cz/public/site/bis.cz/content/vyrocni-zpravy/2008-vz-cz.pdf.

European region.[448] The specifics of these activities, and of the individuals involved, are still a matter of debate. The primary focus of Russia's intelligence services has been to help the Russian Federation obtain economic influence in Czech strategic industries, particularly in the energy sector, due to the Czech Republic's dependence on Russia's energy supplies. Heavy industry has been another industry of interest to the Russian Federation.

During the early 2000s, Russia's intelligence services focused on building a system of "influence agencies" through which the Russian Federation could influence the Czech—government's decisions on a local level, spread disinformation, delegitimize the Czech government if needed by sowing mistrust in the Czech government's decisions among the Czechs, and make foreign allies and partners question the trustworthiness of the Czech Republic as an ally.[449] Russian intelligence services actively recruited Czech citizens to create opportunities for them to penetrate Czech government and private spheres utilizing contacts the KGB developed during the Cold War. In some instances, the cooperation between former KGB affiliates and Russian intelligence services continued seamlessly.[450] It is apparent that Russia had built the information infrastructure that it

---

[448] Czech Security Information Service, "Bezpečnostní informační služba: Zpráva o činnosti za rok 1998 a 1999" (Annual Report of the Security Information Service for 1998 and 1999).

[449] Czech Security Information Service, "Bezpečnostní informační služba: Zpráva o činnosti za rok 2000" (Annual Report of the Security Information Service for 2000), June 1, 2001, https://www.bis.cz/public/site/bis.cz/content/vyrocni-zpravy/vyrocni-zprava-2000.pdf.

[450] Czech Security Information Service, "Bezpečnostní informační služba: Zpráva o činnosti za rok 2009" (Annual Report of the Security Information Service for 2009), 2010, https://www.bis.cz/public/site/bis.cz/content/vyrocni-zpravy/2009-vz-cz.pdf.

activated during the U.S.-Czech radar discussions years before official negotiations started.

The Russian Federation's intelligence services have always been the most active foreign intelligence services operating in the Czech Republic.[451] Their activities are beyond compare to activities of any other foreign intelligence services on Czech territory with regard to the scale of operations and the number of operatives in the Czech Republic.[452] The Russian Federation has been exercising aggressive political influence to get its intelligence operatives accredited as diplomats in the Czech Republic, appointed as intelligence operatives that were dismissed from other democratic nations, and threatened disproportionate retaliatory measures when the Czech government considered not accrediting them.[453] That is why a large number of Russia's intelligence officers in the Czech Republic are protected by diplomatic immunity, which makes it easier for them to bribe, threaten, and corrupt Czech citizens.[454] Their numbers have traditionally been unusually high relative to Russian career diplomats; about half of the Russian Federation's diplomatic representation in the Czech Republic consists of intelligence officers.[455]

---

[451] Czech Security and Information Service, "Bezpečnostní informační služba: Zpráva o činnosti za rok 2004" (Annual Report of the Security Information Service for 2004), 2005,
https://www.bis.cz/public/site/bis.cz/content/vyrocni-zpravy/vyrocni-zprava-bezpecnostni-informacni-sluzby-za-rok-2004.pdf.

[452] "Bezpečnostní informační služba: Zpráva o činnosti za rok 2009" (Annual Report of the Security Information Service for 2009).

[453] Ibid.

[454] "Bezpečnostní informační služba: Zpráva o činnosti za rok 2004" (Annual Report of the Security Information Service for 2004).

[455] Czech Security and Information Service, "Bezpečnostní informační služba: Zpráva o činnosti za rok 2005" (Annual Report of the Security Information Service for 2005), 2006,
https://www.bis.cz/public/site/bis.cz/content/vyrocni-

The disparity in the number of Russia's intelligence officers in the Czech Republic and Czech intelligence officers in Russia makes it very difficult for the Czech government to address Russia's activities that are incompatible with diplomatic conventions even when these activities are uncovered.[456] When the Czech Republic banishes Russian intelligence officers for espionage, Russia can banish the same number of Czech intelligence officers from Russia—a problematic situation, since a much larger number of Russian intelligence officers in the Czech Republic than Czech intelligence officers in Russia means that the Czech Republic could be left without any intelligence operatives in Russia. The Russian Federation retaliated against Czech diplomats when the Czech government refused to grant visas to Russian intelligence officers posing as academics and tourists in 2013.[457]

The situation has been exacerbated by the Czech Republic's participation in the Schengen Area, which allows the Russian Federation's officers to leave the country at a minute's notice in the case of problems.[458] When that happens, the removed Russian officers are replaced

---

zpravy/vyrocni-zprava-bezpecnostni-informacni-sluzby-za-rok-2005.pdf.

[456] Czech Security Information Service, "Bezpečnostní informační služba: Zpráva o činnosti za rok 2010" (Annual Report of the Security Information Service for 2010), 2011,
https://www.bis.cz/public/site/bis.cz/content/vyrocni-zpravy/2010-vz-cz.pdf.

[457] Czech Security Information Service, "Bezpečnostní informační služba: Zpráva o činnosti za rok 2013" (Annual Report of the Security Information Service for 2013), 2014,
https://www.bis.cz/public/site/bis.cz/content/vyrocni-zpravy/2013-vz-cz.pdf.

[458] Czech Security Information Service, "Bezpečnostní informační služba: Zpráva o činnosti za rok 2012" (Annual Report of the Security Information Service for 2012),
https://www.bis.cz/public/site/bis.cz/content/vyrocni-zpravy/2012-vz-cz.pdf.

immediately, putting the Czech counterintelligence officers in a position of dealing with an unknown, rather than a known, "evil." In addition to Russian intelligence officers working in the Czech Republic under the pretense of being career diplomats, the Russian Federation sends its intelligence officers as tourists and academics.

The Czech Republic does not have good options for dealing with the disparity. If it wants to maintain its intelligence presence as a part of its diplomatic mission in the Russian Federation, it must continue accepting Russia's intelligence officers as diplomats (or grant their visas as "students" or "scientists"). The Czech intelligence services are under-resourced relative to the number of targets, and while they generally maintain good working relationships with allied intelligence services, these too run into the problem of too many targets and too few resources. Under such circumstances, it is likely that some of Russia's activities slip under the radar despite the best counterintelligence efforts.

In 2000, the Russian disinformation campaign focused on questioning the benefits of the Czech Republic's membership in NATO and on arguing that costs associated with the Czech Republic's foreign missions and military modernization would be better spent on social programs. In Russia's mind, the Czech Republic joining NATO was a grievance and a threat to Russia's interests—but also an opportunity for Russia to tap into pre-existing networks on Czech territory and create new channels through which Russia could obtain information about other NATO member states and influence its perceived adversaries in NATO. To that end, Russia's intelligence officers tried to penetrate the Czech Ministry of Defense. That was a natural avenue of penetration for the Russian Federation. Today's Czech Army is a legacy institution to the Czechoslovak Army that closely collaborated with the Soviet Union. The Czech Army transformed and professionalized in the 1990s, in no small part thanks to the Czech Republic joining NATO, but some of its old Communist-trained cadres, potentially more sympathetic to the Russian Federation's goals, remained in place. Czech Defense Minister Vlasta Parkanová referred to them in a 2008 interview, pointing to differences between this "old guard" and a new generation of officers that joined the Czech Army after the end of the Cold War.[459]

Russia's Activities During U.S.-Czech Ballistic Missile Defense Discussions and Negotiations

The 2003 Czech National Security Strategy noted ballistic-missile and weapons-of-mass-destruction proliferation as a threat to Czech interests, but the document did not mention the United States or potential ballistic missile defense cooperation with it. [460] Nevertheless, both countries were discussing potential cooperation on this issue. Moreover, these initial discussions were run from within the Czech Ministry of Defense.

In fall 2003, the United States provided the Czech Ministry of Defense with technical requirements for a potential ballistic missile defense site. The exchange started extensive expert-level discussions that continued into 2004. It is unlikely that the Russian Federation would not have known about these discussions, although at that time,

---

[459] Jiří Kubík, "Parkanová: Milenec by mi prošel, písnička o radaru ne" (Parkanová: I Could Get Away with a Lover, But Not with a Song About a Radar), *MF Dnes*, July 20, 2008,
https://www.idnes.cz/zpravy/domaci/parkanova-milenec-by-mi-prosel-pisnicka-o-radaru-ne.A080719_160539_domaci_abr.

[460] Czech Government, "Bezpečnostní strategie České republiky" (Czech National Security Strategy), 2003,
https://www.dataplan.info/img_upload/7bdb1584e3b8a53d337518d988763f8d/bezpecnostni-strategie-cr.pdf.

Russian intelligence officers' primary goal was to advance Russian economic interests on Czech territory.[461]

Russia's diplomatic mission also focused on creating a positive image of Russia among Czech citizens by organizing public cultural activities and through supporting pro-Russian media on Czech territory. Russia reportedly used public cultural activities to seek out sympathetic Czech citizens for the Russian intelligence services to recruit.[462] Russia also focused on penetrating the Czech journalistic scene. Even today, Russian-speaking journalists accredited in the Czech Republic are often Russian intelligence officers and are active in spreading disinformation and propaganda among the rest of the Czech media.[463] Russia's intelligence activities over time resulted in the Czech media's general lack of resistance to Russia's influence and propaganda, helping to create a permissive environment for Russian influence operations.[464] This is not to suggest that all Czech media are controlled by the Russians, but evidence of Russia's influence in the Czech media sphere is in plain sight: a lack of solid and serious reporting, with few exceptions, on Russia's influence operations during the radar debate and discussions between the Czech Republic and the United States.

Russia has no trouble recruiting people willing to cooperate with it in the Czech Republic. Its intelligence

---

[461] Czech Security Information Service, "Bezpečnostní informační služba: Zpráva o činnosti za rok 2004" (Annual Report of the Security Information Service for 2004), 2005.

[462] Czech Security Information Service, "Bezpečnostní informační služba: Zpráva o činnosti za rok 2005" (Annual Report of the Security Information Service for 2005), 2005.

[463] Czech Security Information Service, "Bezpečnostní informační služba: Zpráva o činnosti za rok 2012" (Annual Report of the Security Information Service for 2012), 2013.

[464] Ibid.

services have been particularly interested in former Czechoslovak Communist Party members who obtained professional success in the economic, political, or public spheres, and people who obtained education in the Soviet Union, on the presumption that they are more likely to cooperate due to their positive experience during formative student years. It is worth noting that only those with the correct party "pedigree" were permitted and selected to study in the Soviet Union during the Communist era. Another pool of interesting candidates to the Russian intelligence services have been Czech citizens of Russian origin and Russians living in the Czech Republic long-term, and former members of the KGB who kept their network in the Czech Republic fresh and continue to draw on it for their business activities.[465] There really is no such thing as a former KGB intelligence officer, as even these "former" officers are expected to continue to work to benefit the Russian Federation and be active in its intelligence operations.[466]

The United States planned on placing a radar in a military training area formerly occupied by the Warsaw Pact military. This meant that the Russian Federation had an opportunity to activate its former members who often retired in the vicinity of what became a Czech Army military training area after the fall of the Soviet Union. These people were generally more sympathetic to the Russian Federation than to the United States; after all, they

---

[465] Czech Security Information Service, "Bezpečnostní informační služba: Zpráva o činnosti za rok 2003" (Annual Report of the Security Information Service for 2003), 2004, https://www.bis.cz/public/site/bis.cz/content/vyrocni-zpravy/vyrocni-zprava-bezpecnostni-informacni-sluzby-za-rok-2003.pdf.

[466] "Bezpečnostní informační služba: Zpráva o činnosti za rok 2006" (Czech Security Information Service, 2007), https://www.bis.cz/public/site/bis.cz/content/vyrocni-zpravy/2006-vz-cz.pdf.

had prepared to fight the United States all of their professional military careers.[467]

Russia's intelligence officers managed to build an extensive network of contacts in the Czech political sphere, particularly among Czech politicians, including Members of Parliament and their assistants, and members of political parties responsible for their respective party's foreign policy and security agendas.[468] The challenge for the Czech government workers and politicians has been that Russian intelligence services have multiple missions. For example, Russia's Federal Security Service's main task is domestic intelligence activities, but it also conducts counterintelligence operations and can perform intelligence-related work abroad. This means that what might appear as a legitimate interaction with a Russian intelligence officer on an area of a common interest (for example counterterrorism) might serve other, nefarious, purposes about which a Czech target has no idea.[469] Similarly, interactions between Czech scientists and their Russian counterparts can advance Russia's interests without a Czech target knowing.[470] These overlapping agendas further underscore the point regarding Russia's lack of clear lines between legitimate intelligence activities

---

[467] Karel Ferschmann, "Starostové chtěli informace o radaru aneb jak to skutečně bylo" (Mayors Wanted Information About Radar and What Really Happened), *Obec Němčovice* (blog), September 23, 2007, https://www.nemcovice.cz/starostove-chteli-informace-o-radaru-aneb-jak-to-skutecne-bylo/.

[468] Czech Security Information Service, "Bezpečnostní informační služba: Zpráva o činnosti za rok 2008" (Annual Report of the Security Information Service for 2008), 2009.

[469] Czech Security Information Service, "Bezpečnostní informační služba: Zpráva o činnosti za rok 2012" (Annual Report of the Security Information Service for 2012), 2013.

[470] Czech Security Information Service, "Bezpečnostní informační služba: Zpráva o činnosti za rok 2012" (Annual Report of the Security Information Service for 2012), 2013.

and covert influence operations—a point hard to comprehend in democratic societies with comparatively clearly outlined responsibilities and obligations among different parts of the government and the society.

Russian intelligence services also learned to draw on networks developed by Russia's organized crime networks, active even in the early 1990s, during times of forced relative inactivity for the Russian intelligence services, a result of the lack of resources and chaos in the period after the break-up of the Soviet Union.[471] These networks have been valuable for identifying individuals willing to sell out and provide certain benefits, or access to Russia's intelligence services. Russia's organized crime has been generally focused on economic crime and on targeting local governance structures (to obtain advantages for Russian-backed firms in competitions for government contracts, or to legalize the stay of certain personnel on Czech territory, for example through pro-forma marriages). Russian organized crime has used Czech citizens as fronts for its interaction with Czech government institutions, as legal advisors, and as fronts for purchasing real estate. Organized crime groups benefit from historical roots to Czech territory, knowledge of laws and norms that are applicable to foreigners, ties to official structures, and know-how about how to corrupt Czech officials and citizens.[472]

The Czech Security Service's 2007 annual report hints at a nefarious connection between Czech politics and business, stating that organized crime utilized "financial experts and

---

[471] Czech Security Information Service, "Bezpečnostní informační služba: Zpráva o činnosti za rok 2005" (Annual Report of the Security Information Service for 2005), 2006.

[472] Czech Security Information Service, "Bezpečnostní informační služba: Zpráva o činnosti za rok 2002" (Annual Report of the Security Information Service for 2002), June 1, 2003), https://www.bis.cz/public/site/bis.cz/content/vyrocni-zpravy/vyrocni-zprava-2002.pdf.

people with extensive client ties to certain former and current politicians and high-level government officials."[473] (The report does not specify who these financial experts and other people were.)

Russia's comprehensive activities mean that it is likely that Russian intelligence services have used these networks for the purposes of influencing perceptions of U.S.-Czech radar negotiations on multiple levels simultaneously. The connection between Russia's organized crime and Czech local levels of governance is troubling because evidence of Czech officials' improper conduct in connection to Russia's organized crime can leave them vulnerable to blackmail by Russian intelligence officers.[474] These connections also present a long-term threat to Czech democracy and to the alliance with the United States, because local politics is a source for future high-level government officials. Compromising materials, even several years old, can afford Russia a great deal of influence among future top politicians.[475]

U.S.-Czech ballistic missile defense discussions had become a matter of public knowledge by summer 2006. The Russian Federation made it its diplomatic and intelligence priority to stop a U.S. radar deployment to the Czech

---

[473] Czech Security Information Service, "Bezpečnostní informační služba: Zpráva o činnosti za rok 2007" (Annual Report of the Security Information Service for 2007), 2008, https://www.bis.cz/public/site/bis.cz/content/vyrocni-zpravy/2007-vz-cz.pdf.

[474] Czech Security Information Service, "Bezpečnostní informační služba: Zpráva o činnosti za rok 2010" (Annual Report of the Security Information Service for 2010), 2011.

[475] Czech Security Information Service, "Bezpečnostní informační služba: Zpráva o činnosti za rok 2011" (Annual Report of the Security Information Service for 2011), 2012, https://www.bis.cz/public/site/bis.cz/content/vyrocni-zpravy/2011-vz-cz.pdf.

Republic.[476] The Czech Security Service's 2006 annual report broadly refers to Russia's "active measures" campaign and lists its execution as one of Russia's significant priorities for that year.[477] Russia's active measures encompassed manipulation of media events, outputs, and reports, as well as abuse of cultural and social events to support Russia's power-politics interests on Czech territory.[478] It is plausible that Russian intelligence services took advantage of the rising No Bases Initiative movement founded in summer 2006. The movement organized public demonstrations in several Czech cities and organized public petitions against a radar. These events were extensively covered in the Czech media. The No Bases Initiative was also suspected of accepting Russian money and of significant media help from firms potentially affiliated with the Russian Federation.[479]

Russia was joined in its anti-radar campaign by an unlikely partner after the June 2006 elections to the Czech Chamber of Deputies. The Czech Social Democratic Party lost to the Civic Democratic Party and became an opposition party. The loss marked the beginning of the end of the Social Democrats' support for ballistic missile defense cooperation with the United States — and, according to some, the

---

[476] Military Intelligence Service, "Výroční zpráva o činnosti Vojenského zpravodajství 2008" (Annual Report of the Military Intelligence Agency), 2009, https://www.vzcr.cz/uploads/41-Vyrocni-zprava-2008.pdf.

[477] Czech Security Information Service, "Bezpečnostní informační služba: Zpráva o činnosti za rok 2006" (Annual Report of the Security Information Service for 2006), 2007.

[478] Ibid.

[479] ČTK and Jan Markovič, "Rusko nás neplatí, popírají odpůrci radaru reportáž ČT" (The Russians Are Not Giving Us Money, Opponents of the Radar Dispute Czech Television's News Segment), *MF Dnes*, November 27, 2007, https://www.idnes.cz/zpravy/domaci/rusko-nas-neplati-popiraji-odpurci-radaru-reportaz-ct.A071127_124402_domaci_mr.

beginning of the end of a Czech non-partisan agreement on a pro-American and transatlantic direction of Czech foreign policy after the end of the Cold War. In this context, it is important to recall that the Czech government led by the Social Democrats had *endorsed* ballistic missile defense cooperation with the United States prior to 2006, oversaw technical discussions between the two countries, and narrowed down a potential site selection for a U.S. ballistic missile defense component on Czech territory. The Social Democrats' previous support for the U.S. radar made it easier to deflect (rare) accusations of Russia's undue influence activities regarding the radar.

Russia continued its activities against a potential U.S. radar deployment on Czech territory in 2007. Russia's activities were focused on contacting, infiltrating, and influencing groups and individuals, particularly those active in civic movements, politics, and the media, who could affect Czech public opinion.[480] In 2007, the Czech Security Service judged Russia's active measures as "reaching an extremely high intensity and sophistication."[481] The Czech Security Service also made clear that a majority of members of these movements were unwitting collaborators and exploited victims rather than active collaborators.[482] Russia's influence on these segments of the population can be seen by their rather uninformed parroting of Russia's talking points against a U.S. ballistic missile defense system, sometimes also appearing in the misinformed arguments that the U.S. arms control

---

[480] Czech Security Information Service, "Bezpečnostní informační služba: Zpráva o činnosti za rok 2007" (Annual Report of the Security Information Service for 2007), 2008.

[481] Ibid.

[482] Czech Security Information Service, "Bezpečnostní informační služba: Zpráva o činnosti za rok 2008" (Annual Report of the Security Information Service for 2008), 2009.

community makes to influence the domestic debate on ballistic missile defense in the United States.

The following exchange (translated from Czech by the author of this book) between Defense Minister Parkanová and a Czech journalist, published in *iDnes.cz* in 2008, illustrates the difficulties of speaking openly about Russia's involvement in anti-radar activities:

[In response to the journalist's question about why the government's radar campaign isn't particularly effective in changing the Czechs' minds]

Defense Minister Parkanová: "...Then we add scare tactics, targeted disinformation campaigns, which were not spontaneous but organized from somewhere."

Journalist: "From where? By whom? Do you know something we don't?"

Defense Minister Parkanová: "Now I'm getting myself into a dumb situation in which I'll either have to be secretive or accuse one of the superpowers. I almost need to backtrack. Or I'll be in a position of a character from *Yes, Minister* [the British TV comedy series] who would say, whenever he'd get in trouble, that it was a matter of a state secret. But seriously, there are things that cannot be made public, but it is impossible to not see them."[483]

It is clear that the superpower that Defense Minister Parkanová meant was the Russian Federation. The key question is why the Czech government wouldn't speak more openly of Russia's involvement in anti-radar and anti-American campaigns.

Countering Russia's disinformation proved very difficult for the Czech government largely due to the technical nature of arguments in support of ballistic missile defense cooperation with the United States, security classification of some information regarding an X-band

---

[483] Jiří Kubík, "Parkanová: Milenec by mi prošel, písnička o radaru ne" (Parkanová: I Could Get Away with a Lover, But Not with a Song About a Radar).

radar that made it harder to factually counter disinformation, and a general lack of understanding of defense issues among the Czech population. The Czech government found itself surprised by the strength of Russia's opposition to U.S.-Czech ballistic missile defense cooperation, which left it unprepared to deal with Russia's disinformation campaign.

Russia's broader goal was to rehabilitate its influence in former Warsaw Pact countries and to strengthen isolationist sentiment in the United States. Russia's efforts with that respect were independent of the outcome of U.S.-Czech ballistic missile defense negotiations.[484] Russia's early influence efforts and its engagement on the issue of U.S.-Czech ballistic missile defense cooperation make the Czech government's lack of preparedness with respect to its own communication efforts regarding U.S.-Czech ballistic missile defense cooperation even less comprehensible.

Russia's exploitation of civic movements and internationalist movements continued in 2008, but the Russian Federation conducted fewer active measures that year because it did not want to draw undue attention to its invasion of Georgia.[485] To the pro-transatlantic segment of Czech politics, Russia's invasion of Georgia underscored the dangers of Russia's political influence on Czech territory and the importance of hosting a U.S. radar as a hedge against it. The sentiment was particularly strong due to the 70th anniversary of the Munich Agreement, the 60th anniversary of the Communist take-over of Czechoslovakia, and the 40th anniversary of Czechoslovakia's occupation by the Warsaw Pact army. After Russia's invasion and

---

[484] Czech Security Information Service, "Bezpečnostní informační služba: Zpráva o činnosti za rok 2007" (Annual Report of the Security Information Service for 2007), 2008.

[485] Czech Security Information Service, "Bezpečnostní informační služba: Zpráva o činnosti za rok 2008" (Annual Report of the Security Information Service for 2008), 2009.

occupation of Georgia, the Czech government completely failed to capitalize on the public's anti-Russian sentiments to make a stronger case for U.S.-Czech ballistic missile defense cooperation as a hedge against Russian aggression.

The Czech Security Service's 2009 annual report offered what could be read as a subtle rebuttal to the Obama Administration's "reset" policy with Russia. The report stated that the Czech Security Information Service "does not get to pick its adversaries, nor does it dictate how they operate. They pick the Czech Republic and methods of their works, regardless of the state of the world in its many changes and varieties, and with an emphasis on their own interests and needs."[486] The report also classified Russia's intelligence activities on Czech territory as "contrarian and at times adversarial."[487] The Czech presidency of the European Union led to an increase in Russia's intelligence officers' attempts to connect with Czech politicians.

Russia's attempts to influence Russian expatriates living in the Czech Republic were particularly notable in 2009.[488] At that point in time, the Russians could draw on a variety of connections in Czech local government and resources to make life "uncomfortable" for civic organizations that were not interested in serving Russia's government's interests.[489] On the bright side, a significant portion of the Russian-speaking community on Czech territory seems uninterested in catering to Vladimir Putin's whims.[490]

---

[486] Czech Security Information Service, "Bezpečnostní informační služba: Zpráva o činnosti za rok 2009" (Annual Report of the Security Information Service for 2009), 2010.

[487] Ibid.

[488] Ibid.

[489] Ibid.

[490] Czech Security Information Service, "Bezpečnostní informační služba: Zpráva o činnosti za rok 2012" (Annual Report of the Security Information Service for 2012), 2013.

U.S.-Czech missile defense cooperation would undoubtedly open another opportunity for Russia to potentially obtain more information about U.S. and Czech high-tech and defense sectors. In the Czech Republic, Russia's task of turning people to cooperate with it is made easier by a general lack of loyalty to the Czech state, particularly on the part of Czech government officials.[491] That makes them more likely to collaborate to advance Russia's questionable interests, which in turns undermines the public's belief in the Czech government.[492] Russia's use of institutions, lobbying and networking companies, unions, and law firms that exercise influence on Russia's behalf exacerbates these problems.[493] The Czech Republic has a less developed regulatory environment regarding functioning and transparency of non-profit organizations, which makes it easier to abuse them to advance Russia's influence under the guise of legitimate activities.

Another aspect of the problem is the general Czech inability to clearly condemn collaboration with authoritarian and foreign powers. The Czech Republic did not go through decommunization after the end of the Cold War, and most Communist officials were never held accountable for their participation and maintenance of Czechoslovakia as an authoritarian state subjected to Soviet influence during the Cold War. Today, similar tendencies are apparent in a general Czech unwillingness to condemn re-entry of people with questionable career histories to civil service.[494] It is a vicious cycle. Frustration with the Czech government and the state of civil service can motivate some to collaborate with Russia's intelligence officers, making the

---

[491] Ibid.
[492] Ibid.
[493] Ibid.
[494] Ibid.

repetition of the entire cycle easier during the next go-around.[495]

After the demise of U.S.-Czech ballistic missile defense cooperation announced by President Obama in September 2009, Russia's intelligence activities strengthened focus on their traditional priority of boosting prospects for Russia's economy and obtaining influence in strategic industries via acquisition of selected firms and shares in them (particularly in the energy sector). These activities increased with respect to Russia's efforts to obtain insight into Czech research and development.[496] They continue in similar shapes and forms until today, with a primary focus on securing economic advantages for Russian firms (controlled by the Russian state) and control of strategically important Czech industries.

Conclusion

For various reasons, not all of which are related to Russia's intelligence operations, the Russian Federation was able to claim victory in the case of U.S.-Czech ballistic missile defense cooperation. There are several factors that make the case unique and that made Russia's job easier.

The environment in the Czech Republic is unusually permissive with respect to collaboration with Russian intelligence officers on all levels of the government and in the public, business, and private spheres. This largely has to do with pre-existing relations, a consequence of the Soviet occupation of Czechoslovakia during the Cold War. Pre-existing relations make people more susceptible to collaboration. An additional unique aspect of the Central

---

[495] Ibid.

[496] Czech Security Information Service, "Bezpečnostní informační služba: Zpráva o činnosti za rok 2009" (Annual Report of the Security Information Service for 2009), 2010.

and Eastern European region is penetration by Russia's organized crime and subsequent utilization of these networks by Russian intelligence. This factor will continue to play an important role in the future as local politics feeds national politics.

The fragile situation after the June 2006 election resulted in the Czech Social Democrats distancing themselves from their previous active support of U.S.-Czech ballistic missile defense cooperation, giving legitimacy to those who opposed it, and making it easier for the Russian Federation to spread disinformation about U.S.-Czech ballistic missile defense cooperation—such as the radar being aimed at Russia's ballistic missiles. Paroubek, leader of the Czech Social Democratic Party, and the previous government's Prime Minister, latched on to any visible issue to distinguish himself from Topolánek, the new Prime Minister and leader of the Civic Democratic Party. "The visible issue at the time happened to be the radar issue," according to then-Deputy Director Chalupecký.[497] Between January 2007 and March 2009 when the Czech government fell, the fragile government coalition faced no fewer than five no-confidence votes. As these no-confidence votes piled up, the government grew weaker and internally more divided, making prospects of obtaining parliamentary consent to ballistic missile defense agreements with the United States increasingly difficult. The whole episode was a luck of the draw rather than a pre-meditated scenario run by the Russian intelligence services. The Russian intelligence services, however, were able to exploit the situation and seized the opportunity skillfully.

One difference between Russia's operations in the Czech Republic during radar discussions and negotiations is that social media were relatively nascent, and so Russia could not fully utilize their potential. Russia was involved

---

[497] Author interview with then-Deputy Director Chalupecký.

in producing online content and ensuring that its story lines were visible, but social media today are undoubtedly a more significant and cheaper toolkit in Russia's intelligence operations than they were 10 years ago.

The Czech government's silence regarding Russia's influence operations on its territory was puzzling. At the early stages of U.S.-Czech ballistic missile defense cooperation and discussions, it is possible that the Czech government felt some pressure, even if informal, from the United States to avoid drawing attention to Russia as a problem, because the United States was interested in pursuing its own cooperative policy toward Russia, including finding joint solutions to ballistic missile threats. After Russia's invasion of Georgia in 2008, the Czech government's silence regarding Russia's activities on Czech soil was a missed opportunity to alert the Czech public to Russia's nefarious activities.

The United States could offer only limited help to Czech authorities in countering Russia's influence operations on Czech territory. There are too many targets to focus on, and it is easy for them to slip under the radar. Russia is geographically much closer to the Czech Republic than is the United States. The United States to some degree lacks historical connections to the Czech Republic, although today, the United States has undoubtedly more links to the Czech Republic than during the Cold War. The case also underscores the need for U.S. intelligence and law enforcement to keep track of Russia's activities and its potential influence on U.S. allies.

Lastly, it is reasonable to assume that Russia is attempting similar measures and employing similar tactics in other countries, including the United States. Social media and interconnectivity allow it to utilize its intelligence networks in a collaborative and mutually enforcing manner. The United States must craft a persuasive message to compete with Russia-peddled lies. Some of Russia's propaganda originated in the United States among arms control circles and was used in the Czech Republic to add credibility to Russia's propaganda without making it look like it came from Russia. For example, Czech opponents of ballistic missile defense cooperation met with U.S. and other international experts opposing U.S. missile defense programs who parroted Russia's talking points on the issue, and then these Czech opponents presented their arguments with added credibility in the Czech Republic for having met with the "experts." If given an opportunity, Russia would likely utilize similar approaches in the future.

Chapter Six
Assessing the Importance of Different Factors in U.S.-Czech Ballistic Missile Defense Cooperation

A great deal of world politics is a fundamental struggle, but it is also a struggle that has to be waged intelligently.

Zbigniew Brzezinski
"One on One," *Al Jazeera*, 2010

Chapter Six evaluates how different factors impacted U.S.-Czech ballistic missile defense cooperation and assesses their relative importance. Such an understanding is useful in order to better comprehend current and future U.S. missile defense cooperative efforts with other nations.

The Threat: It's Not What You Think

U.S.-Czech ballistic missile defense cooperation illustrates that the more threatened a nation feels, the more it will be interested in cooperating with another allied nation. This is not a particularly insightful statement, but what is new is that the U.S.-Czech ballistic missile defense case study shows that allies need not fully share their understanding of a threat for their defense cooperation to proceed as if they did.

North Korean and Iranian ballistic missile threats played a lesser role in the Czech public discourse about U.S. missile defense plans in Europe, as evidenced by public statements of the Czech government's representatives. The Czechs were simply not as concerned about the Iranian ballistic missile threat as were the Americans. An idea that an Iranian or North Korean ballistic missile could land on a

Prague castle or another target in Europe was alien to most Czechs. The European Union's trade efforts with Iran at the time also contributed to a perception that Iran (and by extension its ballistic missile program) is not as threatening as the Bush 43 Administration depicted it.

U.S. missile defense opponents did not believe that North Korea or Iran presented a ballistic missile (or other) threat to the Czech Republic or NATO in a way that required placement of U.S. missile defense components in Europe on the timeline advocated by the U.S. and the Czech governments. Other NATO countries with ballistic missiles were a non-issue for the Czech and the U.S. governments, illustrating the importance of balance of threat and states' perceptions rather than focusing on military capabilities alone. The Czechs have not considered French, German, or U.S. ballistic missiles a military threat. Only fringe and insignificant parts of the Czech political spectrum (usually leftist activists) saw NATO as a military threat to the Czech Republic's interests.

While Russia's threats to use nuclear weapons against missile defense sites were viewed with concern in the Czech Republic, they didn't quite change Czech hearts and minds. Russia's threats provided a rationale to proceed with U.S.-Czech missile defense cooperation efforts to those who supported them — and to stop them, to those who opposed them. The Czech government went out of its way to ease Russian concerns, even considering allowing Russian inspectors to occasionally visit a U.S. radar site. As stated above, these proposals generated much negative publicity from the opposition parties and from the Czech population in general.[498]

There is additional supporting evidence that the Czech government was not really concerned about military

---

[498] Ministerstvo zahraničních věcí ČR (Czech Ministry of Foreign Affairs), "Zahraničních politika České republiky dokumenty 4/2008" (Czech Foreign Policy Documents 4/2008).

threats: resources that it spent on the Czech Republic's defense. Figure 5 illustrates the Czech Republic's defense budget expenditures as a share of GDP during the time of ongoing informal and formal ballistic missile defense discussions and negotiations with the United States.[499] The overall trendline is decreasing. It would be the opposite had the Czech government felt an urgent military threat.

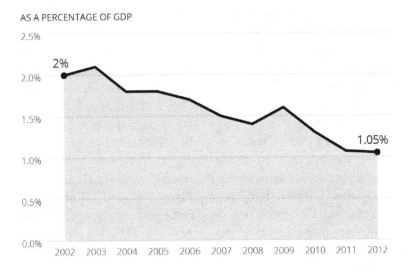

Fig. 5. **Czech Republic Defense Spending**

Source: NATO.

This suggests that while ballistic missile threats played some role in the Czech government's decision to participate in a U.S. ballistic missile defense program, at least on the official level, they were not a primary driver of its motivations to do so. The Czech leadership perceived Russia's political influence on Czech territory as a threat to

---

[499] North Atlantic Treaty Organization, "Information on Defence Expenditures," July 10, 2018,
https://www.nato.int/cps/en/natohq/topics_49198.htm.

the Czech Republic, and the placement of a U.S. defense asset on Czech territory was intended to counter it.

Czech Fear of Abandonment

Alliance literature on abandonment to some extent anticipates the dynamic of allies becoming bolder in their public statements as they become more certain of their patron's support—and that dynamic is evident in the case of U.S.-Czech ballistic missile defense cooperation.[500] The closer the conclusion of negotiations on a U.S. radar on Czech territory, the more willing was the Czech government to speak about the Russian Federation as a threat. The fear of abandonment was present in the Czech government's effort to get a U.S. permanent military presence on Czech territory. The Czech government was motivated by the Czech Republic's historical experience of being abandoned by other states that were supposed to guarantee its security in the face of a threat—such as France and the United Kingdom during World War II. A permanent U.S. presence on Czech territory would be the ultimate guarantee that the Czech Republic would not be left at the mercy of stronger states to its geographical left and right.

International relations literature also anticipates an increase in a state's desire to ally with others as its threat perception increases.[501] While this dynamic was apparent on the part of the Czech government, the Russian Federation's threats did not significantly influence the Czech public's willingness to participate in a U.S. defense

---

[500] See, for example, Glenn H. Snyder, "The Security Dilemma in Alliance Politics," *World Politics*, Vol. 36, No. 4 (1984), pp. 461–95, https://doi.org/10.2307/2010183.

[501] See, for example, Stephen M. Walt, *Origins of Alliances* (Ithaca, NY: Cornell University Press, 1987).

plan, partly because the threats were so outrageous that it was hard for the Czechs to take them seriously: A preemptive nuclear strike on Czech territory in retaliation for hosting a U.S. radar site? Hard for the Czechs to consider this a "real" threat.

The Czech public did not make a connection between a U.S. radar deployment and a hedge against Russia's political influence in a way that would make it more supportive of U.S.-Czech ballistic missile defense cooperation. The covert nature of Russia's influence operations on Czech soil made it hard for the Czech government to frame the radar as a hedge against Russia's political influence. The Czech government was unable to "capitalize" on Russia's direct meddling in Czech politics and security, which certainly was not popular among the Czech population, particularly after Russia's invasion of Georgia in 2008. Compounded by the Czech government's somewhat incoherent argumentation in favor of U.S.-Czech missile defense cooperation, the Czech government never recovered from ceding communication grounds to much better organized, "louder," and more visible opponents of U.S.-Czech missile defense cooperation.[502]

Asymmetries in U.S.-Czech Relations

The alliance between the Czech Republic and the United States is marked by profound asymmetries in political, military, diplomatic, economic, and manpower resources. The Czech Republic's bargaining power has always been weaker than that of the United States. Most important, if the United States hadn't invested in ballistic missile defense

---

[502] Milan Vodička, "Co měla říct vláda lidem, aby jich bylo víc pro radar?" (What Should the Government Have Said to Achieve More Public Support for the Radar?), *MF Dnes*, July 9, 2008, https://www.idnes.cz/zpravy/domaci/co-mela-rict-vlada-lidem-aby-jich-bylo-vic-pro-radar.A080708_201303_nazory_abr.

capabilities, there would be nothing to negotiate about because the Czech Republic would not be interested in developing its own ballistic missile defense program. In that sense, the United States had a final say on ballistic missile defense cooperation with the Czech Republic. No system, no negotiations. As a related matter, the Czech Republic was also limited in the kinds of contributions it could make to U.S. and NATO ballistic missile defense architecture. With respect to the United States, the Czech Republic could contribute its geographical location, and it could bear some infrastructure costs related to a U.S. radar site. It could potentially contribute some advanced technologies, particularly in a field of radar technologies.

Geopolitically, the Czech Republic does not have a viable path to countering Russia's military threat, and countering its political influence is difficult, too. That is why the Czech Republic has valued NATO and the United States as the cornerstone of Czech political and military security. Given the Czech historical experience, relying on French or German security guarantees is problematic. It is also worthwhile to keep in mind that the Czechs are one of the most skeptical nations regarding the European Union, and (generally speaking) they do not consider the EU's viability as a defense guarantor to be as credible as that of NATO.

The United States has the capacity to supply assistance to NATO (and to the Czech Republic, by extension) in the case of conflict, and has pledged to do so since NATO's founding. U.S. options are limited by its capacity and political will, but time and again the United States has demonstrated that it can mobilize its resources and defeat adversaries even across the Atlantic Ocean. The dynamic of the U.S. relationship with the Russian Federation informs U.S. actions in Europe, particularly given Russia's large nuclear weapons arsenal and superiority in tactical nuclear weapons on lower steps of the escalatory ladder.[503]

Czech Dependence

The Czech Republic can be considered dependent on others for its security. International relations literature measures a state's dependence on an ally by that state's need for military assistance; the degree to which an ally fills that need; and alternative ways of meeting the need, whether by increasing one's own military preparedness, allying with someone else, acquiring additional resources by military action, or conciliating an adversary.[504] The Czech Republic does not have viable realignment alternatives to NATO (and the United States as its principal guarantor) if it wants to preserve the democratic and pro-Western character of its society and foreign policy. It could, to some degree, and at a likely cost to the democratic character of its institutions, pursue conciliatory policies toward Russia, but the Czech Republic's post-Cold War foreign policy has aimed to avoid having to do that. For the Czech political leadership, having a U.S. radar base on Czech territory was an additional guarantee that the situation would stay that way. Increasing the Czech Republic's military preparedness, even if the Czech Republic funded its defense at a much higher than the current rate, would not make up for a massive disparity between the Czech and the Russian military forces. The Czech Republic cannot realistically acquire additional resources by military action.

---

[503] U.S. Department of Defense, "Nuclear Posture Review 2018," February 2018, https://media.defense.gov/2018/Feb/02/2001872886/-1/-1/1/2018-NUCLEAR-POSTURE-REVIEW-FINAL-REPORT.PDF.

[504] Glenn H. Snyder, *Alliance Politics* (Ithaca, NY: Cornell University Press, 2007), p. 167.

The theme of Czech dependence on other states, voluntary and involuntary, is woven through the country's history from its early inception, be it dependence on the Habsburgs, on the Germans, or on the Soviets. The Czech Republic's security and political dependence on NATO and the United States was one of the most important factors that influenced the Czech government's decision to negotiate on a U.S. radar site on Czech territory. The Czech fear of abandonment is closely related to its historical experience and its security dependence on others.

The U.S.-Czech missile defense cooperation fulfilled intrinsic, strategic, and reputational interests for the Czech Republic. High-level U.S. attention and the international visibility that came with it was considered prestigious in foreign policy circles, particularly for a state as (relatively) small as the Czech Republic. The country's representatives were pleased with the perception that the Czech Republic is "punching above its weight" in the international arena. The Czech leadership saw U.S.-Czech ballistic missile defense cooperation as advancing the moral values of freedom and democracy for which the Czechs have fought since the end of the Cold War. They saw it as increasing the Czech Republic's security within a broader transatlantic area.

Economic Benefits and U.S.-Czech Ballistic Missile Defense Cooperation

Did the Czech government care whether the Czech Republic economically benefitted from cooperating with the United States on missile defense? It turns out potential economic benefits of hosting a U.S. radar site on Czech territory were secondary at best to the Czech Republic's primary interest of increasing its security vis-à-vis Russia's political threat. "Economic cooperation with the United States didn't play a primary role in Czech considerations to participate in the U.S. missile defense project," according to Jakub Čimoradský.[505]

The Czech government's initial briefing to the Chamber of Deputies' Committee on Foreign Affairs mentioned potential economic benefits, but they were relatively unimportant in terms of their role in U.S.-Czech negotiations.[506] Economic benefits potentially stemming from U.S.-Czech missile defense cooperation were perhaps relevant for Czech construction companies, and were assumed to provide opportunities to strengthen defense science and technology cooperation between the two countries.[507] But the United States was not (and is not) a major trade partner or an investor for the Czech Republic whose primary markets are in the EU. Practical barriers to cooperation between the United States and the Czech Republic, for example the need for Czech defense contractors to obtain U.S. security clearances before conducting official business, made progress on these issues very difficult in reality.

That is not to say that economic cooperation proposals were entirely without a purpose. Economic motivations "were important on the local level from both infrastructure and employment perspectives, if the locals agreed with the plan," according to former First Deputy Minister Pojar.[508] The Czech government (and the United States) used economic incentives to foster positive responses to a radar plan among the local population in the vicinity of a presumed radar site. The government representatives often

---

[505] Author interview with Jakub Čimoradský, Deputy Head of the International Law Section of the Czech Ministry of Defense.

[506] "Zahraničních politika České republiky dokumenty 10/2006" (Ministerstvo zahraničních věcí ČR, October 2006), https://www.mzv.cz/public/fb/a/61/73298_492014_Dokumenty_mes icniku_ZP2006_10.pdf.

[507] "Zahraničních politika České republiky dokumenty 10/2006."

[508] Author interview with former First Deputy Minister Pojar.

mentioned economic opportunities and infrastructure improvements that would increase the quality of life in a relatively poor region.

In the early stages of U.S.-Czech radar negotiations, the Czech government pledged to provide as much as 1.4 billion Czech koruna (CZK), about $70 million, for local infrastructure improvement projects.[509] The Czech government said the region would receive this funding regardless of whether a U.S. radar would be built. Even then, the devil was in the details because the Czech government pledged to provide only about CZK200 million to CZK250 million ($10 million to $12.5 million, of the total pledged amount) and stated that the rest would come from EU funds.[510] The Czech government could not guarantee that the EU would provide the rest of the funding, or any funding for that matter, which is why some called the government's promises disingenuous. Others also pointed to the fact that infrastructure improvement projects were due for modernization regardless of whether a radar would be built, and were therefore not some benefit or concession to the region on the part of the Czech government.[511]

---

[509] Milena Štráfeldová, "Vláda slibuje obcím v Brdech stovky milionů korun" (Government Promises Villages in Brdy Hundreds of Millions of Crowns), Radio Praha, September 5, 2007, https://www.radio.cz/cz/rubrika/zpravy/vlada-slibuje-obcim-v-brdech-stovky-milionu-korun.

[510] Jan Jiřička, "Brdy oplakaly stovky milionů za radar, vláda se k Topolánkovu slibu nemá" (Brdy Mourned Hundreds of Millions for the Radar, the Government Is not Going to Fulfill Topolánek's Promise), *iDnes.cz*, January 29, 2011, https://www.idnes.cz/zpravy/domaci/brdy-oplakaly-stovky-milionu-za-radar-vlada-se-k-topolankovu-slibu-nema.A110124_121933_domaci_jj.

[511] Petr Holub, "Miliarda za radar rozdělena. Půjde do brdské kanalizace" (One billion Koruna Divided. It Will Fund Brdy's Sewer System), *Aktuálně.cz*, February 7, 2008, https://zpravy.aktualne.cz/domaci/miliarda-za-radar-rozdelena-pujde-do-brdske-kanalizace/r~i:article:520459/.

The Czech government's funding promises were undoubtedly meant as a "carrot" with which it tried to obtain local support for a U.S. radar plan. The Czech government used the economic assistance as a stick, too. In the summer of 2008, it allocated CZK1 billion ($50 million) in subsidies to two regions in the vicinity of the presumed radar base. Out of this funding, the village Trokavec, closest to the potential U.S. radar site, was allocated the lowest amount.[512] Its mayor, Jan Neoral, was one of the most outspoken opponents of a U.S. radar plan and one of the public faces of the No Bases Initiative. After the fall of the Topolánek government and the cancellation of the radar plan by the Obama Administration, local villages got less than 5 percent of the overall pledged funding on the grounds that it was necessary to reprioritize this funding to assist villages in other regions impacted by the 2009 and 2010 floods.[513]

The United States bore a disproportionate cost of its missile defense program relative to its NATO allies, including the Czech Republic, which makes perfect sense given that the primary mission of this system was to protect the U.S. homeland. But looking exclusively at dollar costs omits important ways in which smaller allies contribute to joint projects. For example, the Czech government spent significant political capital on radar negotiations with the United States and on trying to get the agreements through the Czech Chamber of Deputies despite the large public opposition. It is difficult, if not impossible, to place a monetary value on the Czech government's political capital, but that contribution was nevertheless significant.

The legacy of the Czech government's diplomatic contribution to get other NATO allies to recognize the

---

[512] Ibid.

[513] Jiřička, "Brdy oplakaly stovky milionů za radar, vláda se k Topolánkovu slibu nemá" (Brdy Mourned Hundreds of Millions for the Radar, the Government Is Not Going to Fulfill Topolánek's Promise).

usefulness of a U.S. ballistic missile defense system for NATO as a whole, and to get the project more accepted by other European nations, continues to be important today, even as U.S. missile defense architecture changed and U.S. missile defense assets are being deployed to Poland and Romania.

Alliance Politics, Public Opinion, and the Danger of Overlapping Narratives

U.S.-Czech ballistic missile defense cooperation exhibits most marks of Richard Neustadt's common attributes of alliance crises: muddled perceptions, disappointed expectations, and domestic bureaucratic politics.[514] Muddled perceptions are apparent from the way the Czech government communicated the issue to its constituents. Disappointed expectations are apparent from the way the Czech government reacted to the Obama Administration's announcement to cancel the U.S. radar plan. Bureaucratic politics is apparent from a lack of information about U.S.-missile defense discussions provided to Czech parliamentarians before the U.S.-Czech official negotiations started.

The Czech Republic considered a NATO dimension of U.S.-Czech ballistic missile defense cooperation to be significant domestically and internationally. Involving NATO in debates about a U.S. radar site in the Czech Republic was a natural step for a smaller state that was interested in additional negotiating strength vis-à-vis a much larger United States, as a prominent international relations theory would predict.[515] Doing so had the additional benefit that a U.S. ballistic missile defense plan

---

[514] Richard Neustadt, *Alliance Politics*, 1970, pp. 55 and 65.

[515] Robert Keohane and Joseph Nye, *Power and Interdependence*, 3rd ed. (London: Longman Publishing Group, 2001).

would be accepted by other NATO members, even those that were initially skeptical of U.S. missile defense project on European territory, and those that were increasingly unhappy about U.S. military operations in Iraq and Afghanistan. Domestically, however, the overlap caused confusion among the Czech general public and complicated the government's communication efforts.

It is not farfetched to suggest that President Obama's cancellation of the radar site contributed to a crisis in relations between the two countries. Former First Deputy Minister Pojar summed up the general challenge:

> The Americans were politically insensitive to events in the Czech Republic. For example, after years of silence they renewed the whole project right in the middle of an election campaign in the spring of 2006. In January 2007, they called to ask the Czech Republic to host the site just a few hours before the Czech [Prime Minister Topolánek's] government faced a very narrow vote of confidence in the Czech Parliament. Last, but not least, President Obama made a phone call to the Czech prime minister to announce cancellation of the project at around 1 a.m. Czech time. If they were more sensitive to the Czech political calendar, things could be easier.[516]

This is not to say that the Czech government conducted its communications campaign well.

Prior to 2006, public opinion was a fairly insignificant factor in the Czech government's conduct of ballistic missile defense cooperation with the United States. Figure 2 (page 197) shows polls conducted by the Public Opinion Research Centre (Centrum pro výzkum veřejného mínění), a research institute affiliated with the Czech Academy of Sciences. The

---

[516] Author interview with former First Deputy Minister Pojar.

first such poll measuring Czech views of U.S. plans to build a missile defense site in the Czech Republic was conducted in September 2006, at the onset of the public debate about a radar site. A majority of respondents, 36 percent and 26 percent respectively, were "firmly" and "mostly" against U.S. plans to build a missile defense site in the Czech Republic.[517] Only 5 percent and 19 percent, respectively, were in "favor" or "mostly in favor" of the plan.[518]

This poll was conducted before the Americans officially asked the Czech Republic to host a U.S. radar and before the Czech general public obtained more information about the project. Other private companies conducted public polls, usually at the request of different actors, including political parties, but these public polls do not have the scope and consistency of polls conducted by the Public Opinion Research Centre. Still, they were generally not very far off from the Center's data.

Even as information about a U.S. missile defense plan became more widely available, the overall public opposition to Czech participation in it remained about the same. Figure 2 depicts responses between September 2006 and June 2009. The percentage of undecided respondents fell below the initial 14 percent in September 2006 and January 2007, to below 10 percent in April 2007, which suggests that as the missile defense question became more widely discussed in public discourse, more respondents formulated their opinion on the matter.[519]

---

[517] Červenka, "Americké protiraketové základny v ČR a Polsku z pohledu domácí veřejnosti" (U.S. Missile Defense Bases in the Czech Republic and Poland from a Perspective of the public), p. 4.

[518] Ibid.

[519] Červenka, "Jak občané hodnotí rozhodnutí vlády USA odstoupit od plánu na vybudování protiraketové radarové základny v ČR?" (How do Czech citizens assess the cancellation of a U.S. decision to build a radar in the Czech Republic?), Public Opinion Research Centre, November 30, 2009, p. 2.

Fig. 2. **Support for a U.S. Missile Defense Site in the Czech Republic**

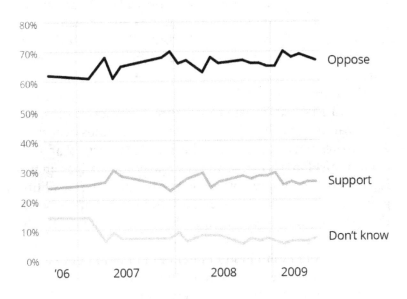

Note: Some figures have been interpolated.
Source: Centrum pro výzkum veřejného mínění (Public Opinion Research Centre).

The opposition to a U.S. missile defense site never fell below 60 percent, albeit calling it "growing" as Secretary of Defense Gates calls it in his memoirs is somewhat misleading.[520] The opposition to the radar site fluctuated over time. According to the polls, only between 20 percent and 30 percent of the respondents agreed that the Czech Republic should host a U.S. missile defense site.

Figure 6 illustrates that the Czech government's communications efforts to get the general public to support Czech participation in a U.S. missile defense plan in Europe were unsuccessful. Special Government Envoy Tomáš

---

[520] Robert Gates, *Duty: Memoirs of a Secretary at War* (New York: Vintage, 2015), p. 402.

Klvaňa argued that opposition to the radar site was emotional and disproportionate to the demands placed on the Czech Republic by the United States. He indicated he was aware that the opposition prevailed because the government's communications strategy was reactive and lagging behind the curve.[521] But Russia's influence operations on Czech territory also contributed to those outcomes.

Data from four polls conducted between September 2006 and May 2007, listed in Figure 6, indicate increased polarization regarding the issue along party lines over time. This makes sense considering the Social Democrats' and the Communist Party's efforts to distinguish themselves on this issue, among many other issues, from the coalition government. Figure 6 also makes apparent that the Civic Democrats were successful in communicating the importance and benefits of U.S.-Czech missile defense cooperation to their base voters because over time, their voters increased their support for the idea of missile defense cooperation between the United States and the Czech Republic—from 40 percent in September 2006 to 47 percent in February 2007, to 53 percent in April 2007, to 62 percent in May 2007.[522] Other political parties were similarly successful in unifying their respective voter bases along the lines of arguments preferred by their respective political leaderships.

According to a February 2007 poll, 54 percent of respondents believed that the radar site would have "largely negative" or "decidedly negative" consequences

---

[521] Tomáš Klvaňa, "Czech Republic: Missile Defense 'Based on Capability,' Not Threats," Radio Free Europe Radio Liberty, August 13, 2007, https://www.rferl.org/a/1078128.html.

[522] Červenka, "Americké protiraketové základny v ČR a Polsku z pohledu domácí veřejnosti" (U.S. Missile Defense Bases in the Czech Republic and Poland from the Perspective of the Public), p. 5.

for Czech security.[523] The second leading issue of concern were "largely negative" or "decidedly negative" consequences for Czech sovereignty raised by 38 percent of respondents, and the third large issue of concern, mentioned by 37 percent of respondents, were "largely negative" or "decidedly negative" consequences for relations with other states.[524] Concerns over Czech security and sovereignty are a powerful legacy of Czech historical experience as a state at the mercy of other states; a legacy that made it easier to tap into this sentiment by opponents of U.S.-Czech ballistic missile defense cooperation and for the Russians to use in their influence operations.

With a significant percentage of respondents easily identifying negatives related to Czech participation in the U.S. missile defense plan, what were the benefits for the Czech Republic that respondents raised as relevant? Seventy-six percent of respondents mentioned a "decidedly positive" or "largely positive" impact on Czech relations with the United States, and 52 percent argued that Czech participation in the U.S. missile defense plan would have a "positive" impact on the country's relationships with other NATO member states.[525] About 24 percent of respondents thought that the Czech Republic hosting a U.S. radar would have "decidedly positive" or "largely positive" impacts on international arms control, while 19 percent thought it would have a "decidedly negative" or "largely negative" impact on international arms control.

---

[523] Ibid., p. 7.
[524] Ibid.
[525] Ibid.

Fig. 6. **Attitudes Toward a Missile Defense Base/Radar in the Czech Republic, by Party Preferences**

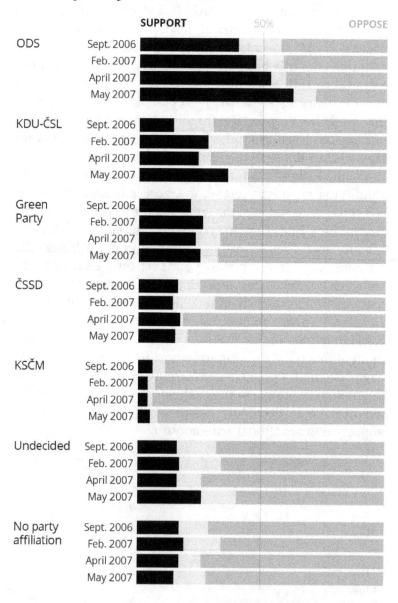

Source: Centrum pro výzkum veřejného mínění (Public Opinion Research Centre).

Potential economic benefits associated with Czech participation in U.S. missile defense plans were not a significant factor in negotiations, even as the government was pushing its U.S. counterparts to allow Czech companies to bid on radar site construction contracts and ensuring that Americans working on the project would be subject to Czech taxation law.[526]

The opposition to hosting a U.S. radar site was stronger on a local level than on a nation-wide level. Many municipalities held public referenda about whether the Czech government should agree to host a U.S. radar. The first referendum was held in Trokavec on March 17, 2007.[527] It was held about two weeks before the Czech government sent its official affirmative response regarding its interest to begin negotiations about a potential radar placement. Opponents argued that the government was not providing them with enough information about U.S.-Czech ballistic missile defense negotiations, and, while that was the case in some respects, many opponents were simply not interested in a fact-based discussion on the issue.

The referendum showed that the "not in my backyard" sentiment was strong in Trokavec, with a majority of voting citizens, 71 out of roughly 100, against the radar.[528] Trokavec citizens gave their local representatives the mandate to use all available means within the bounds of law to prevent the building of a U.S. radar site in the Brdy military training area.[529] The results of local referenda were symbolic and not legally binding for the Czech government.

During U.S.-Czech radar negotiations, more than 20 local villages conducted referenda and public polls that all

---

[526] Gates, *Duty: Memoirs of a Secretary at War*, p. 167.

[527] "Skóre proti radaru? V Trokavci 71:1" (Tally Against the Radar? In Trokavec 71:1), *Aktuálně.cz*, March 17, 2007, http://archive.vn/lsg3H#selection-1163.0-1163.35.

[528] Ibid.

[529] Ibid.

ended up in opposition to the radar.[530] Some mayors disputed the utility of local referenda that cost the villages resources for which the municipal councils had not budgeted, and that were not binding on the government but mayors were bound to mandate referenda in response to their constituents' pressure.[531]

Most Czechs welcomed the Obama Administration's decision to cancel the radar in the Czech Republic. In October 2009, 48 percent of respondents were "decidedly satisfied" with President Obama's decision to abandon the plan to build a radar site in the Czech Republic.[532] Another large segment of respondents, 32 percent, were "mostly satisfied" with the Administration's decision. This means that even those who previously supported Czech participation in U.S. missile defense plans welcomed the Obama Administration's radar cancellation. Only 10 percent and 2 percent, respectively, were "mostly dissatisfied" or "decidedly dissatisfied" with the Obama Administration's announcement.[533]

Over half of the respondents, 52 percent, thought the Obama Administration's decision would have a "decidedly positive" or "largely positive" impact on the security of the Czech Republic and its citizens.[534] Only about 9 percent total thought that the Obama Administration's decision would

---

[530] "Starosta Příbrami má strach z radaru" (Příbram Mayor Is Scared of the Radar), *Hospodářské noviny*, June 16, 2007, https://domaci.ihned.cz/c1-21412460-starosta-pribrami-ma-strach-z-radaru.

[531] "Radar nechceme, řekli v referendu Mirošovští" (We Don't Want a Radar, the Citizens of Mirošov Village Said in a Referendum).

[532] Červenka, "Jak občané hodnotí rozhodnutí vlády USA odstoupit od plánu na vybudování protiraketové radarové základny v ČR?" (How Do Czech Citizens Assess the Cancellation of the U.S. Decision to Build a Radar in the Czech Republic?), Public Opinion Research Centre, November 30, 2009.

[533] Ibid., p. 2.

[534] Ibid.

have a "largely negative" or "decidedly negative" impact on the security of the Czech Republic and its citizens. About 33 percent did not think the decision would affect the Czech Republic's and its citizens' security one way or another.[535]

About 18 percent of respondents thought that the Obama Administration's decision would have a "largely negative" or "decidedly negative" impact on relations with the United States, and a large majority of 71 percent thought that the decision would either have a positive or no impact on Czech relations with the United States.[536] This meant that in the minds of a majority of Czech citizens, the missile defense site question was not particularly relevant when considered in the context of the totality of relations between the Czech Republic and the United States.

The Americans followed the Czech polls regarding the radar issue. At least a part of the U.S. government recognized Russia's influence operations on Czech territory. The Bush 43 Administration was aware of the difficulties that the Czech government faced in pursuing missile defense cooperation in light of the public's opposition.[537] For example, toward the end of 2008, Secretary Gates became convinced that the Czech political opposition would prevent the construction of a radar in the Czech Republic, or that political circumstances would delay such a construction by "many years."[538] Secretary Gates appeared too eager to substitute public opinion polls for the government's future position on a contemporary controversial issue. But foreign and defense policies usually do not make or break elections for the ruling government. Even in the Czech Republic, where the radar issue had more visibility than other foreign policy and defense issues, this

---

[535] Ibid.
[536] Ibid.
[537] Gates, *Duty: Memoirs of a Secretary at War*, p. 162.
[538] Ibid., pp. 399 and 400.

visibility was a consequence of a unique post-election situation with a fragile governmental majority relying on the votes of two renegade parliamentarians from an opposition party, which made it difficult to find a majority vote on any issue, especially as the Topolánek government grew internally weaker over time. If the Czech government was driven by public opinion the way Secretary Gates assumed, it would not even start negotiations with the United States.

The unique situation after the June 2006 election meant that the Czech government was never quite sure whether it had a majority of votes in the Czech Chamber of Deputies on a certain issue. The uncertainty translated into the potential for a single issue, like missile defense, and a single vested coalition parliamentarian, to "make or break" the ruling coalition. The U.S.-Czech radar cooperation happened to enjoy larger visibility than many other issues (including domestic ones), which made it perfectly suited for exploitation by Czech opposition parties to distinguish themselves from the ruling coalition.

The opposition parties' involvement gave legitimacy to a civic movement opposing the U.S. radar base. The opposition movement was helped by resources and organizational networks from the Russian Federation and caught the Czech government unprepared, allowing the opposition to seize the communications initiative against the radar. The Czech government did not recover from the initial surprise, and while it is not clear that even a perfect campaign would have changed a majority of the Czech population's negative perception of the plan, the Czech government representatives' public relations errors, such as a pro-radar song set to an old Soviet-propaganda tune, and the dilettantism on the part of some proponents of the radar made the government's task of obtaining support for U.S.-Czech ballistic missile defense cooperation that much more difficult.

The Russian Federation's involvement in the issue is obvious but remains very politically sensitive to speak about among Czech politicians and the Czech public. The U.S. and Czech governments wanted to avoid any appearance of a ballistic missile defense system being "aimed" at Russia, which likely made it more difficult for the Czech government to speak about Russia's activities on Czech territory. The Czech government's efforts to host a U.S. radar site as a counter to Russia's political influence made it an important target for the Russian Federation. Russia's successful influence operations in concurrence with the Obama Administration's regrettable announcement to cancel the plan to place a radar in the Czech Republic left a legacy of mistrust toward the United States among proponents of strong transatlantic relations, and emboldened anti-American sentiment in the Czech Republic. This legacy will shape U.S.-Czech relations for years to come, although due to a lack of solid alternatives, the United States remains the Czech Republic's best bet for securing its place among democratic nations.

Conclusion and Lessons Learned

Chapter Six assessed the broader relevance of U.S.-Czech ballistic missile defense cooperation for U.S. foreign policy and defense cooperation with other states. Alliances will continue to be important in U.S. foreign policy as well as in the foreign policies of other states. So will ballistic missile defense cooperation, as technological developments make ballistic missiles more available and defenses against them more of a priority for governments around the world. The chapter offers several important lessons stemming from the case of U.S.-Czech ballistic missile defense cooperation.

The first lesson is to be aware that countries do not have to perceive a threat the same way in order to cooperate on missile defense, and that the outcome of their cooperation can be the same as if they did. The Czech government's threat perception was one of the most important factors influencing its willingness to cooperate on ballistic missile defense with the United States. While the United States was concerned about North Korean and Iranian ballistic missiles, the Czech government was not worried about an adversarial missile landing on Czech territory. It adopted the U.S. threat interpretation on an official level, even as its primary motivation for cooperation with the United States was to balance Russia's *political* influence, which made U.S.-Czech ballistic missile defense cooperation an opportune target for the Russian Federation's influence operations. After all, a U.S. radar in the Czech Republic and a few interceptors in Poland would have no appreciable capability against Russia's large and advanced ballistic missile arsenal.

The Czech government hoped that hosting a permanent U.S. military presence, however small, would send a signal to Russia that the Czech Republic was no longer part of the Eastern bloc, and that whatever claim on Czech politics that Russia might think it had, was gone. This element was particularly significant at the outset of discussions, in the context of a relative newness of the Czech Republic as a NATO member state. By signaling that the Czech Republic is now a provider of security in a broader transatlantic context, the Czech government wanted to firmly anchor the Czech Republic in the Western political and military structures. The public debate about U.S.-Czech ballistic missile defense cooperation was conducted at the tail end of a crisis in transatlantic relations between the United States and some NATO member states following the U.S.-led operation in Iraq. The Czech government valued a U.S. ballistic missile defense system for its unifying aspect.

A focus by the United States and the Czech Republic on different threats resulted at times in communications dissonance. Iran and North Korea were too distant to be considered a threat by most Czechs. Czech citizens did not understand why they should be concerned about countries that have never been a security issue for this part of the world. They felt secure in general, as the overall decline curve of the Czech defense budget in Figure 6 illustrated. Russia's political threat was real, but also difficult to discuss publicly, a situation that continues to some degree today because of the covert and often illegal nature of Russia's influence operations in the country. The situation was not helped by the fact that the U.S. and Czech governments wanted to avoid any appearance of a ballistic missile defense system being "aimed" at Russia.

The second relevant lesson is that economic considerations may be secondary at best when it comes to high-stakes security cooperation with other states. The Czech government tried to leverage the radar plan to open opportunities for high-tech defense cooperation with the United States, but practical obstacles, such as the need for U.S. clearances, for Czech firms' participation in U.S. defense contracts made its execution challenging. Some of these efforts continued independently even after U.S.-Czech missile defense cooperation practically ceased. Economic motivations played an important role on a local level in the Czech government's efforts to increase support to projects in villages in the vicinity of a future radar site. Despite the government saying that this funding would be provided independently of the radar, once the Topolánek government fell, subsequent governments did not feel bound by their predecessor's promises. The cancellation of an X-band radar component in the Czech Republic in September 2009 removed any remaining pressures on the Czech government to continue with the distribution of promised funding.

The third relevant lesson is that governments' communications strategies must be kept as simple as possible. Parallel narratives about why a country cooperates on defense with another country must be managed carefully, as they can become counterproductive to the goals of communication campaigns. A favorable perception of NATO among the Czechs did not make a U.S. radar on Czech territory more acceptable to them. Introducing overlapping arguments created confusion as the Czech government tried to frame the issue in NATO terms to the Czech public. Technical issues related to the missile defense system's integration in NATO and what it would mean in practice were only in the early stages of the Alliance discussions, which made it difficult for Czech government officials to be clear about the nature of U.S.-Czech ballistic missile defense cooperation in the NATO context.

NATO-ization of U.S.-Czech ballistic missile defense cooperation held a fragile government coalition together, and was beneficial internationally because it made the idea of a U.S.-led NATO ballistic missile defense system more acceptable to NATO countries that were initially skeptical about the plan or outright opposed it. As these countries accepted a U.S. missile defense system as a capability contributing to NATO's overall security, they raised fewer public objections to U.S.-Czech missile defense cooperation. When they complained about U.S.-Czech ballistic missile defense cooperation, the Czech government could easily deflect the criticism by pointing out that its cooperation is consistent with NATO goals to which their governments agreed.

The fourth relevant policy lesson is that in an era of social media and an almost-real-time media cycle, governments ought to be careful to plan their communications strategies before information about discussions and formal negotiations become public knowledge. Not doing so risks lagging behind the curve if the opposition gets the first chance to frame the issue. The Czech government was late in launching a public relations campaign to communicate the importance of its cooperative efforts with the United States to the public. This made its public relations strategy reactive, defensive, and ultimately not particularly effective.

Granted, governments might wish to keep quiet about their efforts regarding defense cooperation with another state, for example because such cooperation might be considered too controversial by the general public should it get publicized. But governments ought to *think* about communications strategies and campaigns before they need them, because, if they do not, by the time they need them it will be too late to think about most effective ways to communicate an issue.

Governments must also keep in mind that technical issues do not lend themselves to catchy Twitter-length explanations. The confusion stemming from a general lack of understanding of ballistic missile defense issues made it yet more difficult for the Czech government to counter negative public perceptions and disinformation campaigns about the radar. The case illustrates the difficulties that democratic governments face when they publicly discuss issues that are of technical nature and usually not prominent in public discourse. National security issues are inherently complex and interconnected. In connection with modern technologies, they are ripe for exploitation by adversaries, as in the case of Russia's disinformation campaign against U.S.-Czech ballistic missile defense cooperation.

The fifth relevant policy lesson is that domestic politics matters, including its nuances. A detailed understanding of an alliance partner's domestic politics ought to inform the timing of major announcements, visits, and contents of major speeches, and make politicians and diplomats sensitive to what is said in off-hand comments. One does not obtain such a detailed understanding by doing a two-year rotation on a country desk at the State Department.

What is required is the nurturing of government career paths that build (and reward) regional expertise over time.

In the case of U.S.-Czech ballistic missile defense cooperation, there appeared to be a tendency on the part of U.S. policymakers to consider low public support of U.S.-Czech radar cooperation to mean that it would not succeed. But while defense issues in general are emotionally charged, they usually do not make or break elections. In the case of the Czech Republic, defense cooperation was conducted on a professional bureaucratic level and, in a sense, separately from popular sentiments. Unique post-electoral conditions led to an unprecedented popularization of a foreign policy issue and a disruption of an across-the-parties-line agreement on Czech foreign policy after the break-up of the Soviet Union. As such, a reliance just on public opinion polls would have been misleading. In this context, it is important to keep in mind that any political capital that a government spends in pursuing a domestically unpopular defense and foreign policy issue should be considered a legitimate contribution to allied cooperation.

The Czech government's inability to get the Chamber of Deputies to approve agreements between the two countries in a timelier manner may have cost the Czech Republic an opportunity to host a U.S. radar site. As time passed, the Topolánek government grew weaker and internally more divided making obtaining a parliamentary consent practically impossible. Had the construction of the site been more advanced at the time when the Obama Administration started to reconsider its plans, it would have been more difficult for the Administration to cancel it.

The sixth relevant policy lesson applies to small countries and has to do with the danger of centering bilateral relations with a larger country prominently around a single issue. The Obama Administration announced the cancellation of a radar site in the Czech Republic after years of discussions and negotiations with the Czech Republic, thousands of workhours of many people in both the U.S. and the Czech government, and after it invested millions of dollars in educating constituencies in the United States and the Czech Republic on the merits of the plan. After the Obama Administration's cancellation, and with a limited capability to pursue an alternative plan, the Czech Republic found itself in a situation in which it had to promptly find new themes and topics on which bilateral cooperation with the United States would continue. Switching bilateral agendas is likely easier for larger countries with more resources and better administrative capabilities than it is for smaller countries with more limited means to pursue foreign policy.

Lastly, U.S.-Czech missile defense cooperation underscores the need to invest in educated and resilient societies, so that they will not be easily susceptible to adversarial influence operations. Russia's influence operations on NATO-member states' territories are ongoing and have likely increased in sophistication since the days of U.S.-Czech missile defense cooperation. The Czechs were not particularly successful in countering Russia's disinformation campaign, nor did the Americans appear sensitive to Russia's activities on Czech territory. Joint coordination and strengthening information sharing, specifically regarding Russian influence operations, would be beneficial to the Alliance as a whole.

Index

abandonment concerns, Czech Republic 18-19, 145-146, 151, 157, 179, 186-190
'active measures' campaign on NATO member territory, Russian Federation 114, 166-167, 173-182
affecting factors, alliance politics 11-23, 45-49, 53-83, 86-87, 113-114, 130-137, 153-157, 183-211
agent networks
    Russian Federation 127, 160-167, 169-171, 180-182, 187, 204-205
    see also influence operations; intelligence
alliance politics
    affecting factors 11-23, 45-49, 53-83, 86-87, 113-114, 130-137, 153-157, 183-211
    asymmetry of expectations in alliance politics 15-17, 187-190, 194-195, 211
    decision making ix, 13-15, 23, 25-40, 55-82, 86-157, 167-182
    definitions ix-x, 1-2, 15, 16-17, 59-60, 157, 194-195
    dependencies on other countries 11, 14, 15-17, 18-19, 63-64, 131-132, 186-190, 194-195
    economic issues xiv-xv, 3-5, 11-18, 60-62, 113-114, 130-137, 155-157, 162-168, 185-186, 190-194, 207-208
    historical background xiv, xvi, xvii, xix-xx, 2-5, 14, 15-17, 18-19, 41, 44-82, 83-157, 159-211
    importance ix, xii, xiv-xv, 1-23, 195-211
    international relations xii, xiv-xv, xvi, 1-23, 58-62, 70-71, 76, 82-89, 143-145, 155-157, 186-187, 206-207
    lessons learned xiv-xv, xvii, xxi, 16-17, 79-80, 100-102, 197-198, 205-211
    military forces xi, 1-19, 75-78, 87-93, 104, 111, 138-139, 155-157, 160-170, 176-177, 181-190
    motivations 11-23, 41, 44-82, 88-157, 167-182, 184-211
    President George W. Bush 39-40, 50, 62, 65-66, 80-81, 103, 111, 140, 145-146, 151, 184, 203
    President Obama xiv, xvi, xvii, 16-17, 83, 111-112, 138-140, 143-157, 177, 193-196, 202-205, 210-211
    public perceptions 11, 19-23, 44-45, 53-75, 81-90, 96, 101-109, 113-124, 134-142, 147-148, 163-182, 193-211
    theoretical understanding ix-x, 1-23, 186-211
    threat assessments 2-19, 45-49, 55-62, 67-69, 81-82, 85-93, 97-98, 153-157, 167-187, 205-207
allied territory xii-xiii, xiv, 4-9, 15-16, 38-40, 41-82, 86-157, 167-211
    interceptors xiv, 34, 39-40, 47-48, 53, 55-60, 65, 76-82

radars xiii, xiv, xvi, xvii, xix–xx, 9, 16–17, 41, 45–46, 52–56, 62–82, 86–157, 159–211
Russian 'active measures' campaign on NATO member territory 114, 166–167, 173–182
see also Status of Forces Agreement
anti-American sentiment 62–69, 104, 106–107, 169–170, 176, 195, 206
Anti-Ballistic Missile Treaty of 1972 (ABM) xi–xii, xiv, 25, 29–30, 31–32, 35–40
asymmetry of expectations in alliance politics 15–17, 187–190, 194–195, 211

ballistic missile defense ix–xvii, 2–23, 25–40, 41, 44–82, 83–157, 167–182, 183–211
    Ballistic Missile Defense Organization (BMDO) 34, 36
    components ix, xiii, xiv, 15, 96–97, 138, 157, 184–185
    debate cons 53–55, 62–82, 86–95, 100–107, 110–116, 123–139, 143, 147–151, 159–182, 186–211
    debate pros 58–62, 70–87, 91–96, 105–106, 116, 130–131, 138–139, 143–149, 176–177, 186–211
    definition ix, 15, 96–97, 157, 184–185
    historical background xiv, xvi, xvii, xix–xx, 2–5, 14, 15–16, 18–19, 25–40, 41, 44–82, 83–157, 167–211
    President George W. Bush ABM Treaty withdrawal xi–xii, 25, 36–40, 45–46, 62, 145–146, 151
    President Obama xiv, xvi, xvii, 16–17, 83, 111–112, 138–140, 143–157, 177, 193–196, 202–205, 210–211
    Strategic Defense Initiative (SDI) 26, 30–34
    technological issues xiii, 4–14, 25–40, 50–62, 84–85, 92–93, 102–103, 145–147, 152–157, 184–192, 208
Ballistic Missile Defense Agreement (BMDA) 91, 98, 102–103, 107–108, 113–115, 124–125, 126–138, 140–141, 142–143, 146, 148–152
ballistic missile defense cooperation xii–xiii, xiv, 4–5, 8–9, 15–16, 38, 39–40, 41, 44–82, 86–157, 167–211
    conceptualization 2–23
    definition 2–11, 15, 96–97, 157
    historical background xiv, xvi, xvii, xix–xx, 2–5, 14, 15–16, 18–19, 20–21, 36, 40, 41, 44–82, 83–157, 167–211
    importance ix, xii, xiv, 1–23, 195–211
    lessons learned xiv–xv, xvii, xxi, 16–17, 79–80, 100–102, 197–198, 205–211
    smaller country disadvantages xii–xiii, xiv, xvi, 3–7, 13–19, 63–64, 131–132, 147–148, 183–187, 194–195, 211
    threat assessments 2–19, 45–49, 55–62, 67–69, 81–82, 85–93, 97–98, 153–157, 167–187, 205–207
ballistic missiles

Index

capabilities xiii, 13–14, 25–40, 55, 62, 65, 97, 123, 184–185, 187–189, 206
    technological issues xiii, 4–14, 25–40, 50–62, 84–85, 92–93, 102–103, 145–147, 152–157, 184–192, 208
    see also missile defense
Baluyevsky, Yuri 67, 80, 87–89, 126–127
bilateral alliances 2, 59–60, 73, 77–79, 88–89, 91–92, 102–103, 124–125
    definition 2, 59–60, 73, 77–79
    see also alliance politics
blackmail concerns
    dependencies on other countries 63–64, 97
    Russian Federation 172–173
Boletice military training area site location considerations 51, 57
Brdy military training area site location considerations 51, 102–110, 115–116, 192–194, 201–202
    Soviet Union military operating area history 104
Brilliant Pebbles program 33
    see also Global Protection Against Limited Strikes
Bucharest summit in 2008, North Atlantic Treaty Organization (NATO) xiv, 115, 116–125
burdens, ballistic missile defense cooperation 4–6, 8
Bush, President George W. 25, 36–40, 45–46, 50, 62, 65–66, 80–81, 103, 111, 140, 145–146, 151, 184, 203
    ABM Treaty withdrawal 25, 36–40, 45–46, 62
    Poland 140, 145–146
    President Obama's plan abandonment decision in September 2009 145–146, 151, 157, 179, 193–194, 207
    U.S. Visa Waiver Program (VWP) 137
    X-band radars 80–81, 103, 111, 140, 184

California, interceptors xiv, 77, 81
capabilities/contributions assessments xi, 6–13, 59–60, 62, 116–127, 153–154, 157, 166–167, 187–189, 206
Chamber of Deputies 42–45, 54–57, 69–70, 74, 83–87, 90–91, 119, 135–143, 173–174, 191–193, 204, 210
    committees 90–91
Christian and Democratic Union-Czechoslovak People's Party 48–49, 52–69, 83–84, 95, 200
Civic Democratic Party (ODS) 57–58, 69–73, 83–84, 103–105, 108–109, 128, 133–134, 153, 173–174, 180, 198–200
co-production/co-development cooperation 5, 10–11, 113, 130–137, 140, 152–156, 188, 191–192, 207
coalition governments
    Czech Republic 43–44, 52–70, 79, 83–84, 93, 103–104, 112–113, 119, 133–134, 140–141, 180–181, 203–204
    see also elections of governments; governments

coalition pressures, public perceptions 19-20, 62-63
coercion tools xii-xiii, 15-16, 17
communications strategies xv, 16-17, 31-32, 64-65, 73-74, 87-89, 95-96, 100-109, 113-114, 122, 134, 176-177, 187, 194-211
    media penetration 159-160, 168-169, 173, 174-175, 178, 180-181, 204-205, 208-209
    mistakes 16-17, 64-65, 73-80, 89-90, 100-102, 106-109, 113-114, 122-124, 134, 176-177, 187, 194-211
    recommendations 208-209
    Special Government Envoy 100-102, 197-198
    see also public relations
Communist Party xvii, 63-64, 70, 74, 76, 95, 147-148, 169, 198-200
Constitutional Court, Czech Republic 44, 135-136
consultations, ballistic missile defense cooperation 4-7, 47, 54-69, 85-86, 151-152, 192
Conventional Forces in Europe Treaty (CFE) 111
cooperation
    affecting factors 11-23, 45-49, 53-83, 86-87, 113-114, 130-137, 153-157, 183-211
    conceptualization 2-23
    consultations 4-7, 47, 54-69, 85-86, 151-152, 192
    economic issues xiv-xv, 3-5, 11-18, 60-62, 113-114, 130-137, 155-157, 162-168, 185-186, 190-194, 207-208
    importance ix, xii, xiv, 1-23, 195-211
    lessons learned xiv-xv, xvii, xxi, 16-17, 79-80, 100-102, 197-198, 205-211
    levels 2-11, 155-157
    motivations 2-23, 41, 44-82, 88-157, 167-182, 184-211
    pitfalls ix, xii, 16-17, 79-80, 205-211
    recommendations xvii, xxi, 205-211
    see also alliance politics; ballistic missile defense cooperation
corruption 61, 141, 164-165, 171-172, 180
    see also organized crime
costs 8, 13-14, 27, 29-30, 33, 35-36, 107, 114, 166-167, 185-186
Czech Communist Party of Bohemia and Moravia 47, 63-64, 70, 74, 76, 95, 135, 147-148, 169, 198-200
Czech intelligence services 85-86, 164-166
    see also agent networks; intelligence
Czech Ministry of Defense 1-5, 46-57, 85-86, 91-100, 103-107, 118-119, 136, 141-143, 154-155, 166-168, 191
    roles 100, 105-107, 167-168
    site location impact assessment studies 105-108, 115-116
Czech Ministry of Foreign Affairs 45, 47-58, 68-69, 76-79, 85-87, 90-95, 98, 100, 113, 119, 126-127, 134-135
    roles 100

Czech Ministry of Health 107-108
Czech Ministry of the Interior 85-86
Czech National Security Council (NSC) 45-46, 85-86, 90-91, 102, 167-168
Czech Republic ix-x, xiii-xvii, 2-5, 14, 15-17, 36, 40, 41-82
  abandonment concerns 18-19, 145-146, 151, 157, 179, 186-190
  Chamber of Deputies 42-45, 54-57, 69-70, 74, 83-87, 90-91, 119, 135-143, 173-174, 191-193, 204, 210
  coalition governments 43-44, 52-70, 79, 83-84, 93, 103-104, 112-113, 119, 133-134, 140-141, 180-181, 203-204
  command and control conflicts 123-124, 128-129, 149-150
  Constitutional Court 44, 135-136
  corruption 61, 141, 164-165, 171-172, 180
  dependencies on other countries 11, 14, 15-17, 18-19, 63-64, 131-132, 186-190, 194-195
  domestic scandals 2, 155
  early warning missile defense site discussions in 2011 154-156, 157
  economic issues xiv-xv, 3-5, 11-18, 60-62, 113-114, 130-137, 155-157, 162-168, 171-172, 179, 185-186, 190-194, 207-208
  elections 42-44, 52-58, 63-64, 69-70, 93, 133-135, 142-145, 153, 157, 173-174, 195, 203-204
  end of collaboration in 2011 xvi, xvii, 2, 154-156
  executive branch of government 42, 44, 86-87, 133-136
  Fischer government (May 8, 2009-July 13, 2010) 142-153, 196
  floods of 2009/2010 193
  government systems 41-82, 135-136
  Gross government (August 4, 2004-April 25, 2005) 52-53
  interceptor suggestions 76-77
  legislative branch of government 42-44, 69-70, 83-84, 86-87, 91-92, 102-103, 133-136
  motivations 11-23, 41, 44-82, 88-157, 167-182, 184-211
  NATO accession in 1999 119-121
  NATO membership x, xv, xvii, 14-19, 45-49, 54-74, 76-82, 84-100, 114-128, 138, 153-157, 161, 166-167, 184-211
  NATO-ization of U.S.-Czech cooperation 78-79, 91, 92-93, 118-127, 208
  Nečas government (July 13, 2010-July 10, 2013) 153-156
  no-confidence votes 43-44, 83-84, 141-142, 180-181, 195, 207
  oil supplies 127, 163
  Paroubek government (April 25, 2005-September 4, 2006) 52-69, 71-72, 160, 173, 180, 196
  pivotal moment following June 2006 election 57, 63-64, 70, 173-174, 180, 195, 204
  population-protection priorities xiv-xv, 188-190

President Obama xiv, xvi, xvii, 16–17, 83, 111–112, 138–140, 143–157, 177, 193–196, 202–205, 210–211
presidential powers 42, 44–45, 74, 86–87
prime ministers 43, 52–70, 71–72, 84, 109–110, 123–124, 128, 141–142, 144–145, 180, 195, 207
referenda 55, 63, 74–76, 86–87, 90–91, 103–104, 120–121, 201–202
Russian Federation tourism/travel 160, 165–166
Russian oil supply cuts to the Czech Republic in 2008 127
Russian-speaking community 177–178
Schengen Area membership from December 21, 2007 160, 165–166
Senate 42–43, 86, 133–134, 137–138
site locations 41, 45–46, 50–52, 53–74, 76–82, 84, 86–157, 167–182, 191–211
Špidla government (July 15, 2002-August 4, 2004) 46–52
technology transfers 60–61, 152–153
Topolánek's first government (September 4, 2006-January 9, 2007) 69–83, 84, 180, 196–200
Topolánek's second government (January 9, 2007-May 8, 2009) 70, 79, 83–142, 180, 193, 195–201, 204, 207, 210
U.S. 'diplomatic offense' in October/November 2009 149–150
U.S. Office of Naval Research in Prague 152
visas for U.S. travel 86–87, 136–138
Czech Security Information Service 159–182
    see also intelligence
Czech Social Democratic Party 46–79, 95, 102–103, 110, 126–127, 133–135, 141–148, 153, 173–174, 180, 198–200
Czechoslovakia
    Soviet occupation 63–64, 166–167, 175–176
    World War II 64, 186

debate cons 53–55, 62–82, 86–95, 100–107, 110–116, 123–139, 143, 147–151, 159–182, 186–211
    anti-American sentiment 62–69, 104, 106–107, 169–170, 176, 195, 206
    letter from local mayors in 2007 106–107, 130–131
    local mayors 106–107, 130–131, 193, 201–202
    opposition/support statistics 21, 72, 121, 139, 147, 195–203
    see also League of Mayors; negotiations; No Bases Initiative
debate pros 58–62, 70–87, 91–96, 105–106, 116, 130–131, 138–139, 143–149, 176–177, 186–211
    opposition/support statistics 21, 72, 121, 139, 147, 195–203
decision making ix, 13–15, 23, 25–40, 55–82, 86–157, 167–182
    alliance politics ix, 13–15, 23, 25–40, 55–82, 86–157, 167–182
    early warning missile defense discussions in 2011 154–156, 157
    U.S. command and control conflicts 123–124, 128–129, 149–150
defense policy ix–xvii, 49–82, 85–157

Index

overview of the book ix–xvii
see also alliance politics
dependencies on other countries
    alliance cooperation affecting factors 11, 14, 15–17, 18–19, 63–64, 131–132, 186–190, 194–195
    blackmail concerns 63–64, 97
    see also asymmetry of expectations in alliance politics
disinformation campaign, Russian Federation 82, 114, 124, 159–180, 187, 209–211
Dodge, Paul 123
domestic policy x, xv–xvi, 8, 10, 16–17, 19–23, 36, 76–82, 85–157, 170–182, 205–211
    economic issues 17–18, 157
    Fearon's two-level games analysis 19–20
    mistakes 16–17, 100–102, 197–198, 205–211
    recommendations 209–211
    see also foreign policy

early cooperation, U.S.-Czech ballistic missile defense cooperation (2002–2011) 36, 40–82, 84, 118, 122, 156–157, 167–168, 174, 181, 192
early warning ballistic missile defense data centers xiv, 2, 9, 154–155, 157
    see also radars
economic issues
    alliance cooperation affecting factors xiv–xv, 3–5, 11–18, 60–62, 113–114, 130–137, 155–157, 162–168, 185–186, 190–194, 207–208
    domestic policy 17–18, 157
    foreign direct investment 17–18, 157
    funds-providing issues 4–6, 81, 107, 159–160, 173–174, 185–186, 192–193, 207
    Russian Federation 162–164, 168, 171–172, 179
    tax incentives 18, 133
elections of governments 19–22, 41–44, 52–58, 63–64, 69–70, 93, 110, 133–135, 142–145, 153, 157, 173–174, 195, 203–204
    pivotal moment following June 2006 election 57, 63–64, 70, 173–174, 180, 195, 204
energy sector, Russian Federation 127, 163, 179
environmental issues 69, 89, 92–96, 102–107, 115–116, 125–126, 128–130
    Ballistic Missile Defense Agreement (BMDA) 129–130
    narrowing down technical site investigations 92–96, 104–107, 109–110, 114–115, 125–126, 129–130, 174
    radars 69, 92–96, 102–107, 115–116, 125–126, 128–130
    site locations 69, 92–96, 102–107, 115–116, 125–126, 128–130
European Phased Adaptive Approach (EPAA), definition 146–148
executive branch of government 42, 44, 86–87, 133–136

see also Czech Republic; governments

Fischer government (May 8, 2009-July 13, 2010) 142-153, 196
foreign policy ix-xvii, 1-2, 19-23, 35-36, 44-82, 85-157, 159-182
    decision making 23, 25-40, 55-82, 86-157, 167-182
    see also alliance politics; domestic policy; national security
Freedom Union-Democratic Union (US-DEU) 52-69

Gates, Robert 66, 80, 82, 97-98, 108-109, 131-132, 146, 148-149, 197, 201, 203-204
Global Protection Against Limited Strikes (GPALS)
    definition 32-33
governments
    authoritarian/democratic contrasts 19, 42-43, 63-64, 127
    elections 19-22, 41-44, 52-58, 63-64, 69-70, 93, 110, 133-135, 142-145, 153, 157, 173-174, 195, 203-204
    public perceptions 11, 19-23, 44-45, 53-75, 81-90, 96, 101-109, 113-124, 134-142, 147-148, 163-182, 193-211
    see also coalition governments; Czech Republic; elections of governments; foreign policy
Green Party 71, 79, 83-84, 93, 104-105, 119, 200
    see also environmental issues
Gross government (August 4, 2004-April 25, 2005) 52-53
Ground-Based Midcourse Defense interceptors (GMD) xiv, 34, 65, 77-78, 80-82, 87-92, 96-97, 111, 140-149, 194

historical background
    ballistic missile defense xiv, xvi, xvii, xix-xx, 2-5, 14, 15-16, 18-19, 25-40, 41, 44-82, 83-157, 167-211
    ballistic missile defense cooperation xiv, xvi, xvii, xix-xx, 2-5, 14, 15-16, 18-19, 20-21, 36, 40, 41, 44-82, 83-157, 167-211
    Global Protection Against Limited Strikes (GPALS) 32-33
    Ground-Based Midcourse Defense interceptors (GMD) xiv, 34, 65, 77-78, 80-81
    National Missile Defense Act of 1999 (NMDA) 35-36
    radars xiv, xvi, xvii, xix-xx, 2, 16-17, 41, 45-46, 52-56, 62-82, 83-157, 167-211
    regional (shorter-range) ballistic missile defense 33-34, 38, 147-148, 149-150, 151-152
    Strategic Defense Initiative Organization (SDIO) 31-34
    Strategic Defense Initiative (SDI) 31-34
    U.S.-Czech ballistic missile defense cooperation (2002-2011) xiv, xvi, xvii, xix-xx, 2-5, 14-21, 36, 40, 41, 44-82, 83-157, 167-211
hit-to-kill interceptor technologies

Index

impact assessments, radars 94, 103–108, 115–116
influence operations by the Russian Federation xv, xvii, xx, 6–7, 38, 53–69, 71–73, 80–109, 111–114, 126–127, 138–147, 157–182, 187, 198, 204–211
    agent networks 127, 160–167, 169–171, 180–182, 204–205
    media penetration 159–160, 168–169, 173, 174–175, 178, 180–181, 204–205, 208–209
    organized crime 161–162, 171–172, 180
    recommendations and lessons learned 211
    tactics 87–88, 92–93, 104, 111, 126–127, 131, 159–182, 187, 198, 204–211
    see also Russian Federation
intelligence xi, 6, 9–10, 61, 85–86, 91–92, 127, 159–182, 187, 204–205, 211
    Czech intelligence services 85–86, 164–166
    KGB 163–164, 169
    see also agent networks; influence operations
interceptors xiv, 34, 39–40, 47–48, 53–60, 65, 76–82, 89–90, 146–147, 194
    Alaska xiv, 77, 81
    California xiv, 77, 81
    European Phased Adaptive Approach (EPAA) 146–148
    Poland xiv, 65, 77–78, 80–82, 87, 89, 92, 96–97, 111, 140, 143–149, 194
    Romania 146–147, 194
    see also ballistic missile defense cooperation; site locations
international relations
    affecting factors 11–23, 58–62, 70–71, 76, 82, 86–87, 88–89, 143–145, 155–157, 186–187, 206–207
    alliance politics xii, xiv–xv, xvi, 1–23, 58–62, 70–71, 76, 82–89, 143–145, 155–157, 186–187, 206–207
interviews ix, 14–15, 40, 46, 50, 56–82, 90, 98–101, 115, 118–119, 137–141, 146–155, 167, 180, 191, 195
Iran
    threat assessments xi–xii, xiv, 39, 49–50, 55, 59, 61, 66, 68, 81, 100, 110–111, 146–148, 151, 183–184, 206–207

KGB 163–164, 169
    see also agent networks; intelligence
Klaus, President Václav 74, 80, 86, 101

League of Mayors 103–104, 106–107, 130–131, 193
    see also debate cons
Lee, Jesse 146
legislative branch of government 42–44, 69–70, 83–84, 86–87, 91–92, 102–103, 133–136
    see also Czech Republic; governments
lessons learned xiv–xv, xvii, xxi, 16–17, 79–80, 100–102, 197–198, 205–211
levels of ballistic missile defense cooperation 2–11, 155–157

Libavá military training area site location considerations 51

media penetration
    Russian Federation 159–160, 168–169, 173, 174–175, 178, 180–181, 204–205, 208–209
    social media era xv, 180–181, 208–209
missile defense
    definition ix, 25–29, 96–97, 157
    historical background xiv, xvi, xvii, xix–xx, 2–5, 14–19, 25–40, 41, 44–82, 83–157, 167–211
    overview of the book ix–xvii
    see also ballistic missile defense; national security
Missile Defense Agency (MDA) 26, 56–57, 94–95, 109–110, 113, 150
motivations, ballistic missile defense cooperation 2–23, 41–82, 88–157, 167–182, 184–211
multilateral alliances
    definition 2, 59–60
    see also alliance politics

NATO-ization of U.S.-Czech cooperation 78–79, 91, 92–93, 118–127, 208
Nečas government (July 13, 2010-July 10, 2013) 153–156
negotiations
    between 2007 and 2009 xvi, xvii, 70, 79, 83–157
    BMDA conclusion announcement in April 2008 117–118, 124–125
    debate cons 53–55, 62–82, 86–95, 100–107, 110–116, 123–139, 143, 147–151, 159–182, 186–211
    debate pros 58–62, 70–87, 91–96, 105–106, 116, 130–131, 138–139, 143–149, 176–177, 186–211
    January 19, 2007 negotiations formal start 83, 84–90, 194, 201
    political boundaries 93–94
    public perceptions 11, 19–23, 44–45, 53–75, 81–90, 96, 101–109, 113–124, 134–142, 147–148, 163–182, 193–211
    Status of Forces Agreement (SOFA) 91–92, 98, 102–103, 110, 113–115, 131–133, 148–149
No Bases Initiative 53–54, 63, 74, 113–115, 147–148, 173–174, 193
    Russian Federation funds 173
    see also debate cons
no-confidence votes, Czech Republic 43–44, 83–84, 141–142, 180–181, 195, 207
North Atlantic Treaty Organization (NATO) x–xi, xiv, xv, xvii, 6–8, 14–19, 37–49, 54–69, 73–93, 96–100, 114–128, 138, 153–167, 184–211
    ABM Treaty withdrawal 37–40, 62
    Article V x, 60, 153–154
    ballistic missile defense capability from 2012 123
    Bucharest summit in 2008 xiv, 115, 116–125

Czech Republic x, xv, xvii, 14–19, 45–49, 54–74, 76–82, 84–100, 114–128, 138, 153–157, 161, 166–167, 184–211
  member capabilities/contributions assessment xi, 6–8, 59–60, 78–79, 96–97, 116–127, 153–154, 157, 166–167, 188
  Prague Summit Declaration in 2002 48
  Riga summit in 2006 122
  Russian 'active measures' campaign on NATO member territory 114, 166–167, 173–182
  Russian Federation xvii, 62, 114, 157, 161, 166–167, 173–182
  Strategic Concept of 2010 153–154
  see also alliance politics
North Korea
  threat assessments xi–xii, 14, 34–35, 39, 49–50, 55, 68, 100, 110, 183–184, 206–207
nuclear weapons
  arms race 26–29, 30–31, 34–35, 37–38, 67, 97, 188–190
  costs 27, 107
  historical background 25–40
  proliferation trends xi–xii, 7–8, 27, 34–35, 45–49, 55
  stockpiles 26–27, 62, 97, 138, 188–189, 206

Obama, President Barack xiv, xvi, xvii, 16–17, 83, 111–112, 138–140, 143–157, 177, 193–196, 202–205, 210–211
  Ballistic Missile Defense Review (BMDR) 150–151
  cancelled missile defense plans xiv, xvi, xvii, 16–17, 83, 138–140, 143–157, 177, 179, 193–196, 202–205, 210–211
  critique xiv, xvi, xvii, 83, 111, 138, 143–151, 157, 177, 193, 195–196, 202–205
  European Phased Adaptive Approach (EPAA) 146–148
  missile defense plans 145–149, 150–151, 157, 177, 195–196, 202–205, 210–211
  phone call announcement of cancellation 195
  Poland xiv, 143–149, 194
  President George W. Bush 43 plan abandonment decision in September 2009 145–146, 151, 157, 179, 203, 207
  public perceptions 147–148, 205
  Romania 146–147, 194
  Russian Federation 'reset' policy 144–147, 177–178, 181
opposition/support statistics 21, 72, 121, 139, 147, 195–203
  see also influence operations by the Russian Federation; organized crime
  Russian Federation 161–162, 171–172, 180

pacifist tendencies, Czech Republic 75
Parkanová, Vlasta 91, 95–96, 103, 132–133, 167, 175

Paroubek government (April 25, 2005-September 4, 2006) 52-69, 71-72, 160, 173, 180, 196
Paroubek, Prime Minister Jiří 52-69, 71-72, 84, 110, 141-142, 144-145, 180, 196
pitfall avoidance
    missile defense cooperation ix, xii, 16-17, 79-80, 205-211
Pojar, Tomáš 56-57, 58, 71-72, 75, 78-79, 85, 101, 151, 191-192, 195
Poland x, xiv, 20, 49-50, 63-65, 77-82, 87, 89, 92, 96-97, 111, 137, 140, 143-149, 194
    ballistic missile defense xiv, 20, 49-50, 63, 65, 77-78, 80-82, 87, 89, 92, 96-97, 111, 140, 143-149, 194
    Czech Republic 77-78, 80-82, 89, 92, 96-97, 111, 140, 143-149
    Ground-Based Midcourse Defense interceptors (GMD) xiv, 65, 77-78, 80-82, 87, 89, 92, 96-97, 111, 140-149, 194
    interceptors xiv, 65, 77-78, 80-82, 87, 89, 92, 96-97, 111, 140, 143-149, 194
    President George W. Bush 140, 145-146
    President Obama xiv, 143-149, 194
    President Putin 96-97
    Russian Federation 146-147
    U.S. Visa Waiver Program (VWP) 137
Prague Summit Declaration in 2002, North Atlantic Treaty Organization (NATO) 48
pre-ABM treaty missile defense efforts 25-29
pre-emptive threats
    Russian Federation 87-88, 92-93, 111, 126-127, 187
presidential powers in the Czech Republic 42, 44-45, 74, 86-87
prime ministers in the Czech Republic 43, 52-70, 71-72, 84, 109-110, 123-124, 128, 141-142, 144-145, 180, 195, 207
    see also individual prime ministers
public perceptions 11, 19-23, 36, 44-45, 53-75, 81-90, 96, 101-109, 113-124, 134-148, 163-182, 193-211
    alliance cooperation affecting factors 11, 19-23, 53-75, 81-90, 96, 101-109, 113-114, 118-124, 134-142, 147-148, 163-182, 193-211
    NATO-ization of U.S.-Czech cooperation 118-121, 208
    opposition/support statistics 21, 72, 121, 139, 147, 195-203
    President Obama 147-148, 205
    Russian Federation 159-163, 168-169, 177, 184-187
    U.S.-Czech ballistic missile defense cooperation (2002-2011) 20-22, 44-45, 56-75, 81-90, 96, 101-109, 113-124, 134-142, 147-148, 163-182, 193-211
    see also debate cons; debate pros; referenda
public relations 3, 81, 101-102, 113-114, 124, 130-131, 134-135, 142, 168-169, 195-196, 208-209
    see also communications strategies; public perceptions

Putin, President Vladimir 37, 96–97, 117–118, 127–128, 144–145, 162–163, 177
- intelligence funding 162
- oil supply cuts to the Czech Republic in 2008 127
- radars 96–97, 117–118, 127–128, 144–145, 177
- *see also* Russian Federation

radars xiii, xiv, xvi, xvii, xix–xx, 2, 9, 11, 16–17, 41, 45–46, 52–56, 62–82, 83–157, 159–211
- beam safety concerns 69, 92–96
- environmental issues 69, 92–96, 102–107, 115–116, 125–126, 128–130
- impact assessments 94, 103–108, 115–116
- letter from local mayors in 2007 106–107, 130–131, 193
- No Bases Initiative 53–54, 63, 74, 113–115, 147–148, 173–174, 193
- pollution concerns 106–107, 125–126, 129–130
- President George W. Bush 80–81, 103, 111, 140, 145–146, 151, 184, 203
- President Obama xiv, xvi, xvii, 16–17, 83, 111, 138–140, 143–157, 177, 193–196, 202–205, 210–211
- President Putin 96–97, 117–118, 127–128, 144–145, 177
- Russian Federation xvii, xx, 65–66, 80–82, 86–90, 92, 112–113, 134, 138–139, 144–147, 167–182, 184–185
- *see also* ballistic missile defense cooperation; site locations

ratification of agreements 137–138, 140–141, 142–143, 151

recommendations
- ballistic missile defense cooperation xvii, xxi, 205–211
- *see also* lessons learned

referenda 55, 63, 74–76, 86–87, 90–91, 103–104, 120–121, 201–202
- North Atlantic Treaty Organization (NATO) 76, 120–121

research and development 5, 37–38, 113, 136–137, 151–153, 179, 188, 191–192

retaliation threats
- Russian Federation 87–88, 92–93, 111, 126–127, 131, 164–165, 187
- *see also* influence operations

Rice, Condoleezza 97, 126–127

Riga summit in 2006, North Atlantic Treaty Organization (NATO) 122

Romania 39, 146–147, 194
- interceptors 146–147, 194

Rumsfeld, Donald H. 36, 38–39

Russian Federation xv, xvii, xx, 6–7, 33–40, 46, 53–71, 80–93, 96–113, 117–118, 134, 144–147, 159–182, 184–211
- 'active measures' campaign on NATO member territory 114, 166–167, 173–182
- agent networks 127, 160–167, 169–171, 180–182, 187, 204–205
- blackmail concerns 172–173
- business sector links 127, 162–163, 171–172

capabilities 62, 65–66, 97, 144, 188–189, 206
disinformation campaign 82, 114, 124, 159–180, 187, 209–211
economic issues 162–164, 168, 171–172, 179
energy sector 127, 163, 179
Federal Security Service 170–171
KGB 163–164, 169
media penetration 159–160, 168–169, 173, 174–175, 178, 180–181, 204–205, 208–209
oil supplies to the Czech Republic 127, 163
Poland 146–147
pre-emptive threats 87–88, 92–93, 111, 126–127, 187
President George W. Bush ABM Treaty withdrawal 37–40, 46, 62
President Obama's 'reset' policy 144–147, 177–178, 181
public perceptions 159–163, 168–169, 177, 184–187
radars xvii, xx, 65–66, 80–82, 86–90, 92, 112–113, 134, 138–139, 144–146, 167–182, 184–185
retaliation threats 87–88, 92–93, 111, 126–127, 131, 164–165, 187
Romania 146–147
social media era 180–181
see also Anti-Ballistic Missile Treaty of 1972; influence operations; Soviet Union

Schwarzenberg, Karel 60, 91, 92, 112–113, 126–127, 129
Senate
  Czech Republic 42–43, 86, 133–134, 137–138
site construction stoppage in February 2009, President Obama 143–144, 151–152
site locations 41, 45–46, 50–52, 53–74, 76–82, 84, 86–157, 167–182, 191–211
  early warning ballistic missile defense data centers xiv, 2, 9, 154–155
  impact assessments 94, 103–108, 115–116
  letter from local mayors in 2007 106–107, 130–131, 193
  local mayors 106–107, 130–131, 193, 201–202
  narrowing down technical investigations 92–96, 104–105, 109–110, 114–115, 129–130, 174
  No Bases Initiative 53–54, 63, 74, 113–115, 147–148, 173–174, 193
  pollution concerns 106–107, 125–126, 129–130
  President Obama xiv, xvi, xvii, 16–17, 83, 111, 138–140, 143–157, 177, 193–196, 202–205, 210–211
  Russian presence concerns 97, 108–109
  selection criteria 102–105
  sovereignty concerns 62–64, 132–133
  see also radars
smaller country disadvantages xii–xiii, xiv, xvi, 3–7, 13–19, 63–64, 131–132, 147–148, 183–187, 194–195, 211
social media era xv, 180–181, 208–209

see also communications strategies; media penetration
sovereignty concerns, U.S.-Czech ballistic missile defense cooperation (2002-2011) 62-64, 132-133
Soviet Union ix-x, 16, 26-31, 60-67, 93, 96-97, 104, 118-119, 130, 159-162, 166-169, 181, 210
    Brdy military training area site location considerations 104

    see also Russian Federation
Špidla government (July 15, 2002-August 4, 2004) 46-52
statistics x, 5, 13-14, 21, 72, 121, 139, 147, 185-186, 192-193, 195-202
    funds-providing issues 185-186, 192-193, 207
    opposition/support statistics 21, 72, 121, 139, 147, 195-203
Status of Forces Agreement (SOFA) 8-9, 91-92, 98, 102-103, 110-115, 131-133, 137-143, 148-152
    costs 8, 133
    definition 8, 131-133, 137-138
    duration agreement 133
    negotiations 91-92, 98, 102-103, 110, 113-115, 131-133, 148-149
    ratification of agreements 137-138, 140-141, 142-143, 151
    text of the agreement 131-133
    U.S. bilateral SOFA 91-92, 98, 102-103, 131-133, 148-149, 151-152
Strategic Concept of 2010, North Atlantic Treaty Organization (NATO) 153-154
Strategic Defense Initiative Organization (SDIO) 26, 31-34
    roles 31-32
Strategic Defense Initiative (SDI) 26, 30-34
    acquisition initiatives 31-32
    'Star Wars' name 34
Strategic Offensive Reductions Treaty (SORT/Moscow Treaty) 37, 62, 97

technological issues xiii, 4-14, 25-40, 50-62, 84-85, 92-93, 102-103, 145-147, 152-157, 184-192, 208
    research and development 5, 37-38, 113, 136-137, 151-153, 179, 188, 191-192
    social media 180-181, 208-209
    transfers 9-10, 60-61, 152-153
theoretical understanding, alliance politics ix-x, 1-23, 186-211
threat assessments 2-19, 45-49, 55-62, 67-69, 81-82, 85-93, 97-98, 153-157, 167-187, 205-207
    Iran xi-xii, xiv, 39, 49-50, 55, 59, 61, 66, 68, 81, 100, 110, 146-148, 151, 183-184, 206-207
    North Korea xi-xii, 14, 34-35, 39, 49-50, 55, 68, 100, 110, 183-184, 206-207
    overestimated threats critique 68, 151, 183-184, 206-207

Topolánek's first government (September 4, 2006-January 9, 2007) 69–83, 84, 180, 196–200
Topolánek's second government (January 9, 2007-May 8, 2009) 70, 79, 83–142, 180, 193, 195–201, 204, 207, 210
Topolánek, Prime Minister Miroslav 66, 69–148, 180, 193, 195–201, 204, 207, 210
   no-confidence vote on March 25, 2009 141–142, 180, 195, 207
Trokavec
   referendum on March 17, 2007 201
Tvrdík, Jaroslav 47, 49

U.S. Congress 10, 20, 28, 29, 32–33, 37, 39–40, 115, 150–151
U.S. Department of Defense (DoD) xiii, 8, 36, 39–40, 108–109, 151–152, 189
U.S. Department of State 8, 29, 150
U.S. global status 6, 13–14, 18, 33, 67–69, 122–124, 148–149, 187–188
   anti-American sentiment 62–69, 104, 106–107, 169–170, 176, 195, 206
   ballistic missile defense cooperation 6, 18, 148–149, 187–188
U.S. Secretary of Defense 1, 27–29, 30, 34, 36–40, 46–47, 50, 66, 79–82, 97, 108–109, 146

U.S. Visa Waiver Program (VWP) 86–87, 136–138
U.S. withdrawal from the Anti-Ballistic Missile Treaty of 1972 xi–xii, 25, 36–40, 45–46, 62
U.S.-Czech ballistic missile defense cooperation (2002-2011) ix, xiii–xvii, 2–5, 11, 14, 15–19, 36, 40, 41, 44–82, 83–157, 167–211
   asymmetry of expectations in alliance politics 15–16, 187–190, 194–195, 211
   conclusion of negotiations 116–142
   debate cons 53–55, 62–82, 86–95, 100–107, 110–116, 123–139, 143, 147–151, 159–182, 186–211
   debate pros 58–62, 70–87, 91–96, 105–106, 116, 130–131, 138–139, 143–149, 176–177, 186–211
   definition xiv–xv, 156–157
   draft agreements in 2007 106–107
   early cooperation 36, 40–82, 84, 118, 122, 156–157, 167–168, 174, 181, 192
   early warning missile defense site discussions in 2011 154–155, 157
   end of collaboration in 2011 xvi, xvii, 2, 154–156
   historical background xiv, xvi, xvii, xix–xx, 2–5, 14–21, 36, 40, 41, 44–82, 83–157, 167–211
   lessons learned xiv–xv, xvii, xxi, 16–17, 79–80, 100–102, 197–198, 205–211
   public perceptions 20–22, 44–45, 56–75, 81–90, 96, 101–109, 113–124, 134–142, 147–148, 163–182, 193–211

signed agreements in 2008 126–137
sovereignty concerns 62–64, 132–133
see also ballistic missile defense cooperation; Czech Republic; interceptors; radars; site locations; Status of Forces Agreement

Vondra, Alexandr 58–59, 75, 77, 109–110, 154–155

wars 1, 18–19, 25–26, 33, 63, 65, 67–69
weapons of mass destruction (WMD) xii, 41, 49–51, 118–119

X-band radars xiv, xvi, xvii, 2, 16–17, 41, 45–46, 52–56, 62–82, 83–157, 167–182
   beam safety concerns 69, 92–96
   inspections 66, 94–96, 107–108, 116, 184–185
   President George W. Bush 80–81, 103, 111, 140, 184
   President Obama xiv, xvi, xvii, 16–17, 83, 111, 138–140, 143–157, 177, 193–196, 202–205, 210–211
   see also radars

About the Author

Michaela Dodge, Ph.D., is a Research Scholar at the National Institute for Public Policy (NIPP). Prior to joining NIPP, Dr. Dodge worked at The Heritage Foundation from 2010 to 2019. She left Heritage to serve as Senior Defense Policy Advisor for Senator Jon Kyl from Arizona from October to December 2018.

Dr. Dodge's work focuses on U.S. nuclear weapons and missile defense policy, nuclear forces modernization, deterrence and assurance, and arms control. Additionally, she was a Publius Fellow at the Claremont Institute in 2011, and participated in the Center for Strategic and International Studies PONI Nuclear Scholars Initiative Program.

Dr. Dodge received a Ph.D. from George Mason University in 2019. She earned her Master of Science in Defense and Strategic Studies from Missouri State University in 2011. At Missouri State, Dr. Dodge was awarded the Ulrike Schumacher Memorial Scholarship. She received her Bachelor in International Relations and Defense and Strategic Studies from Masaryk University in the Czech Republic.

CPSIA information can be obtained
at www.ICGtesting.com
Printed in the USA
LVHW082015201220
674376LV00003B/4